THE **MARZANO ACADEMI**

LEADING A
COMPETENCY-BASED
ELEMENTARY
SCHOOL

Robert J.
MARZANO

Brian J.
KOSENA

with
BARBARA HUBBS

MARZANO
Resources

555 North Morton Street
Bloomington, IN 47404
888.849.0851
FAX: 866.801.1447

email: info@MarzanoResources.com
MarzanoResources.com

Printed in the United States of America

Library of Congress Cataloging-in-Publication Data

Names: Marzano, Robert J., author. | Kosena, Brian J., author.
Title: Leading a competency-based elementary school : the Marzano Academies
    model / Robert J. Marzano, Brian J. Kosena.
Description: Bloomington, IN : Marzano Resources, 2021. | Includes
    bibliographical references and index.
Identifiers: LCCN 2021043156 (print) | LCCN 2021043157 (ebook) | ISBN
    9781943360413 (paperback) | ISBN 9781943360420 (ebook)
Subjects: LCSH: Competency-based education--United States. | Education,
    Elementary--United States. | Elementary school administration--United
    States.
Classification: LCC LC1032 .M38 2021 (print) | LCC LC1032 (ebook) | DDC
    370.11--dc23
LC record available at https://lccn.loc.gov/2021043156
LC ebook record available at https://lccn.loc.gov/2021043157

Production Team

President and Publisher: Douglas M. Rife
Associate Publisher: Sarah Payne-Mills
Managing Production Editor: Kendra Slayton
Editorial Director: Todd Brakke
Art Director: Rian Anderson
Copy Chief: Jessi Finn
Senior Production Editor: Laurel Hecker
Content Development Specialist: Amy Rubenstein
Copy Editor: Mark Hain
Proofreader: Jessi Finn
Text and Cover Designer: Abigail Bowen
Editorial Assistants: Charlotte Jones, Sarah Ludwig, and Elijah Oates

ACKNOWLEDGMENTS

To begin, this book could not have been written without the support and encouragement of Pamela Swanson, superintendent of Westminster Public Schools (WPS). Through her leadership, WPS and John E. Flynn, a Marzano Academy, have pioneered many of the competency-based principles highlighted in the pages of this book. In addition, Oliver Grenham and Jeni Gotto provide daily guidance without which John E. Flynn, a Marzano Academy, could not be the great school it is. Which brings us to the final and maybe most important acknowledgment: the students, faculty, and staff of John E. Flynn, a Marzano Academy, are the real heroes of this book. They are responsible for the teaching, learning, and leadership strategies this book exhibits. Never has a group of people been more dedicated to making a new and different type of school model work. It is our honor to serve the Flynn school community and we appreciate its willingness to be daring and innovative in the shared pursuit of finding a better way to educate children.

TABLE OF CONTENTS

CHAPTER 1

Indicators That Address the Psychological, Social, and Emotional Context of the School 13

CHAPTER 2

Indicators That Address Competency-Based Instruction 49

ABOUT THE AUTHORS

Robert J. Marzano, PhD, is cofounder and chief academic officer of Marzano Resources in Denver, Colorado. During his fifty years in the field of education, he has worked with educators as a speaker and trainer and has authored more than fifty books and two hundred articles on topics such as instruction, assessment, writing and implementing standards, cognition, effective leadership, and school intervention. His books include *The New Art and Science of Teaching, Leaders of Learning, Making Classroom Assessments Reliable and Valid, The Classroom Strategies Series, Managing the Inner World of Teaching, A Handbook for High Reliability Schools, A Handbook for Personalized Competency-Based Education,* and *The Highly Engaged Classroom.* His practical translations of the most current research and theory into classroom strategies are known internationally and are widely practiced by both teachers and administrators.

Dr. Marzano received a bachelor's degree from Iona College in New York, a master's degree from Seattle University, and a doctorate from the University of Washington.

To learn more about Dr. Marzano, visit www.MarzanoResources.com.

Brian J. Kosena, EdD, is the founding principal of John E. Flynn, a Marzano Academy, a preK–8 school of innovation in Westminster Public Schools, located in Westminster, Colorado. The first campus of the Marzano Academy network, Flynn continues to serve as the instructional laboratory school for both Westminster Public Schools and Marzano Academies. Dr. Kosena has been an educator since 2006, with a background as a principal, instructional technology coordinator, and high school social studies teacher. His educational experiences range from teaching in a private Jesuit high school to being a principal of a predominantly low-income minority public elementary, as well as a preK–8 innovation school. He has also taught graduate-level and teacher-licensure courses in the Denver metro area.

Dr. Kosena is a strong advocate for competency-based education (CBE). In addition to working in Westminster Public Schools, a national leader in CBE design, Dr. Kosena has formally researched CBE instructional practices and implementation in school settings. He regularly attends and presents at CBE conferences, helping share his experiences while encouraging a wider adoption of CBE across all public school systems. His work has helped identify common challenges for CBE schooling, as well as find practicable solutions.

Dr. Kosena received a bachelor's degree in international affairs from the University of Colorado Boulder, a master's degree in secondary education from the University of Phoenix, and a doctorate in educational leadership and equity from the University of Colorado Denver.

To book Brian J. Kosena for professional development, contact pd@MarzanoResources.com.

Barbara Hubbs, MEd, is a competency-based educator and school leader with over fifteen years of experience working in schools. She currently serves as the assistant principal at John E. Flynn, a Marzano Academy, in Westminster, Colorado, an innovation school in Westminster Public Schools. Her previous experience includes roles as an instructional coach, an English language learner teacher, and an elementary teacher. Before entering administration, Ms. Hubbs taught multiple levels in a competency-based system, providing unique insights into the high-leverage instructional practices schools must implement to be successful in a competency-based environment. In addition, as an administrator at a Marzano Academy, she understands the importance school leadership has in ensuring successful instruction across every classroom.

Ms. Hubbs received a bachelor's degree in elementary education from the University of Northern Arizona and a master's degree in multicultural education from the University of Colorado Boulder.

Introduction

This book is about leadership in elementary schools. Of course, there are many books with a similar focus. The elementary school leadership addressed in this book, however, is focused on a particular type of school that we refer to as a *Marzano Academy* or simply as the *academy model*. While this book is certainly designed for schools that are pursuing the official process of becoming a Marzano Academy, it is also intended for schools that do not wish to pursue that process but do wish to implement some of the components of the Marzano Academies model within their current system. Schools that wish to go through the formal process should contact MarzanoAcademies.org.

Traditionally, the term *academy* has been used to describe secondary schools, but it is now used across the K–12 continuum. Regardless of the grade level referenced, educators frequently use the term to describe a school that is designed to produce students who have mastered specific areas of knowledge and skill, such as an academy for the arts, an academy for science, an academy for literature, and so on. By convention, then, in the United States, the term *academy* generally means that a school has a primary and somewhat narrow focus.

The academy model we describe here is, to a certain extent, the antithesis of the traditional approach to academies. Instead of having a primary, narrow academic focus, it is designed to develop a wide and interconnected array of knowledge and skills that allows students to pursue any endeavor they so choose and to succeed in that pursuit.

The History and Foundations of the Marzano Academies Model

The Marzano Academies model, as described in this book, is the product of decades of interrelated efforts to translate research and theory into practice starting with efforts in the 1980s to integrate direct instruction in thinking skills into the K–12 curriculum (for instance, Marzano et al., 1988). Such efforts have proceeded up to the present, with works that cover a wide variety of topics, including instruction, leadership, curriculum, assessment, vocabulary, standards, grading, high reliability organizations, professional learning communities, personalized competency-based education (PCBE), student motivation, social-emotional learning, teacher and leader evaluation, and taxonomies of knowledge and skill, to name a few. In short, the model presented here is the integration of numerous research and theory efforts over multiple decades, all of which were developed such that every piece is designed to fit with every other piece. This type of systematic planning is in contrast to the efforts in many schools to put together separate and sometimes disparate programs designed independently by different experts and organizations. While such efforts are well intended and have a certain intuitive appeal, they often fail because the selected initiatives might clash and cancel each other out, even though all are effective in their own right. Throughout this book, we systematically reference and describe the previous works on which the Marzano Academies model is based so that readers might consult those original sources, if they so choose.

Marzano Academies brings all these pieces together into a comprehensive model that produces consistent, high-quality education. This model is a departure from traditional structures of schooling in a number of ways. First, it is a competency-based system. *Competency-based education* (CBE) refers to the practice of promoting students to the next level only when they have demonstrated mastery of the academic content at the previous level. Time is not a factor—a student can progress at an accelerated rate in one subject and take more time in another. For example, a student might be working on fourth-grade English language arts content and sixth-grade mathematics content. Students are organized into classes and groups by their ability, rather than by age, allowing teachers to provide more targeted, effective instruction. CBE ensures that students actually learn before advancing, so they master the content the school considers important at each level and are prepared for the next one.

Second, to determine the content that students will learn at each level, the Marzano Academies model defines its academic program in a highly precise manner. For each topic that students must master, a *proficiency scale* delineates the progression of learning, from basic knowledge and skills, to the target level that students are expected to reach, to opportunities for advanced applications. A manageable set of proficiency scales for each content area at each level ensures consistency—students master the same content and skills no matter which teachers they learn from. Proficiency scales show exactly what students need to know and how they will get there. Furthermore, teachers assess students, score work, and report grades based on proficiency scales. Feedback to students lets them know where on the scale their current level of knowledge falls, making it easy for them to see what they need to do to improve. When grades are reported, it is not as an omnibus percentage or letter grade, but rather as a set of individual scores for each topic that the student is currently working on.

To support students in learning the academic content defined by proficiency scales, the Marzano Academies model also employs a robust, schoolwide vocabulary program. Vocabulary is foundational to learning in general, and direct vocabulary instruction is the best way to ensure that all students know the words they need to know to be successful in school and in life (see Marzano, 2020, for a discussion of the research). At the elementary level, the focus is on acquisition of basic and advanced high-frequency terms—that is, words that appear often in general language use. Thus, students have a base vocabulary that prepares them to learn domain-specific academic vocabulary (for example, technical terms related to science) in secondary school.

A third way that the Marzano Academies model differs from a typical traditional school is its recognition that effective education goes beyond academic content. The model includes directly teaching cognitive and metacognitive skills, such as analytical thinking, problem solving, impulse control, and collaboration. These skills are as essential to preparedness for life and career as academic content, so age-appropriate learning progressions for each skill are defined through proficiency scales. Students learn information and processes related to each one, and teachers give feedback on students' mastery thereof.

The Marzano Academies model also includes social-emotional components. The community of the school sets the environment for learning, and the quality of that community impacts the quality of students' education. Thus, this model emphasizes relationships and a sense of belonging among students, teachers, leaders, and other stakeholders. In addition to regular social-emotional learning on topics like mindfulness and empathy, students in a Marzano Academy participate in inspiring programs like those presented by Rachel's Challenge, an anti-bullying organization that focuses on kindness and compassion (www.rachelschallenge.org).

The final unique component we will mention here is the Marzano Academies approach to instruction. An *instructional model* defines in detail the practices associated with excellent teaching. The Marzano Academies instructional model includes forty-nine elements of effective instruction for CBE, ranging from content-delivery elements like recording and representing content to elements related to the classroom context, such as showing value and respect for all learners. With support from school leaders, teachers are expected to set goals and develop their abilities relative to the elements of the instructional model. Instruction in the Marzano Academies model also includes the systematic use of strategies known to improve students' retention of information, such as cumulative review.

While the Marzano Academies model may seem complex, its components form a coherent whole that drives toward a single goal: the highest quality education for all learners. The structure that allows school leaders to manage these seemingly different initiatives in a cohesive, integrated fashion is the concept of a high reliability organization.

High Reliability Leadership

The academy model utilizes a high reliability approach to leadership. While there has been a great deal written about leadership in K–12 education, until recently there has been relatively little written about *high reliability* leadership in education. The high reliability process used in the academy model is outlined in the book *Leading a High Reliability School* (Marzano, Warrick, Rains, & DuFour, 2018).

At its core, a high reliability perspective involves monitoring the relationship between the actions that an organization takes to enhance its effectiveness and the extent to which these actions do, in fact, produce their desired effects. In the literature on high reliability organizations, those actions an organization engages in are referred to as *leading indicators*, and the concrete results produced from monitoring the effects of the leading indicators are referred to as *lagging indicators*.

Leading and lagging indicators are the operational cornerstones of the high reliability process employed in the academy model. There are sixteen leading indicators that constitute the Marzano Academies model. We refer to them as school-level indicators. Those sixteen leading indicators are as follows (Marzano Academies, n.d.).

1. **Safe, Orderly, and Supportive Environment:** The school has programs and practices in place that provide students, parents, and staff with a sense of safety, order, and support.

2. **Student Efficacy and Agency:** The school has programs and practices in place that help develop student efficacy and agency.

3. **Inspiration:** The school has programs and practices in place that are designed to inspire students by providing opportunities for self-actualization and connection to something greater than self.

4. **Personal Projects:** The school has programs and practices in place that allow students to engage in projects of their own design.

5. **Instruction and Teacher Development:** The school has a Marzano Academies–approved instructional model that it uses to provide feedback to teachers regarding their status and growth on specific pedagogical skills.

6. **Blended Instruction:** The school procures online resources and engages teachers in activities that help them develop online resources for score 2.0, 3.0, and 4.0 levels on proficiency scales.

7. **Cumulative Review:** The school has programs and practices in place that ensure students continually review and revise critical content and practice various forms of assessment relative to that content.

8. **Knowledge Maps:** The school ensures that students use knowledge maps as tools to comprehend and write various types of texts.

9. **Measurement Topics and Proficiency Scales:** The school has well-articulated measurement topics with accompanying proficiency scales for essential academic content.

10. **Cognitive and Metacognitive Skills:** The school has well-articulated measurement topics and accompanying proficiency scales for cognitive and metacognitive skills that are systematically taught and assessed throughout the curriculum.

11. **Vocabulary:** The school has programs and practices in place to ensure that all students have a working knowledge of tier one, tier two, and tier three vocabulary.

12. **Explicit Goals for Students' Status and Growth:** The school has explicit goals for students' status and growth at the individual-student level and at the whole-school level.

13. **Assessment:** The school has an assessment system that ensures the use of reliable and valid classroom assessments that measure each student's status and growth on specific measurement topics.

14. **Reporting and Grading:** The school has a reporting and grading system that depicts both status and growth for individual students and allows for students to work at multiple levels across different subject areas.

15. **Collective Responsibility:** The school has programs and practices in place that ensure teachers collectively provide instruction, support, and assessments on measurement topics regardless of whose class students are primarily assigned to.

16. **Flexible Scheduling:** The school employs scheduling practices that allow students to receive instruction, support, and evaluation on measurement topics at any level in any subject area.

Note that each of the sixteen indicators references programs or practices. As previously described, this is the essence of a leading indicator. A school is executing some program or practice for distinct purposes. These sixteen leading indicators for the academy model represent non-negotiable interventions in which the school must engage. They also represent sixteen areas for which concrete data must be generated. These data are the basis for establishing lagging indicators. In effect, lagging indicators are the quantitative evidence that the desired effect of a leading indicator has been produced. To illustrate, consider the second leading indicator for the academy model, student efficacy and agency: the school has programs and practices in place that help develop student efficacy and agency. The lagging indicator for this leading indicator would be the concrete evidence that students' senses of efficacy and agency are actually increasing. Such evidence might involve concrete choices students are making, examples of student input into the effective running of the school, data from survey questions administered to students, and the like. In effect, the leading indicators are the starting place for implementing high reliability leadership and the lagging indicators are the evidence that validates the efficacy of the leading indicators.

The important and powerful connection between leading and lagging indicators can be used by those following the academy leadership process as a five-step process to high reliability status, as follows.

Step 1: Make sure explicit programs and practices are in place for each of the sixteen leading indicators.

Step 2: Create lagging indicators for the sixteen leading indicators based on the desired effects implicit or explicit in the leading indicators and establish criterion levels for success.

Step 3: Collect data on the lagging indicators.

Step 4: If the school has not met the minimum requirements for a lagging indicator, refocus attention and resources on the actions in the associated leading indicator.

Step 5: Continually collect data on the lagging indicators and respond accordingly.

These steps are implicit in the scale an academy uses to judge its progress on each of the sixteen indicators. To determine the extent to which a school is operating as a high reliability organization, an academy leader uses a five-point scale that ranges from not using (0) to sustaining (4) to evaluate the performance of the school on each of the sixteen indicators. Consider figure I.1.

Level Descriptions	
4 **Sustaining**	The school exhibits all behaviors at the applying level and takes proper action to intervene when quick data indicate a potential problem.
3 **Applying**	The school employs programs and practices that address the academy school-level indicator and can provide lagging indicators to show the desired effects of these actions.
2 **Developing**	The school employs programs and practices that address the academy school-level indicator but cannot provide lagging indicators to show the desired effects of these actions.
1 **Beginning**	The school is in the beginning but incomplete stages of developing programs and practices that address the academy school-level indicator.
0 **Not Using**	The school does not attempt to develop programs and practices that address the academy school-level indicator.

Source: Adapted from Marzano et al., 2018.

FIGURE I.1: Generic scale for high reliability status in the academy model.

For each indicator, an academy leader examines the programs and practices in the school and determines the school's status using this scale. At the not using (0) level of the scale in figure I.1, a school has made no attempt to develop programs and practices that address the indicator. The school has not even begun to take step number 1. Using school-level indicator 1 (safe, orderly, and supportive environment) as an example, at the not using (0) level of the scale, the school would have no plans to implement programs that address the safety, order, and support of the school, or there would be no evidence that individual teachers are using strategies and activities that address this area on their own, even though there is not a schoolwide program in place.

At the beginning (1) level, the school has initiated step 1 by attempting to develop programs and practices but is doing so in an incomplete manner and still has work to do to fully address the indicator. At the beginning (1) level of the scale for school-level indicator 1, the leader would have written plans regarding the implementation of programs and practices that address students' needs for safety, order, and support but there would be little or no evidence that these plans are actually implemented schoolwide, or the school might have a written plan for the implementation of specific programs but there would not be evidence that teachers were implementing these programs with fidelity.

It is only at the developing (2) level where a school has completed step 1. The school has programs and practices in place that address the indicator. Those programs and practices are complete and executed without significant errors or omissions. To be scored at the developing (2) level for school-level indicator 1, not only would the school have written plans for the implementation of programs and practices that address safety, order, and support, but those programs and practices would be implemented with fidelity.

It is interesting to note that discussions of school effectiveness have traditionally stopped here. This phenomenon is discussed at length in the book *Leading a High Reliability School* (Marzano et al., 2018). During the 1980s there was a school-reform movement to identify those programs and practices that had substantial correlations with student achievement. Of course, the literature on high reliability organizations calls those programs and practices *leading indicators*. But the reform of the 1980s stopped at the execution of the identified programs and practices. To this extent, the high reliability movement can be thought of as an extension of those early efforts. This extension starts at the applying (3) level of the scale.

It is at the applying (3) level of the high reliability scale that a school can produce evidence of the effectiveness of its leading indicators. This requires the execution of steps 2, 3, and 4. Step 2 involves the actual creation of the lagging indicator. This requires school leaders to identify the specific type of data that they will collect, along with the criteria for success. For example, in step 2, a school might identify perceptual data collected using surveys from students, teachers, and parents regarding the first school-level indicator: a safe, orderly, and supportive environment. School leaders would then identify the criterion for concluding that the school had addressed this issue, such as 90 percent of students and teachers and 80 percent of parents must respond that the school is a safe, orderly, and supportive environment. Finally, in step 4, the school collects the survey data, analyzes them, and compares them to the criterion for success. If the school has not met the criterion scores, it refocuses attention and resources on the actions inherent in the associated leading indicator. At a later date, school leaders would readminister the surveys. If the scores on the surveys meet the established numerical criteria, then leaders would conclude that the school had reached the applying (3) level. Again using school-level indicator 1 as an example, the school leader might have implemented a specific program that is used each morning for students to get to know each other throughout the year. In addition, the leader would have set the standard that 90 percent of students believe that their peers like them and know them well. With a standard of evidence in place that is being met, the school would conclude that it is at the applying (3) level on the high reliability scale.

At the highest level of the scale, sustaining (4), the school continues to collect data (referred to as *quick data* because they are designed to be quick and relatively easy to collect) to ensure that the school has embraced a continuous improvement process. This is the essence of step 5. For example, the leader ensures the school continues to maintain its standards on school-level indicator 1 by using focus group discussions and quick conversations with teachers, parents, and students. In some situations, the leader might find information about the effects of specific leading indicators by systematically examining school-level reports that are periodically provided by the district on things like incidents of bullying and the like. When a school reaches this level of operation, it is functioning as a high reliability organization.

The continuum depicted in the high reliability scale provides an interesting perspective on the stages a school must work through to maximize its effectiveness relative to a specific indicator. By definition, it is at the developing (2) level of the scale where programs and practices are in place relative to a specific indicator and implemented completely and with fidelity. The developing (2) level might be thought of as the fulcrum of the continuum. At the first two levels of the scale (not using and beginning), a school is in the process of rigorously analyzing a particular indicator and determining how it will deal with it. Reaching the developing (2) level of the scale indicates that a school has comprehensively and thoroughly addressed an indicator. To reach the applying (3) level on the scale, a school must go much further and create lagging indicators with concrete, clear criteria for success. Finally, even after these criteria have been met, the highest level of the scale, sustaining (4), demands that a school continually collect quick data to ensure that implementation is not slipping relative to an indicator. When an elementary school is operating at the applying level (3) or the sustaining level (4) on all sixteen school-level indicators, it is effectively implementing the academy model.

Lagging Indicators

For each of the school-level indicators, leaders must select lagging indicators related to the specific programs and practices the school is implementing for that indicator. To illustrate, the discussion in the previous section used the indicator of a safe, orderly, and supportive environment as an example. This indicator, which we discuss in more detail in chapter 1 (page 14), might include the following programs and practices.

- The safety of the physical plant

- Access to communication devices

- Crisis and emergency procedures

- Systematic practice of safety and emergency procedures

- Programs and practices for belonging and esteem

It's important to note that the leaders using the academy model might focus on very different initiatives than these. Each school leader must identify initiatives that meet his or her immediate needs relative to the indicator of a safe, orderly, and supportive environment. The ones we discuss in this book are only examples of the many possible initiatives on which a school might focus.

To create lagging indicators, leaders would select a few of the programs and practices they are employing that they consider particularly timely and critical for their school. Based on the example programs and practices for school-level indicator 1, school leadership would have a wide variety of lagging indicators from which to select. Figure I.2 (page 8) lists some of those potential lagging indicators.

The first column in figure I.2 lists the programs and practices a school is implementing to address school-level indicator 1. The second column identifies the type of data that school leaders might collect to create a lagging indicator, and the third column describes the criteria that leadership might use to ascertain whether the school has achieved acceptable levels of performance.

It is important to note that the last row in figure I.2 addresses the perceptions of students, teachers, and parents. School leaders can collect perceptual data for each of the sixteen school-level indicators using surveys. Although it is not necessary to have perceptual data for each school-level

Programs and Practices	Lagging Indicator Data	Potential Standard for High Reliability Status
Safety of the physical plant	Physical inspection report of areas critical to safety	100 percent of all critical areas of the physical plant meet safety standards
Access to and use of communication devices	Percentage of teachers and staff that have access to communication devices	90 percent of teachers and staff have access to communication devices and 100 percent of those use them as intended
Systematic practice of safety procedures	The frequency of practice sessions for safety procedures	Safety procedures are practiced bimonthly with 100 percent of practice procedures executed without significant errors or omissions
Specific classroom strategies and programs	The percentage of teachers using specific classroom strategies	100 percent of teachers use specific classroom strategies that enhance students' sense of safety, order, and support
	The percentage of teachers using 180 Connections	90 percent of teachers engage in 180 Connections on a daily basis
		80 percent of teachers use the star student activities
		80 percent of primary teachers use play-based learning
Perceptions of students, teachers, and parents	Surveys of teachers, students, and parents	90 percent of students respond positively that they perceive the school as safe, orderly, and supportive
		100 percent of teachers respond positively that they perceive the school as safe, orderly, and supportive
		70 percent of parents and guardians respond positively that they perceive the school as safe, orderly, and supportive

Source: © 2021 by Robert J. Marzano.

FIGURE I.2: Potential lagging indicators and criteria for school-level indicator 1.

indicator, we highly recommend that leaders generate such data simply because of their timeliness and the utility of the information they provide. Specifically, perceptual data are easy to collect using surveys. They take very little time to administer and provide immediate and easily interpretable results. More important, perceptions are a critical aspect of a school's high reliability status. A school might, in fact, be safe, orderly, and supportive, but if teachers, students, parents, or administrators do not perceive it as such, then it is not, at least for that group in terms of how they feel relative to the school.

When designing perceptual surveys, school leaders must consider several things. First, leaders need to create different surveys for students, for faculty and staff, and for parents. Each of these surveys should be specifically designed to understand how these individual stakeholders perceive the specific indicator. Survey questions like the following might be used for school-level indicator 1, for example.

- Is the school a safe place?

- Is the school an orderly place?

- Does the school have clear routines, procedures, and rules in place?

- Does the school have a crisis plan and are all stakeholders aware of this plan?
- Does the school communicate safety and order issues?
- What types of decisions are made with community input?
- How are school safety and order data collected and communicated?

Regardless of the questions used, the principal needs to determine the minimum thresholds he or she will accept. For example, if 70 percent of parents state the school has clear routines and procedures in place, is this enough? This criterion score might suffice for parents but might not for students and teachers.

A principal will want to set his or her minimum threshold expectations before administering the survey, to ensure that the results don't influence what is considered acceptable. Next, the principal should decide how often he or she will administer the surveys to the school community, and the preferred administrative methods to ensure high participation rates. The principal can easily request every faculty and staff member take the survey during designated planning time, or during an in-service day. If the principal considers these perceptual surveys a priority, he or she can ensure teachers and staff complete them with consistency and fidelity. This is also true for students. The principal can designate a particular day and time that all classrooms will dedicate to administering the survey to all students.

Getting 100 percent of parents to complete a school survey might not be realistic. Knowing this, a principal will need to determine what will be an acceptable number of families to survey. Obviously, the higher the number of completed surveys, the more accurate the findings. One strategy to ensuring higher participation rates among families is to include the survey as part of another school event. One example is to set up several computers with the survey preloaded in the main office during parent-teacher conferences. The school can then direct all parents through the main office as they arrive for their scheduled conference, and can ask parents to take the survey then, or stop back before leaving. Another time to capture the responses of a group of parents is during school registration. Many schools have registration "assembly lines" with specific stations. A principal might include a registration station with computers ready for survey completion. Other school events such as PTA or PTO events, music and theater performances, or awards ceremonies can also be utilized. Finally, a principal might include the survey link in his or her monthly newsletter to parents, explaining the purpose of the survey and asking for parent input. These types of home-based survey administration methods, however, might not yield as high a participation rate as the school-based methods will.

Trim Tab Indicators and Customized High Reliability Scales

Those who engage in boating, aviation, and other similar activities are familiar with the principle of trim tabbing. In boating and aviation, trim tab devices are mechanical systems that allow the person piloting the boat or airplane to make small changes in the controls that have large effects on how the boat or the airplane maneuvers. If you examine the cockpit of a large commercial airplane, you will find small knobs that pilots adjust to control the roll, pitch, and yaw of the airplane. (Roll is rotation around the front-to-back axis, pitch is rotation around the side-to-side axis, and yaw is rotation around the vertical axis of the airplane.) Small movements of these knobs generate big changes in what the plane is doing. At a nonmechanical level, trim tabbing means focusing on small, specific actions that will have the biggest effect on whatever endeavor is being executed.

Trim tabbing within the context of high reliability leadership means selecting a relatively few lagging indicators that will have the biggest impact on the effectiveness of a school relative to the school-level indicator being addressed. Stated differently, it might be somewhat inefficient for a leader to focus on all the potential lagging indicators for an aspect of the model—all those described in figure I.2, for example. Rather, a school leader should select a subset of lagging indicators that will operate as trim tabs for the school. Then, the leader can customize the high reliability scale introduced in figure I.1 (page 5) to reflect the specific ways the school is addressing and monitoring the indicator. To illustrate, assume that a school leader has selected the subset of lagging indicators depicted in figure I.3, which represents a customized high reliability scale for his or her school's approach to school-level indicator 1.

Evidence	
4 **Sustaining** **(quick data)**	Quick data like the following are systematically collected and reviewed. • Focus-group data with students, parents, and teachers • Quick conversations with students, parents, and teachers • Regular reports on incidents of bullying, misbehavior, absenteeism, tardiness, and so on
3 **Applying** **(lagging)**	Performance goals with clear criteria for success like the following are in place. • 100 percent of all critical areas of the physical plant meet safety standards • 100 percent of students participate in 180 Connections and star student programs • 100 percent of teachers use specific classroom strategies that enhance students' sense of safety, order, and support • 90 percent of students respond positively that they perceive the school as safe, orderly, and supportive • 100 percent of teachers respond positively that they perceive the school as safe, orderly, and supportive • 70 percent of parents and guardians respond positively that they perceive the school as safe, orderly, and supportive
2 **Developing** **(leading)**	Concrete programs and practices, such as the following, are in place to develop a sense of safety, order, and support. • The physical plant is designed to maximize student safety and support • Communication devices are available and used by staff and teachers to ensure the safety and comfort of students • Safety procedures are in place and routinely practiced by staff and students • Teachers are trained in 180 Connections, star student programs, and play-based learning • Teachers are trained in specific strategies for their classrooms
1 **Beginning**	• The school has written plans for implementing programs for safety, order, and support but these have not been implemented • Individual teachers employ strategies to foster a sense of safety, order, and support, but there is not a schoolwide emphasis
0 **Not Using**	• The school has no written plans for implementing programs for safety, order, and support • There is no classroom implementation of strategies for safety, order, and support

Source: © 2021 Robert J. Marzano.

FIGURE I.3: Customized high reliability scale for school-level indicator 1.

Also note that at the sustaining (4) level of the customized high reliability scale, school leaders have identified data they can collect relatively quickly regarding this indicator. Those types of data include conversations with various constituent groups, remarks made during focus group discussions, and systematic review of reports that are readily available relative to the school's safety, order, and supportiveness.

High reliability leadership requires focused and prudent use of data. One might say that many elementary school systems are data rich but information poor. They have so many separate reports issued by state agencies, district agencies, and even program vendors that it is impossible for them to comprehend the big-picture implications. In effect, the numerous data translate into little or no useful information. In contrast, the leader who designed the lagging indicator data at the applying (3) level in figure I.3 would have focused and interpretable information about functioning of the school. Such information can be used to make small trim-tab changes in school practice to optimize the effect of the programs and practices relative to this school-level indicator.

How This Book Is Organized

In this book, we organize the sixteen school-level indicators into four categories that constitute chapters 1 through 4. For each indicator, we explain key concepts and present strategies and decision points that elementary leaders can apply in their schools. In addition, the section for each school-level indicator includes suggested lagging indicators and a customized high reliability scale. Chapter 1 includes the first four school-level indicators. These all deal with the psychological, social, and emotional context of the school. Chapter 2 addresses school-level indicators 5, 6, 7, and 8. Collectively, these indicators address effective competency-based instruction in the Marzano Academies model. Chapter 3 addresses school-level indicators 9, 10, 11, and 12. These focus on the curriculum within the model. Chapter 4 covers school-level indicators 13, 14, 15, and 16. Collectively, they address necessary structural changes that schools must make when embracing the model. Chapter 5 deals with leading the type of substantial change required when implementing the Marzano Academies model.

Finally, we should note that this book focuses on elementary schools, which typically encompass kindergarten through grade 5. Generally, we use the terms *primary* to refer to grades K–2 and *intermediate* or *upper elementary* for grades 3–5. However, the grade-level spans within elementary schools are not universal; schools and districts recognize different grades as the end of elementary school and the beginning of middle school. The sixth grade is the most equivocal in terms of where it is placed (National Center for Education Statistics, n.d.). Thus, we occasionally include sixth-grade examples as we discuss the Marzano Academies model at the elementary level.

CHAPTER 1

Indicators That Address the Psychological, Social, and Emotional Context of the School

The psychological, social, and emotional context is foundational to the effective functioning of any elementary school—Marzano Academy or otherwise. The Marzano Academies approach to this important aspect of effective education is grounded in the well-known hierarchy developed by Abraham Maslow (1943, 1954). Maslow's hierarchy originally had five levels: (1) physiology, (2) safety, (3) belonging, (4) esteem within a community, and (5) self-actualization. Later versions (Koltko-Rivera, 2006; Maslow, 1969, 1979) included a sixth level: connection to something greater than self. Briefly, the six levels are referred to as a hierarchy because the higher levels are generally not available without first fulfilling the lower levels. Maslow used the term *needs* to describe the elements of his hierarchy but also alluded to *goals*.

Robert J. Marzano, Darrell Scott, Tina H. Boogren, and Ming Lee Newcomb (2017) adapted Maslow's hierarchy to meet the purpose and focus of the academy model in the book *Motivating and Inspiring Students*. The extent to which students experience the school's context as psychologically, socially, and emotionally supportive is a function of the extent to which the leadership in a school attends to the needs and goals in the hierarchy. Figure 1.1 depicts the organization of all six levels of the model.

Referencing the hierarchy, one might say that elementary students in any given situation are constantly asking themselves the following questions.

- **Level 1:** Is this situation physiologically comfortable?

- **Level 2:** Does this situation provide me with a sense of physical safety?

- **Level 3:** Does this situation provide me with a sense of belonging?

- **Level 4:** Does this situation make me feel like I am valued?

- **Level 5:** Does this situation allow me to work on things related to my personal interests?

- **Level 6:** Does this situation make me feel like I'm a part of something important?

Source: Marzano, Scott, et al., 2017, p. 3.

FIGURE 1.1: Maslow's hierarchy of needs and goals.

The first four school-level indicators in the Marzano Academies model address the levels of the hierarchy to ensure that the school environment supports students' psychological, social, and emotional needs.

School-Level Indicator 1: Safe, Orderly, and Supportive Environment

The leader of an elementary academy must ensure that the school has programs and practices in place that provide students, parents, and staff with a sense of safety, order, and support. These factors deal with the bottom four levels of the hierarchy of needs and goals.

Programs and Practices for Physiological Comfort and Physical Safety

The first two levels of Maslow's hierarchy consider students' physiological needs and physical safety. These needs must be addressed before students can learn effectively.

The lowest level of Maslow's hierarchy involves the most basic of human needs: physiological comfort. If a person is too hungry, thirsty, or tired, he or she must eat, drink, or sleep before focusing attention on anything else. Generally, elementary schools attend to many of these basic physiological needs. Buildings are heated during the winter and often cooled during warmer months, cafeterias provide sustenance, and so on. However, a school leader employing the Marzano Academies model should still monitor and address the physiological needs of students as much as resources will allow and work with students, parents, and outside entities when they are not. Five areas of physiological needs are of particular concern: food, sleep, physical health, mental health, and housing (Marzano, Scott, et al., 2017).

Physical safety is the second level of needs in Maslow's hierarchy. To address safety, virtually all schools have implemented physical and procedural safeguards to protect school buildings from external threats. These include secured entry points, ID badging systems, safety drills, and enhanced security procedures, all of which have produced safer schools. Even with these things in place, the fact remains that some teachers, students, and parents might still perceive their school as unsafe. Bullying, an unsupportive teacher, or even dangerous neighborhood streets can all create the belief that a school is in fact not safe. This difference between actual and perceived safety is not always visible, but could be a limiting factor of a school's academic success. Toward this end, ensuring all school members feel that the environment is safe, orderly, and supportive must be a school's top priority.

The following sections present various considerations for leaders as they establish the foundations of physiological comfort and physical safety for the school environment.

Food

Some elementary students suffer from food insecurity. This is not to say that all students who say they are hungry suffer from this malady. To identify students who have food insecurity, teachers might look for behaviors like rushing food lines, hovering around for seconds, and being extremely hungry on Mondays. If the school leader determines that some students have a problem with food insecurity, there are services such as free meal programs and food pantries that the leader can connect families with. Additionally, staff and faculty might ensure that students have access to food throughout the day. For example, guided by the school leader, each teacher might establish a bin that holds fruit for students to take when they are hungry or let students who may need extra food know that they can come to class a few minutes early to pick up a snack before the majority of the class arrives (Marzano, Scott, et al., 2017).

Sleep

Sleep is a physiological need that, when unmet, can dramatically affect a student's ability to attend to what is occurring in class. While school leaders and individual teachers do not have control over the amount of sleep students get at home, they can emphasize the importance of sleep to students and encourage them to develop healthy sleeping habits. Additionally, the school leader can send communications home emphasizing the importance of proper rest and providing some suggestions for parents and guardians. Strategies in this area include the following (Marzano, Scott, et al., 2017).

- Seat students who tend to fall asleep closer to the teacher's desk so that it is easier to observe them and provide them with intellectual stimulation when they seem to be very tired. Alternatively, seat them by a window to take advantage of fresh air and natural light to help keep students alert.

- Incorporate frequent movement breaks into lessons. If students seem to be dozing off, ask them to briefly walk down the hall to get a drink of water.

- Call on students unexpectedly if they seem to be dozing off. However, it's important not to humiliate them with such questions. Questions should be designed and posed in such a way as to heighten students' interest and alertness.

Physical Health

Physical health represents an obvious and critically important component of students' physiological needs. Three important aspects of health that school leaders should consider are illness, hygiene, and exercise. It's probably safe to say that student physical health will be at the forefront of school leaders' minds due to the COVID-19 pandemic. Of course, there are state and local resources available to schools to help guard against such illnesses, which we do not address here. There are also day-to-day activities leaders and teachers can employ in their schools and classrooms (Marzano, Scott, et al., 2017).

- Encourage students to wash their hands frequently. This can be facilitated by keeping hand sanitizer in an easily accessible area of the classroom.

- Teach students preventative behaviors like properly covering their mouths and noses when coughing and sneezing. It is also useful to make tissues easily accessible.

- Systematically sanitize the classroom. Disinfect high-touch surfaces (such as countertops, desks, keyboards, phones, faucets, doorknobs, and handles) on a regular schedule. Keep adequate cleaning supplies on hand in the classroom.

Of course, even when these precautions are followed, students will inevitably get sick. School leaders should ensure that teachers encourage students to stay at home when they are sick or have symptoms of colds or flus. When students are sick in class, they should be sent to the nurse's office away from other students before going home. School leaders may also want to send home a sickness policy at the beginning of the year informing parents of the school's preferences and protocols.

Hygiene is fairly easy to reinforce in the elementary classroom. If a teacher needs to address hygiene issues with a specific student, he or she should speak to the student privately. The teacher should emphasize that he or she is concerned for the student, but be direct and honest in the conversation. The following are some strategies teachers might employ (Marzano, Scott, et al., 2017).

- Teach all students about positive hygiene behaviors and their importance.

- When students have poor hygiene, meet with them individually to give them instructions for specific behaviors that support good hygiene.

- After meeting with students about hygienic behaviors, reinforce positive changes in their behavior.
- Keep hygiene items (such as toothbrushes, toothpaste, combs, brushes, shampoo, deodorant, and menstrual products) on hand in the school or classroom.

Exercise is the final aspect teachers might address regarding students' physical health. School leaders can initiate programs that involve exercise such as walk- or bike-to-school days, recreational sports, school field days, and extended recess periods. Teachers can incorporate physical activity into class time through physical activity breaks that provide opportunities for students to move.

Mental Health

Mental health is another important aspect of students' physiological well-being. School guidance counselors should be consulted if any students exhibit mental health issues. Leaders and teachers should consider student behaviors like the following as possible indicators of mental health issues that would trigger contacting a school counselor.

- Appearing sad or withdrawn for more than two weeks
- Trying to physically harm themselves
- Being involved in fights or trying to hurt others
- Displaying out-of-control behavior that can hurt themselves or others
- Not eating
- Displaying severe mood swings

While mental illness may only affect a few members of a class, all students experience worry to some degree. Elementary students might worry much more than teachers realize. Common worrisome topics for students include their academic performance, relationships with their peers, a family member's health, and local or world events. Teachers can use strategies like the following to address students' worries (Marzano, Scott, et al., 2017).

- Be supportive of students when they express their worries, but avoid reinforcing their fears. This requires recognizing the difference between being supportive and reinforcing students' fears. Use language such as, "I hear you and what you're saying," instead of "That is very scary," or "I can see why you think that."
- Teach students about the physiology behind fear. Explain that worry is a natural neurological process. At the elementary level, teachers can describe the fight-or-flight response.
- Explain to students the difference between healthy and unhealthy worry. Emphasize that all people worry and that it is a natural human response. Differentiate between healthy worry and unhealthy worry by asking students to compare the amount of time they ruminate on specific worries versus other topics.
- Ask students to verbalize their worries by writing them down or saying them aloud. This can dispel fear and highlight worries that are unrealistic. Have students consider the probability of certain outcomes and brainstorm behaviors that can prevent negative outcomes.
- Help students externalize their worries through fictional characters. For example, teachers of young students might introduce the Worry Monster as a bully who makes people feel bad.

Housing

Homelessness and housing insecurity are the final aspect of students' physiological needs that leaders should be aware of. While educators cannot alleviate students' unmet housing needs, leaders can help teachers be aware of students' circumstances and strive to make the classroom as comfortable for them as possible while demonstrating compassion for their situation. Consider the following strategies (Marzano, Scott, et al., 2017).

- When discussing students who are experiencing homelessness or talking to students about their housing circumstances, take care to do it away from other students to avoid embarrassing these students.

- Assess and stabilize students' basic needs. If students' needs related to physiology and safety are not being met, meet with appropriate administrators and staff to ensure that they are.

- Avoid asking students to take work home with them if you know or believe that they are experiencing homelessness. Furthermore, avoid asking students to bring in food, photos, or other items from home.

The Security of the Physical Plant

An academy leader should conduct an analysis of existing safety systems, which must include elements that pertain to both actual and perceived safety. A principal might start by determining how secure the entry points are to the building. Many schools, especially those in older buildings, have numerous exterior doors, sometimes even within each classroom. Although convenient, this can be a safety hazard. Every exterior entry point should be considered a potential liability. A principal should discern whether every door needs to be used or if some can be permanently locked.

After an analysis of physical security is complete, any exterior access points that will be used should have strict security protocols. Teachers should have keys or fobs that they bring with them when supervising recess or taking a class outside for a learning activity. Under no circumstance should a door be left propped open. This can be tempting to do, especially if food deliveries or other types of in-and-out access are required, but a propped door is an unsecured access point to the building, and convenience should never be prioritized over safety.

Communication Devices

A principal should ensure that every staff member can easily communicate with necessary personnel. Most schools are already equipped with intercom systems. The school's public address (PA) system should be routinely inspected to ensure every speaker is working properly. Beyond the ability to communicate with classroom teachers from the office, the PA system should also be utilized to initiate lockdown and lockout alerts. Many newer schools have an interconnected PA system with fire alarms and automatic door-lock mechanisms. This is a nice feature to have and can be retrofitted into older buildings. In an actual emergency situation, having doors automatically secure and automated notifications broadcast across the PA system allows the principal and school personnel to focus on other immediate needs.

Finally, providing every staff member with a handheld walkie-talkie can provide a lot of safety benefits to a school. Teachers can easily communicate with the principal, office staff, or school psychologist without needing to stop instruction in the classroom or send a student to deliver a message. At minimum, every adult who accompanies students outside should have a handheld radio at all times. Whether it be recess staff needing to communicate with one another while at different ends of the playground, the physical education teacher notifying the office staff of an injured student, or school personnel communicating during an emergency, walkie-talkies are cost-effective communication tools every school should utilize to ensure safety and order.

Crisis and Emergency Procedures

A principal should ensure the building crisis and emergency plan is in place, updated regularly, and communicated to all school personnel. This plan is a critical document for school safety and must include at minimum the following components.

- The building crisis team
- Incident command roles and responsibilities
- Incident command locations
- Predetermined evacuation sites (both on- and offsite)
- Evacuation procedures
- Controlled release and parent reunification processes
- Security procedures
- Media and communication expectations
- Staff training

When drafting a school's crisis and emergency plan, a principal should consider a number of elements. First, the principal should determine which personnel will make up the building's crisis team. Typically, this team includes the members of the school's administration team, the building secretary, the building aides, custodians, the school psychologist, and if available, the school resource officer. This group will be the point people during a crisis, and also hold specific incident command roles. The crisis and emergency plan should identify who these people are, their titles and roles in the building, office and cell phone numbers, and whether they possess a school walkie-talkie or other internal communication device.

In addition, every member of the crisis team will have a specific responsibility during an emergency. The school crisis and emergency plan must state these roles, as well as any procedures these responsibilities must follow. For example, the principal most likely will hold the role of incident lead, with the responsibility of managing all other roles, responsibilities, and emergency processes. Another role is that of community greeter, which includes the responsibilities of greeting and directing parents and helping fill out incident release forms. This role is typically best assigned to front office personnel, or someone who knows many of the parents already and can be a welcoming and familiar face for concerned families as they arrive. If the school community has a high population of English-as-a-second-language speakers, the person who fills this role should be bilingual, if possible, to remove communication challenges that could slow down the crisis procedures.

Emergency procedures should have clear routines built in for all school personnel. Creating a "go-kit" for every classroom is an easy way to ensure every teacher has everything he or she needs in the case of emergency. A go-kit should at minimum include updated class rosters for attendance, safety vests for easy identification of staff personnel, evacuation maps or routes, a copy of the school's crisis and emergency plan, and a card system staff can use for easy communication. An example of a card system would be green and red sheets of paper. After the teacher takes attendance when the evacuation occurs, he or she holds up the green sheet of paper to communicate to the principal all students are accounted for, or a red sheet of paper if a student is missing. This card system allows for easy visual communication in what might be a crowded area.

A well-designed crisis and emergency plan must include both on- and offsite evacuation locations. For emergencies such as a fire, the school's playground area, blacktop, or sports field can often serve as a safe location to evacuate students and staff. Evacuation procedures and maps should properly identify the safest and quickest routes from every room in the school and be posted and easily visible, typically by the classroom door itself. These evacuation routes and locations should be strictly adhered to during every fire drill to ensure automaticity of use in the case of an actual emergency. Although these routes and locations will be used in most evacuations, the plan should also identify alternative exit routes and evacuation points in case particular exits or building locations are not accessible in an actual emergency.

There are some types of emergencies that will require the school to evacuate offsite. These can include hazardous materials spills, or in a worst-case scenario, an active shooter. In these scenarios, the principal will want to identify offsite evacuation locations that include nearby locations within walking distance, such as another neighborhood school, community center, or church. These locations should be considered not just for how close they are but also for the extent to which they can accommodate hundreds of people congregating at once. Available parking, restrooms, and staging areas for parent reunification are all things a principal should consider when choosing an offsite evacuation location.

After the principal designates an offsite location, it is important that he or she communicate with the appropriate people at those sites. Personnel can change from year to year at these locations; a pastor at the local church might agree to be an offsite location for the school one year, but the next year that same church might have a new pastor not aware of the previous agreement. Asking for site permission annually is an important step to keeping a school's crisis and emergency plan updated.

Finally, some school emergencies might require students to be transported to an evacuation location that is not within walking distance. In this case, the principal must clearly identify transportation procedures. Will school district buses be used? If not, what type of transportation will be provided? Where will students load the buses? If the primary transportation site is not accessible, where is the secondary loading area? What site will students be transported to? Is that receiving location aware of the school's evacuation procedures and parent reunification processes? A good crisis plan will include a facility map of the offsite evacuation sites, as well as where students will be housed on arrival, where parents will be greeted, and ultimately where reunification will occur. In addition, all these details must be clearly communicated to all necessary parties, both within the school and at the offsite evacuation location.

One part of the school's crisis and emergency plan that hopefully will never need to be realized is the parent communication and reunification practices. The school's plan needs to consider how families will be greeted on arrival, what will be communicated to them, where they will be staged while waiting for reunification, where reunification will occur, and how families will depart the evacuation site. Understandably, in a real crisis, parents will arrive concerned or upset, demanding information and most likely wanting to see their children immediately. It is important that the principal consider the state of mind of family members on arrival and design communication and procedural responses ahead of time. Along the same lines, local media could arrive at the same time. It is important that the school's crisis plan designates an official public relations representative to provide timely and appropriate information to onsite media. If the school's response and designed protocols for families and media are well thought out and practiced, they will provide the perception that the situation is under control, even if not all information is readily made available. Any degree of disorganization or miscommunication in a crisis scenario will lead to increased anxiety and ultimately detract from the school's ability to follow its established procedures.

Finally, and perhaps most important, is communicating and training all necessary parties in the school's crisis and emergency plan. No matter how well designed, if the plan itself is not accurately communicated to all school personnel and routinely trained for, school personnel will not follow it with automaticity in the case of an emergency. The principal should make the crisis plan readily available, such as on a shared local school drive or cloud-based location like Google Drive. The principal should distribute physical copies of the plan to all school personnel and highlight for each person his or her specific role and responsibilities. The plan itself should be reviewed, updated, and modified annually, if not semiannually, to ensure it remains reliable.

Emergency Procedure Drills

Having safety procedures in place is foundational to a safe, supportive, and orderly climate, but such procedures must be practiced to the point where they can be executed with automaticity. To this end, it is critical that a principal schedule routine drills of all kinds. Drafting this drill schedule and ensuring a strict adherence to it is a prime responsibility of the principal. Some things a principal might consider are how often he or she wants to practice each kind of drill and what to monitor during the drills. For example, fire drills might be scheduled monthly. In that case, it is best to schedule the drill before the end of the month. Adverse weather or other unexpected things can prevent a school from holding its scheduled drill, so building possible makeup days into the drill schedule can ensure a school conducts every drill every month. Creating an appointment on the school's shared calendar can help ensure a drill doesn't get missed; however, a principal might decide not to communicate every instance of an upcoming drill to help the school practice some drills unexpectedly. Practicing alternate exit routes and evacuation points is also important during monthly drills. An easy way to do this is by blocking off a hallway or exterior door with cones before conducting the fire drill to allow teachers and students to practice using alternate evacuation scenarios.

During a drill, it is essential to practice the complete emergency procedure with fidelity. For example, teachers need to take attendance to account for all students after they arrive at their evacuation location and signal the result with the red or green cards from their go-kits. One strategy to help keep attendance practices tight during a drill is for the principal to retain a student in the main office during a drill to see if this student is accounted for during the drill's attendance. Before starting the fire drill, the principal can randomly select a student coming out of the bathroom or walking down the hallway to go to the office during the drill. The classroom teacher of this student should display a red card after taking attendance if he or she is following proper procedures. Although this could be seen as a "gotcha" practice, it will only take once for all teachers to know they must be 100 percent certain of their attendance practices. To mitigate possible negative reactions to this practice, it is useful to forewarn teachers and staff that a student might possibly be used in this way. After this warning, the principal can sometimes hide a student in the office during a drill, and sometimes not. Additionally, if a student is "missing," school leaders should quickly debrief with the teacher and classmates of the "missing" student after the drill to prevent adverse emotional impact.

Communication With Outside Agencies

Regular and routine communication with local law enforcement is critical. Many schools partner with the local police or sheriff's department to provide a dedicated school resource officer for the school. This partnership is a powerful one, especially if the school resource officer is a visible and constant presence at the school. Simply having a police car routinely parked in front of the school communicates the presence of law enforcement in the school and can even deter outside threats. Some schools might not have a school resource officer assigned to their building, but should still have regular communication with their local law enforcement agencies. The principal should attempt to form relationships with local police officers and even have their cell phone numbers saved. Although a 911 call will always be made in the case of an emergency, sometimes the personal relationship with an officer can be utilized in nonemergency situations. An example of this might be an officer stopping by the school to have a conversation with a troubled student, or conducting a welfare check on a family the principal might be concerned about. Regardless of circumstance or severity, the stronger the school's and principal's relationships with local law enforcement agencies are, the better resourced the school will be in creating a safe school environment.

Programs and Practices for Belonging and Esteem

Our comments thus far have dealt with the first two levels of the hierarchy of needs and goals. The next two levels of that hierarchy are a sense of belonging and a sense of esteem. A number of programs and practices can be used to help students feel that they have a place and are valued at school. In this section we consider the following examples: 180 Connections, play-based learning, and star student programs.

180 Connections

Getting to know teachers and other students on a personal level helps all learners feel a sense of belonging within their classroom community. A daily personal-connections program goes a long way to addressing belonging and esteem needs in a systematic way. Here, we consider one such program from Rachel's Challenge, called 180 Connections (Scott & Scott, 2018).

This program provides daily prompts for teachers and students to answer together. These prompts can be superficial, such as "What is your favorite pizza topping?" or more serious like "What is your greatest fear?" Regardless of the prompts used, it is important that every classroom use the same prompt on the same day. When this occurs, students in different homerooms or classes are more likely to discuss their answers with other students later in the day knowing everyone participated in the same daily connection.

In addition to daily prompts, the principal should ensure uniformity exists across all classrooms in relation to the implementation of the program. Following a progression like the one we present here will ensure the school meets the goals of a daily connection program.

1. The teacher displays the daily prompt on the board.
2. The teacher gives the students time to consider their answers.
3. The teacher shares with the entire class his or her own answer.
4. Every student shares his or her answer with at least one partner or table group.
5. Any student who wishes to share his or her answer with the entire class is provided an opportunity to do so.

It is critical that the teachers lead by sharing their answers first. This achieves several goals. First, doing so provides effective modeling on how to appropriately share personal responses. Second, it sets the tone that the classroom is a safe space and everyone should feel comfortable sharing. Third, and most importantly, it helps humanize the teacher to his or her students. When students find commonality with their teacher as well as with their peers, the foundations for strong relationship building are increased.

It is also important that every student share his or her answer with at least one person and listen to at least one answer from another student. Abstaining from participation is not an option. This sends the message that every student's response matters. No one is too good, or too bad, to not contribute. This practice also helps normalize the belief that sharing personal information is a good thing, and ultimately strengthens the classroom community.

Finally, the teacher must provide an opportunity for students to share their answers with the entire class. Unlike the previous step, student participation in this larger setting is voluntary. The teacher should create a classroom routine that encourages students to share their responses. This routine should clearly delineate when a student shares and what an appropriate response to that student's answer will sound like. A routine that works well is to have the class sit in a large circle. The teacher sends around a talking stick or any item that denotes it is the possessor's time to share. After the student shares his or her response, the entire class acknowledges that student by snapping their fingers or clapping their hands. The acknowledgment must be something every student can do at the same time and must be easy to remember. Such a simple routine can eliminate inappropriate responses and ensure all students participate in celebrating their classmates.

Star Students

When a student holds high self-esteem, he or she feels personal and social acceptance by the classroom community, is realistic in assessing personal abilities, is empowered to achieve, and is more readily able to accept recognition from peers and teachers. To achieve this goal, there are practices a school can put in place to help build students' self-esteem. Often utilized in homeroom, a "star student of the week" program is one such way to meet students' needs relative to belonging and sense of esteem. Each week the teacher selects one student to share about himself or herself, answer personal questions, and most importantly, be celebrated by his or her peers. Teachers should encourage students to bring in pictures of family members, hobbies, interests, or anything that illustrates who they are. Teachers should have dedicated wall space for displaying these items for the student's week. Star students should have an opportunity to present to the whole class and relate stories and explanations regarding the artifacts they have brought in, but such presentations should be optional. One of the main goals of this activity is for students to better know their classmates. Discovering unrecognized commonalities is an easy way to create personal connections and help students feel a sense of belonging within their classroom community.

Play-Based Learning

In the preK and primary grades, play-based learning is an effective avenue for students to build their esteem in several ways. First, since the teacher does not structure play-based learning, students can explore ideas and interests independently, thus promoting self-reliance and confidence. This freedom provides students the opportunity to feel in control of their learning by choosing what to learn and how to learn it. It also enables the learner to solve problems as they arise, often without adult assistance. Play-based learning encourages students to collaborate (play together), which increases social skills, peer acceptance, and even critical-thinking ability. Play-based learning can be used on a daily basis. Depending on the academic goals on which it is focused, play-based learning can be relatively brief (for example, if it is designed to provide students experience with a vocabulary term) or relatively long (for example, if it is designed to provide students experience with a complex process like comparing).

Elementary principals should promote play-based learning throughout their schools. In addition to providing teachers appropriate professional development on how to use play-based learning, the principal must ensure physical spaces exist within the school that are conducive to social learning. Designing classrooms with flexible seating or creating designated areas in hallways or the library dedicated specifically to group interactions can encourage play-based learning in real, robust ways.

Routine Classroom Strategies That Provide Students With a Sense of Safety, Order, and Support

In addition to specific programs like those described in preceding sections, teachers can enact a wide variety of classroom strategies and activities to provide students with a sense of safety, order, and support. The following list describes a number of such strategies, which teachers should employ on a systematic basis to ensure that the classroom environment addresses the first four levels of Maslow's hierarchy. *Motivating and Inspiring Students* (Marzano, Scott, et al., 2017) describes these and many other strategies in depth. The school leader should coordinate these efforts by identifying which of Maslow's first four levels will be the focus for teachers during a given month.

Level 1: Physiological Comfort

- On a monthly basis, collect information about students' access to adequate nutritious food by observing students and discussing this issue with them in appropriate ways. If you identify problems with specific students, contact appropriate agencies.

- On a monthly basis, collect information about students' access to adequate sleep by observing students and discussing this issue with them in appropriate ways. If you identify problems with specific students, contact appropriate agencies.

- On a monthly basis, collect information about students' general physical health by observing students and discussing this issue with them in appropriate ways. If you identify problems with specific students, contact appropriate agencies.

- On a monthly basis, collect information about students' general mental health by observing students and discussing this issue with them in appropriate ways. If you identify problems with specific students, contact appropriate agencies.

- On a monthly basis, collect information about students' status relative to homelessness by observing students and discussing this issue with them in appropriate ways. If you identify problems with specific students, contact appropriate agencies.

Level 2: Safety

- Once a semester, review specific emergency procedures and behavior expectations with students.

- At least once a month, assess how classroom design, classroom structure, and the enforcement of behavior expectations create an environment where students are safe.

Level 3: Belonging

- At least once a semester, identify aspects of classroom protocols and practices that communicate to students they are welcome, as well as protocols and practices that might communicate the opposite message.

- At least once a semester, assess the need for interventions for specific students and whether bullying is occurring in the classroom.

- At least once a week, use strategies that contribute to a respectful learning environment, such as demonstrating awareness of important aspects of students' cultures.

- At least once a week, use strategies related to affection or cooperation, such as interacting with students in a relaxed and playful manner.

Level 4: Esteem

- At the beginning and end of the year, ask students to assess their own esteem by examining the ways they view themselves, as well as which characteristics of high self-esteem they tend to exhibit.

- At least once a semester, ask students to reflect on their thoughts and consider how they may contribute to their esteem.

- Focus on students' academic growth and protect students' esteem as much as possible when responding to students who are struggling academically.

- At least once a month, use strategies that make students feel significant and recognized by their teachers and peers, such as acknowledging students' accomplishments and efforts.

High Reliability Leadership for School-Level Indicator 1

In summary, this school-level indicator uses the first four levels of Maslow's hierarchy to ensure that the school is a safe, supportive, and orderly environment. On the surface, the programs and practices for this indicator might appear somewhat disparate—the activities that focus on students' physiological comfort are quite different from those that focus on physical safety, and the strategies that focus on students' sense of belonging and esteem have a dynamic of their own. However, the school leader must keep in mind that all of these strategies have a common purpose, which is to provide students with a strong sense that they are safe, that they are part of a supportive community, and that school operations are orderly and well designed.

The preceding discussion about school-level indicator 1, a safe, orderly, and supportive environment, focused on the following characteristics.

- Programs and practices for physiological comfort and physical safety, such as:
  - Assessment of students' access to food, sleep, physical health, mental health, and housing
  - The security of the physical plant
  - Communication devices
  - Crisis and emergency procedures and drills
  - Communication with outside agencies
- Programs and practices for belonging and esteem, such as:
  - 180 Connections
  - Star students
  - Play-based learning
- Routine classroom strategies that provide students with a sense of safety, order, and support

Figure 1.2 lists some potential lagging indicators for a safe, orderly, and supportive environment. From this list, the leader would select trim tab indicators to create a customized high reliability scale. This is depicted in figure 1.3 (page 26). Note that the introduction (page 1) used figures 1.2 and 1.3 to explain high reliability leadership. We present them again here for continuity of discussion.

Programs and Practices	Lagging Indicator Data	Potential Standard for High Reliability Status
Safety of the physical plant	Physical inspection report of areas critical to safety	100 percent of all critical areas of the physical plant meet safety standards
Access to and use of communication devices	Percentage of teachers and staff that have access to communication devices	90 percent of teachers and staff have access to communication devices and 100 percent of those use them as intended
Systematic practice of safety procedures	The frequency of practice sessions for safety procedures	Safety procedures are practiced bimonthly with 100 percent of practice procedures executed without significant errors or omissions
Specific classroom strategies and programs	The percentage of teachers using specific classroom strategies	100 percent of teachers use specific classroom strategies that enhance students' sense of safety, order, and support
	The percentage of teachers using 180 Connections	90 percent of teachers engage in 180 Connections on a daily basis
		80 percent of teachers use the star student activities
		80 percent of primary teachers use play-based learning
Perceptions of students, teachers, and parents	Surveys of teachers, students, and parents	90 percent of students respond positively that they perceive the school as safe, orderly, and supportive
		100 percent of teachers respond positively that they perceive the school as safe, orderly, and supportive
		70 percent of parents and guardians respond positively that they perceive the school as safe, orderly, and supportive

Source: © 2021 by Robert J. Marzano.

FIGURE 1.2: Potential lagging indicators and criteria for school-level indicator 1.

School-Level Indicator 2: Student Efficacy and Agency

The leader of an elementary academy should ensure that the school has programs and practices in place that help students develop efficacy and agency. In the Marzano Academies model, *efficacy* is defined as a mindset grounded in the belief that with proper focus and effort, an individual can accomplish a great deal, even in areas in which the individual does not believe he or she has natural talent. Where efficacy involves beliefs, *agency* involves action (Marzano, Norford, Finn, & Finn, 2017). Students develop agency by explicit actions and decisions that have a direct and positive effect on their current circumstances.

Evidence	
4 **Sustaining** **(quick data)**	Quick data like the following are systematically collected and reviewed. • Focus-group data with students, parents, and teachers • Quick conversations with students, parents, and teachers • Regular reports on incidents of bullying, misbehavior, absenteeism, tardiness, and so on
3 **Applying** **(lagging)**	Performance goals with clear criteria for success like the following are in place. • 100 percent of all critical areas of the physical plant meet safety standards • 100 percent of students participate in 180 Connections and star student programs • 100 percent of teachers use specific classroom strategies that enhance students' sense of safety, order, and support • 90 percent of students respond positively that they perceive the school as safe, orderly, and supportive • 100 percent of teachers respond positively that they perceive the school as safe, orderly, and supportive • 70 percent of parents and guardians respond positively that they perceive the school as safe, orderly, and supportive
2 **Developing** **(leading)**	Concrete programs and practices, such as the following, are in place to develop a sense of safety, order, and support. • The physical plant is designed to maximize student safety and support • Communication devices are available and used by staff and teachers to ensure the safety and comfort of students • Safety procedures are in place and routinely practiced by staff and students • Teachers are trained in 180 Connections, star student programs, and play-based learning • Teachers are trained in specific strategies for their classrooms
1 **Beginning**	• The school has written plans for implementing programs for safety, order, and support but these have not been implemented • Individual teachers employ strategies to foster a sense of safety, order, and support, but there is not a schoolwide emphasis
0 **Not Using**	• The school has no written plans for implementing programs for safety, order, and support • There is no classroom implementation of strategies for safety, order, and support

Source: © 2020 by Marzano Academies, Inc. Adapted with permission.

FIGURE 1.3: Customized high reliability scale for school-level indicator 1.

Efficacy and agency are directly related to the top two levels of the hierarchy of needs and goals described in figure 1.1 (page 13), self-actualization and connection to something greater than self. When students engage in activities that make them feel self-actualized and connected to something greater than themselves, they are most probably thinking in ways that foster efficacy and acting in ways that promote agency. As described previously, agency refers to actions one takes with specific ends in mind. Self-actualization involves accomplishing goals one considers to be highly important to one's identity in life. The act of accomplishing a goal by definition involves direct action (that is, agency) regarding this goal. Similarly, connecting to a cause greater than oneself like the cessation of global warming by definition requires some type of direct action.

Simple yet revealing questions a principal can ask about his or her school to determine if it fosters student agency are, What role do students play in the teaching and learning process? What responsibilities do they have in the teaching and learning process? Are students active participants or passive recipients within the teaching and learning process? As the principal walks through the classrooms of school, he or she might look for concrete evidence that students have some control over the processes by which they learn and are assessed.

One can make the case that in most traditional classrooms, instruction is teacher-centered and most time is spent providing students with new information in a direct instruction format. Indeed, Robert J. Marzano and Michael D. Toth (2013) reported that based on thousands of classroom observations, they found that about 60 percent of classroom instruction is direct instruction. While direct instruction can be an effective tool, it is frequently executed in ways that impede rather than foster efficacy and agency.

The Marzano Academies model operates from the premise that when people are given some control over and responsibility for a process, they are more likely to care about its outcome. Students are no exception. When a learner is given power to make decisions about his or her learning, the level of personal ownership he or she feels toward his or her learning increases. Student voice and choice are the tools educators can use to develop student efficacy and agency. Voice and choice are closely connected; however, there are important distinctions. While *voice* is focused on creating opportunities for students to provide input into academic issues and cultural issues, *choice* is focused on providing students with concrete alternatives in terms of academic and cultural activities.

Voice

Academy teachers can and should provide students with opportunities to have a say in the learning environment. This can be accomplished in part by providing students with opportunities to give feedback to the teacher on both academic and cultural aspects of the classroom. For example, students can provide feedback on various academic issues including assessments, assignment types, and unit organization. Cultural issues are those that address the values of the students and the teachers and the behaviors that represent those values. For example, when a teacher asks students what they believe the class does well and what the class can improve on to ensure that students are made aware of and respect each other's cultures, that teacher provides students with an opportunity to affect the culture of the classroom. There are a number of tools that provide students with opportunities to exercise their voice regarding academic and cultural matters.

- **Affinity diagrams:** These diagrams help students collect ideas about academic or cultural issues and group them into categories. Once students group related pieces of feedback into categories, they prioritize and narrow the list. This narrowed list then becomes the basis for students to recommend changes in academic or cultural issues. For a detailed discussion of the specifics of affinity diagrams, see *A Handbook for Personalized Competency-Based Education* (Marzano, Norford, et al., 2017).

- **Digital platforms:** There are a variety of digital platforms (Padlet, Edmodo, and so on) available for teachers and students to gather and share ideas. Students can enter their comments regarding specific academic or cultural issues and the teacher can respond in kind. All of these interactions can be done asynchronously and anonymously, if so desired.

- **Parking lot:** The parking lot is a technique that allows students to pose questions or ask about issues that can't be addressed immediately in the classroom but that the teacher will get to as soon as he or she has time. The parking lot can be as simple as a piece of chart paper. The parking lot is typically divided into four categories that help teachers address both general and focused issues. The categories are (1) things that are going well (symbolized by a plus sign), (2) opportunities for improvement (symbolized by a delta or triangle symbol), (3) questions (symbolized by a question mark), and (4) ideas (symbolized by a lightbulb or lightning bolt).

- **Plus or delta:** With this activity, students record positive and negative input regarding what is currently going on in class. Students assign pluses to what is going well in the classroom and deltas to what needs improvement. For example, on a slip of paper with a plus sign, a student might record a message to the teacher regarding how clear the teacher's explanation was regarding an important generalization. Conversely, a student might record a message to the teacher on a piece of paper with a delta sign indicating that the student was confused by the teacher's explanation of something in class. As with the parking lot activity, students can provide feedback at any point and the teacher periodically addresses the plus comments and the delta comments.

- **Exit slips:** Exit slips are short activities that students must complete before they leave the classroom. In effect, submitting an exit slip is a student's "ticket" to leave the class. Exit slips are a chance for teachers to get individual feedback from all students on any topic. They can be used as a quick assessment of learning, a way to get input about the culture of the classroom, or a self-reflection on the day. Exit slips can be used to gather important data as unique issues arise. When exit slips are used for self-reflection, students are typically asked to respond to questions like, What is something you did well in class today and what is something you could have done better?

- **Interactive notebooks:** Interactive notebooks are personal notebooks for students to write in; teachers may also write in them by individual student invitation. Although interactive notebooks have a variety of uses, they are most commonly used as communication tools. For example, teachers might provide students with a prompt like, What suggestions do you have to help me make the classroom run more efficiently? After students have written their responses in their interactive notebooks, the teacher reads them and replies with comments in the notebooks when appropriate. When used well, interactive notebooks promote a healthy dialogue between students and teachers.

- **Brainstorming:** Brainstorming is a widely used tool for gathering input from students. Generally speaking, teachers gather input from a group (either verbally or in writing) in order to get as many ideas on a subject or topic as possible. However, teachers should always be sure to provide a safe environment for each student to contribute.

- **Class meetings:** Class meetings are a chance for groups of students to gather and discuss problems and issues on a regular basis. These meetings should have a routine schedule and a clear structure that promotes honest dialogue about current classroom issues. For example, class meetings might occur once every two weeks with the added provision that students can request extra class meetings, which the teacher can convene at his or her discretion. To ensure productive and respectful meetings, the class should set procedures for how to bring up issues, how to respond to the opinions of others, and so on.

Choice

Choice activities provide students with options for a variety of the actions and events that occur in the classroom. Choice is closely related to voice. Indeed, one might think of choice as a subset of voice. Voice activities are broad in nature in that they provide opportunities for students to express their thoughts and opinions on a wide variety of topics that are part of their classroom experiences. Choice activities involve options from which students must make a selection. As with voice, there are a number of tools that teachers can use to provide choice (Marzano, Norford, et al., 2017).

- **Power voting:** This tool can be used to provide choice in a variety of circumstances in the classroom. Virtually anytime students are making a choice as a group, power voting can be used. It can be employed to select snacks that will be available in class or the types of activities that will be used to demonstrate competence on a specific proficiency scale. There are many different formats of power voting, but the operating principle is that students have multiple votes to cast so that they may weight their input according to their preferences. For example, in an activity called Spend a Dollar, each student has four votes to spend, each worth $0.25. A student might choose to spend all four votes on one choice that is particularly important to him or her, or spread the votes out over several items that he or she finds acceptable.

- **Choice boards:** Choice boards can take the form of any game board that visualizes choices available to students. In effect, choice boards use games and the boards they are played on as the foundation but build academic choice into the game. For example, a teacher might use Monopoly to provide choice to students. As students land on different properties, they are presented with academic choices represented by the squares they land on. Teachers can customize boards to meet a variety of needs, such as homework options, standards or learning goals, and so on.

- **Choice menus:** Choice menus are a fun way to provide opportunities for student choice. Each course of the "meal" represents a different type of choice for students. For example, "appetizers" might present choices regarding introductory content or vocabulary words. "Main course" offerings might be related to the target content that students must master, while "dessert" items can offer extra activities or extensions to help students extend learning in order to achieve a higher level.

- **Preference surveys:** Teachers can easily gather information about students' interests and learning preferences through use of in-class or take-home surveys. These surveys can also provide group feedback on students' preferred styles of learning or assessment. After administering a preference survey, teachers can use the information it provides to structure the types of options that will be provided to students.

- **Digital platforms:** Students can utilize platforms such as TeacherTube, Safari Montage, or Khan Academy to access instruction or activities that pertain to the content they are learning. In this manner, students are able to choose which format and program works best for them.

- **Must-do and may-do lists:** Teachers give students a set of choices, all of which appear on one of two lists. A must-do list covers the expectations all students must meet; the may-do list offers a variety of choices for after students have accomplished the must-do list.

- **Task cards:** A task card lists a task or learning activity for students to complete that is associated with a specific learning target. A task card can simply provide short questions that require students to explain content they have learned or practice a skill or process. A teacher can provide a set of task cards for the set of learning targets that students are currently working on. Students use a task card when they finish another task early or when they have independent working time.

These are all activities that should be standard practice in a school using the Marzano Academies model. In addition, there is one other tool that we believe is one of the most powerful in developing students' efficacy and agency. This tool is the data notebook.

Data Notebooks

Data notebooks are a staple of academies at the elementary level. We will cite the utility of data notebooks directly and indirectly in our discussions of a number of school-level indicators. In effect, the Marzano Academies model is powered by data that are available to constituents all throughout the system. The most granular level of data is students' current performance and past performance on the learning targets at specific levels of specific proficiency scales. One of the most important consumers of these data is students themselves. Data notebooks are the foundational archive for this information. Although data notebooks are most often simple physical binders in which students store their work, their impact on learning comes from the process a well-designed notebook enlists, not its particular form.

When using data notebooks, students must clearly describe the learning targets they are working on in their own words, as well as determine the *success criteria*, or what they will need to do to demonstrate mastery of the learning targets. Students should also record results from a related preassessment that helps them identify their baseline performance and provides a point of reference for them to set specific learning goals. Students' data notebooks should also include action plans regarding specific learning targets. When used with fidelity, a data notebook ensures a high degree of student efficacy and agency by guaranteeing students are aware of learning targets, what success looks like, evidence of baseline performance, as well as personal goals and procedures for tracking individual progress.

One challenge a principal will encounter when implementing student data notebooks is ensuring that notebooks are used across every classroom with every student. When you first introduce the data notebook, some teachers might not believe it makes sense for their subject area, while others might worry the process of student goal setting will take up too much instructional time. A principal must be ready to address every concern of classroom educators and support teachers as they implement the practice, as well as monitor implementation throughout the year. This requires specific, purposeful actions.

First, the principal must clearly communicate the purpose of the data notebooks to the teaching faculty. By focusing on the process of student goal setting and the associated awareness of academic targets and proficiency scales, the conversation surrounding data notebooks becomes about empowering the learner, not about the notebook itself. It is important to keep in mind that the physical form the notebook takes isn't as important as the process it elicits.

Principals can also create data notebook templates for teachers to use. Templates reduce the amount of planning time teachers must engage in and also ensure uniformity across all classrooms. Data notebook templates might include the following sections.

- The learning target or targets a student is working on, as stated by the student
- The success criteria, as determined by the student
- The student's preassessment data
- The student's learning goal or goals for the unit of instruction
- The student's action plan for achieving the learning goals
- Benchmarks used for the student to track progress

- Identified vocabulary lists for the unit of instruction
- An achievement badge system for learning targets the student has mastered
- Local or state assessment results
- The student's career goals and academic curiosities
- Personal projects

The principal should monitor classroom notebook usage to ensure the efficacy and agency of every learner is being supported. For example, a principal can monitor progress toward data notebook implementation by incorporating spot checks while observing classrooms. Randomly selecting a data notebook to inspect while in a classroom is an easy way to discern its frequency of use. If there is evidence of a variety of types of data, tracking of student progress, and meaningful goals set for each unit of instruction, the principal can be sure that the student is utilizing the data notebook. On the other hand, if the last entry in a notebook was several weeks prior or template pages are blank, the principal knows he or she will need to follow up with that teacher to discuss effective notebook practices. Another way to gauge data notebook implementation is to ask students to describe what is in their notebooks. Evidence of use would include students clearly navigating the sections, discussing their goals, and explaining progress-monitoring data. When notebooks are being used well, any student in the classroom should be able to do this.

Finally, a principal can ask teachers to bring several example data notebooks to collaborative team meetings, data cycle meetings (see school-level indicator 9, page 83), or evaluation meetings to elicit conversations about the use of notebooks in their classrooms. Since data notebooks are stored in the classroom, teachers should always have access to any student's notebook. No matter how a principal ensures fidelity of implementation across his or her school, that principal must actively and repeatedly communicate the importance of the data notebooks, as well as monitor every classroom.

Focused Instructional Time

One indirect but far-reaching way to support student efficacy and agency across an entire elementary school is to implement a focused instructional time (FIT) block. FIT is a scheduled class period that teachers can employ from once per week to five times per week. In our discussion of school-level indicator 16, flexible scheduling (page 152), we discuss the use of FIT in depth and recommend it be implemented each day. Although this block can be used creatively for a variety of reasons, including tiered interventions such as response to intervention (RTI), it can also be used as a student-choice period where learners are given the freedom to explore topics of their choosing. Sometimes referred to as *what I need* (WIN) block or "genius hour," a student-choice FIT block allows for self-guided exploration and discovery within the confines of a structured classroom. Students can choose any topic, take on any project, or solve any problem that is important to them. The role of the teacher is to support these endeavors by providing guidance and resources for the student-generated goals.

High Reliability Leadership for School-Level Indicator 2

School-level indicator 2 deals with developing students' senses of efficacy and agency. While efficacy involves the cultivation of specific beliefs, agency involves specific actions. Providing students with activities involving voice and choice should occur on a daily basis. Additionally, involving students in keeping track of their own status and growth using data notebooks provides a fertile environment for developing efficacy and agency.

The previous discussion on school-level indicator 2 emphasizes the following elements regarding student efficacy and agency.

- Voice
- Choice
- Data notebooks
- Focused instructional time

Figure 1.4 lists some potential lagging indicators. Examining the list of potential lagging indicators, the school leader would select a subset that he or she considers as trim tab indicators to create a customized high reliability scale. This is depicted in figure 1.5.

Programs and Practices	Lagging Indicator Data	Potential Standard for High Reliability Status
Voice activities	The percentage of teachers employing specific classroom activities to elicit student voice	90 percent of teachers can provide explicit evidence of their classroom voice activities
Choice activities	The percentage of teachers employing specific classroom activities designed to elicit student choice	90 percent of teachers can provide explicit evidence of their classroom choice activities
Data notebooks	The percentage of students who use data notebooks effectively	90 percent of students regularly make entries in their data notebooks
FIT	The percentage of students who use FIT to work on topics of personal interest	90 percent of students actively engage in FIT to work on projects of personal interest
Perceptions of students, teachers, and parents	The percentage of students, teachers, and parents who perceive that the school promotes their efficacy and agency	90 percent of students respond positively that they perceive the school as developing their efficacy and agency 100 percent of teachers respond positively that they perceive the school as developing students' efficacy and agency 70 percent of parents and guardians respond positively that they perceive the school as developing students' efficacy and agency

Source: © 2021 by Robert J. Marzano.

FIGURE 1.4: Potential lagging indicators for school-level indicator 2.

School-Level Indicator 3: Inspiration

Inspiration is fairly easy to identify when one experiences it. For example, consider an individual reading a story about a woman who overcame poverty, started a multimillion-dollar company, and donated much of her wealth to benefit underprivileged communities. It is likely that the individual reading the story would be inspired. While it's easy to recognize inspiration when we experience

Evidence	
4 **Sustaining** **(quick data)**	Quick data like the following are systematically collected and reviewed. • Walk-through observational data • Quick conversations with teachers and students • Quick conversations with parents
3 **Applying** **(lagging)**	Performance goals with clear criteria for success like the following are in place. • 90 percent of teachers can provide explicit evidence of their classroom voice activities • 90 percent of teachers can provide explicit evidence of their classroom choice activities • 90 percent of students regularly make entries in their data notebooks • 90 percent of students actively engage in FIT to work on projects of personal interest • 90 percent of students respond positively that they perceive the school as developing their efficacy and agency
2 **Developing** **(leading)**	• Teachers have explicit strategies to enhance students' voice and choice • Students have data notebooks and protocols for using them • FIT is scheduled on a regular basis
1 **Beginning**	• The school has written plans for developing student efficacy and agency but there is no implementation of those plans • A few teachers execute their own strategies to develop student efficacy and agency but there is no schoolwide emphasis
0 **Not Using**	• The school has no written plans for developing student efficacy and agency • There is no implementation of efficacy and agency strategies at the classroom level

Source: © 2020 by Marzano Academies, Inc. Adapted with permission.

FIGURE 1.5: Customized high reliability scale for school-level indicator 2.

it, it is not so easy to define or explain it. Psychology scholars Todd M. Thrash, Andrew J. Elliot, Laura A. Maruskin, and Scott E. Cassidy (2010) noted that inspiration is central to many of the human experiences we refer to as profound:

> Many of the experiences that individuals find most fulfilling—peak experiences . . . creative insights . . . spiritual epiphanies . . . and emotions of awe and elevation . . . —cannot be controlled or directly acquired, because they involve the transcendence of one's current desires, values, or expectations. Indeed, life would likely seem bland if one's strivings were never interrupted and informed by such experiences. We propose that *inspiration* . . . is central to each of the above experiences. (p. 488)

Foundational to Thrash and colleagues' description of inspiration is the momentary experience of going beyond one's current circumstances. This is called transcendence. Marzano, Scott, and colleagues (2017) explain that transcendence involves gaining access to one's beliefs about the way one would like the world to be. These beliefs are referred to as *ideals*. Examples of commonly held ideals include the following.

- Hard work and dedication to a project are always rewarding.

- People are intrinsically good.

- If you are dedicated to something, others will come to your aid in times of need.

- Helping others who are in need is a basic human responsibility.

When a person encounters a situation that reminds that person of one or more of his or her ideals, and makes him or her believe they are actually true, that person transcends current circumstances and enjoys the thoughts of the potential future implied by those ideals. This is the moment of inspiration. For example, the story of the philanthropic entrepreneur might provide evidence to a specific person for the validity of her ideal that great wealth can be used to benefit others or that people can overcome negative circumstances that are out of their control.

There are a wide variety of ways to use ideals and stimulate inspiration in an elementary academy. The leader of an elementary academy should ensure that programs and practices specifically designed to inspire students are in place. Inspirational activities should not be occasional or sporadic events. Rather, they should be routine events that students expect and even count on in the academy model. A list of inspirational classroom strategies follows.

Clips From Movies

Movies can be inspirational for both teachers and students. When using clips from movies, teachers should first explain the relevant background information in an age-appropriate manner. For example, a teacher who has decided to show the film *Hidden Figures* in class might begin the discussion by providing a brief review of the American political environment in the 1950s and 1960s. The teacher might describe and explain events surrounding the desegregation of schools beginning in Little Rock in 1957. He or she might emphasize how challenging it was for African Americans during that time to receive the upper-level education the characters in *Hidden Figures* needed to have. Students might be surprised and interested to learn that women have a long history of working for the government in crucial roles requiring deep knowledge of STEM subjects.

After providing students with relevant context, teachers can then provide a purpose for viewing by discussing the nature and function of ideals raised by the film. While watching parts of the movie, students might be asked to write down the ideals they believe the film delivers. For example, students might determine that the movie provides evidence for ideals like the following.

- Any person can achieve any goal he or she sets through hard work and perseverance.

- The ability to work as a part of a team can be life changing.

- Setting an example by doing what is right can change history and create positive results.

After students have articulated the ideals they feel the film exemplifies, the teacher might ask students to relate the ideals they have identified to their personal lives. Questions such as the following might be suitable.

- Have you ever encountered examples of this ideal at work in your own life? When you saw that this ideal could be true, how did it make you feel?

- Can you describe an instance in your life where you felt like the movie's ideals were lacking?

Discussion around the ideals exemplified by movies can provide students with insights about what they value and what inspires them. Such conversations do not have to result in any concrete actions. The conversations and the insights they provide are sufficient.

The following is a list of movies commonly used to inspire students.

- *Akeelah and the Bee*
- *Babe*
- *Beasts of the Southern Wild*
- *The Diving Bell and the Butterfly*
- *Hidden Figures*
- *Life Is Beautiful*

- *Life of Pi*
- *Miracle*
- *The Pursuit of Happyness*
- *Rudy*
- *Slumdog Millionaire*

Stories and Anecdotes

Stories and anecdotes can be flexible sources of inspiration. There are many stories and anecdotes appropriate for inspiration that are readily available to teachers both online and in print. For example, a teacher working with upper elementary and middle school students might choose the myths described in the *Percy Jackson and the Olympians* fantasy series by Rick Riordan as a source of student inspiration. After reading these books, students might be asked to consider some of the events in these stories in terms of the ideals they portray. They might also be asked to compare these ideals with their own.

Teachers might also use nonfiction stories as inspirational sources. For example, a teacher might ask students to read *I Am Malala* by Malala Yousafzai and Patricia McCormick (2016) or read parts of the book to them. Each student would articulate the ideals he or she finds exemplified in Malala's story. The teacher would ask students to identify passages that support the ideal they find to be inspiring. The following is a list of individuals whose personal stories might be considered inspirational.

- Temple Grandin
- Nancy Herz
- Chloe Kim
- Liz Murray
- Randy Pausch

- J. K. Rowling
- Sean Swarner
- Desmond Tutu
- Oprah Winfrey
- Liu Xiaobo

Quotations

Because quotations are generally brief, teachers can incorporate them into lessons in a variety of ways. For example, teachers might simply read or display a quotation at the beginning of class and let students ponder its meaning or the ideal it exemplifies without any discussion. Conversely, teachers might accompany the quote with information about the person to whom it is attributed. Students can also use quotations to consider inspirational themes a teacher may have chosen, such as perseverance, independence, or overcoming obstacles.

Teachers can also engage students in whole-class discussions about the implicit ideals they see in quotations. For example, consider the following quote:

"Follow your inner moonlight; don't hide the madness."
—Allen Ginsberg (Strickland, 1992, p. 47)

While this quote seems simple, students might extract very different ideals from it. For example, one student might say the ideal it exemplifies is that everyone is a little quirky and no one should feel badly about that or ashamed to express their quirkiness. Another student might be curious enough to look up the context of the quotation. He or she might find the interview in which the quote appears, and, after reading the entire interview, the student might determine that the ideal at the center of the quote focuses on the importance of speaking up if one feels injustice is occurring. A rich discussion of ideals might follow.

School leaders can also employ quotations in a schoolwide context quite easily. For example, a powerful practice is to begin each day with a quotation that is broadcast to all students, preferably by another student. Along with reading the quotation, the student might also identify the ideal he or she believes it exemplifies.

Altruistic Class Projects

At the elementary level, it is common for teachers to foster inspiration by engaging students in altruistic class projects. Altruistic projects are activities that are designed to improve life for another individual or group. A critical aspect of altruistic activities is that they are done solely for the benefit of others. These projects have at least two purposes. One is to help other people in some way. The second is to provide students with an opportunity to experience inspiration firsthand. To illustrate, the following is a description of an altruistic project first-grade teacher Katie Fox provided for her students.

TEACHER KATIE FOX'S ALTRUISTIC CLASS PROJECT

Altruistic projects are, without a doubt, one of my favorite things about being a part of the Marzano Academy. I love that they give students the opportunity to think beyond themselves, and about the world around them. They allow students a chance to see what they want to change in our current world and to plan action steps they can actually attempt in order to change it. With my class, I had many talks about what an altruistic project really is. We talked as a large group and in small groups about issues surrounding students and their community.

I was not at all surprised in what my students saw first as something they wanted to change. Being that Rachel's Challenge is such a focus for us as a school and classroom community, the resounding issue they identified was that people in the world just are not as kind as they could be. They offered up suggestions about just telling people to be kind and sticking up for others, but we finally settled on a project they were thrilled about doing: making kindness bracelets to sell for another cause. They really took on the initiative and it was amazing to be able to step back as the teacher and just let my students take the lead. It was one of the most memorable and rewarding experiences for me as an educator.

So what was the plan? My students went out and bought their own supplies: ribbons, string, beads, and so on. They created posters to promote the idea and posted them around the school. They also teamed up and wrote mini broadcasts that they made over the announcements to tell fellow students in the school about their plan and how they hoped they would buy bracelets. They decided that each bracelet should be sold for $2.00 and handed out order forms to each classroom. Before going into the process of making them, the students brainstormed what they wanted the money to support. We finally settled on donating the funds to the Humane Society of Boulder Valley, as my students all really had a love for and appreciation of animals. I called to make sure a donation would work and we were full steam ahead! Students worked on bracelet designs—containing words like *kindness, love, smile, be kind, be the difference,* and so on. When orders started rolling in, the students even took personal requests for favorite colors or design patterns, so that people would be more excited to wear their bracelets proudly.

Students requested to work during their independent time and recess time, and probably would have stayed after school had I let them. We ended up raising over $150, which was donated to the care of animals at the shelter. It was successful on so many levels for the students and for me as a teacher. The students spread kindness to others, they worked together to create something that started as one small idea, they were proud of themselves, and they still talk about it to this day! I remember them saying how fun it was and how they hoped a kindness bracelet would instill kindness in others. Ultimately, they were even more excited to see how their idea helped to support animals in need. If I could do this all over again, I would—it was a great first altruistic project (K. Fox, personal communication, April 2, 2021).

Teachers and students can follow up projects like these with discussion about the ideals that the projects might exemplify.

For all the inspirational activities we've described thus far, leaders should emphasize the importance of having discussions with students about ideals. However, it is important to keep in mind that these represent high-level beliefs students are developing—some, if not many, of which are directly influenced by their homes and culture. Teachers should not challenge these beliefs, particularly at the elementary grade levels. As students mature, they will naturally engage in discussions with their peers about the similarities and differences in their ideals.

Growth Mindset Thinking

Growth mindset thinking is one of the ten metacognitive skills that are part of the Marzano Academies model. We address these skills in depth in the discussion of school-level indicator 10, cognitive and metacognitive skills (page 91). However, the metacognitive skill of a growth mindset is also relevant to inspiration.

Popularized by psychologist Carol Dweck (2006), *growth mindset* thinking is a pattern of thinking based on the assumption that effort is more important than talent when it comes to accomplishing complex goals. This perspective is in sharp contrast to *fixed mindset* thinking, which is based on the assumption that natural abilities are the prime determiners of success in accomplishing complex goals. Although Dweck popularized this notion, it has deep roots that go back many decades (for a deeper discussion, see Marzano, Scott, et al., 2017). Some of the most well-articulated and educationally useful growth mindset strategies were designed by psychologist and educator Martin Seligman (2006). While it is not commonly acknowledged, Seligman's contribution to contemporary practices in growth mindset thinking was substantial.

The details of a growth mindset are complex and sophisticated concepts but teachers can present them to students in abbreviated forms even at the primary level. For example, a teacher might talk to students about the "power of yet." By encouraging students to insert the word *yet* after any negative statement about their ability, the teacher plants the seeds of a growth mindset. For example, if a student says, "I'm not good at math," his or her teacher can respond by saying, "No, you're not good at math *yet*."

A principal can build the power of yet into the ethos of the school by ensuring every teacher explicitly discusses this mindset with his or her students. Another useful activity is for a principal to create a school slogan that highlights the power of yet, and then include it in the daily announcements, in school newsletters, and at parent nights. Students are more likely to believe in the power of yet if teachers, building aides, paraprofessionals, and even parents are repeating this mantra. For a school to comprehensively embrace the development of a growth mindset, it should incorporate that mindset formally into the curriculum. The use of a specific proficiency scale centered on a growth mindset accomplishes just that.

We address the nature and function of proficiency scales for academic content in depth in our discussion of school-level indicator 9 (page 83). Here, we consider proficiency scales only in the context of the growth mindset. Like any proficiency scale, a growth mindset scale includes a progression of score 0.0 through 4.0 learning targets, key vocabulary terms, success criteria, and helpful resources. Figure 1.6 and figure 1.7 depict growth mindset proficiency scales for grades K–2 and 3–5 respectively.

4.0	The student will:
	• Provide a rudimentary description of what it looks like when someone develops a growth mindset

3.5	In addition to score 3.0 performance, partial success at score 4.0 content

3.0	The student will:
	GMT1—When asked by the teacher, accurately recognize when he or she is or is not operating from a positive mindset (for example, the teacher asks, "Are you thinking positively about what you can accomplish in this upcoming task?" and the student correctly evaluates him- or herself)

2.5	No major errors or omissions regarding score 2.0 content, and partial success at score 3.0 content

2.0	GMT1—The student will recognize or recall basic vocabulary associated with growth mindset thinking (for example, *fixed mindset, growth mindset, learning from mistakes, trying*) and perform basic processes such as:
	• Understand that a growth mindset is a positive way to think about what you can accomplish (for example, that you can learn to do almost anything if you are willing to work hard)
	• Recognize situations in which growth mindset thinking might be useful (for example, when you are learning a new skill, when you have a goal that is not easy for you to accomplish)

1.5	Partial success at score 2.0 content, and major errors or omissions regarding score 3.0 content

1.0	With help, partial success at score 2.0 content and score 3.0 content

0.5	With help, partial success at score 2.0 content but not at score 3.0 content

0.0	Even with help, no success

Source: © 2017 by Marzano Resources. Used with permission.

FIGURE 1.6: Growth mindset proficiency scale for grades K–2.

Both of these growth mindset scales follow the same format as the proficiency scales for academic content. The 3.0 level represents what is considered proficiency. At the K–2 level, the expectation is that when cued by the teacher, students recognize if they are currently operating from a growth mindset perspective. At the 3–5 level, the expectation at the 3.0 level is that when cued by the teacher, students can execute a specific process that stimulates growth mindset thinking. The 2.0 level of both scales represents the content that teachers should directly present to students so that they can achieve 3.0 status. For example, in the 3–5 scale, students must understand more advanced vocabulary such as *ability, developed, effort, failure, innate, intelligence.* At the 2.0 level, students should also be able to recognize common mistakes or pitfalls associated with growth mindset thinking (for example, having a growth mindset in one area but a fixed mindset in others, or starting out with a positive attitude but getting discouraged easily).

Growth mindset thinking is one of the metacognitive skills that are a regular part of the Marzano Academies curriculum (see school-level indicator 10, page 91). In this capacity, individual teachers

4.0	The student will: • When cued by the teacher, explain how well he or she operated from a positive mindset
3.5	In addition to score 3.0 performance, partial success at score 4.0 content
3.0	The student will: GMT1—When cued by the teacher, execute a simple teacher-provided strategy for growth mindset thinking (for example, [1] notice how you are thinking about your ability to accomplish the upcoming task, [2] try to change any negative thoughts to positive thoughts [for example, change "I can't do this" to "I can accomplish some good things, if I try"; change "This is going to be boring" to "I can make this fun"; change "This is useless" to "I can learn something valuable from this"], [3] promise yourself that you are going to try your best and not let yourself get discouraged)
2.5	No major errors or omissions regarding score 2.0 content, and partial success at score 3.0 content
2.0	GMT1—The student will recognize or recall advanced vocabulary associated with growth mindset thinking (for example, *ability, developed, effort, failure, innate, intelligence*) and perform basic processes such as: • When asked by the teacher, accurately recognize when he or she is operating from a positive mindset (for example, when asked "Are you thinking positively or negatively about your ability to do this?") • Recognize common mistakes or pitfalls associated with growth mindset thinking (for example, having a growth mindset in one area but a fixed mindset in others; starting out with a positive attitude but getting discouraged easily)
1.5	Partial success at score 2.0 content, and major errors or omissions regarding score 3.0 content
1.0	With help, partial success at score 2.0 content and score 3.0 content
0.5	With help, partial success at score 2.0 content but not at score 3.0 content
0.0	Even with help, no success

Source: © 2017 by Marzano Resources. Used with permission.

FIGURE 1.7: Growth mindset proficiency scale for grades 3–5.

instruct and reinforce this mindset. However, within the context of school-level indicator 3, it is a corollary to inspiration. When school leaders provide activities that inspire students, they can also reference specific aspects of growth mindset thinking (articulated in the proficiency scales) as important skills to develop that will help students manifest what inspires them. In effect, growth mindset thinking becomes a schoolwide emphasis with students, teachers, administrators, and staff working on specific skills for their personal development.

High Reliability Leadership for School-Level Indicator 3

Student inspiration is an often-discussed goal in many elementary schools but is commonly ill-defined and lacking concrete strategies. School-level indicator 3 not only defines inspiration for educators but also provides concrete actions teachers can take that include stories, quotes, and the like. Equally important to inspiring student is fostering their abilities to think in ways that make inspiration operational.

The previous discussion on school-level indicator 3 emphasizes the following elements regarding inspiration.

- Clips from movies
- Stories and anecdotes
- Quotations
- Altruistic class projects
- Growth mindset thinking

Figure 1.8 depicts some potential lagging indicators for each school-level indicator of inspiration. From this list, the leader would select trim tab indicators to create a customized high reliability scale. This is depicted in figure 1.9.

Programs and Practices	Lagging Indicator Data	Potential Standard for High Reliability Status
Movies	The percentage of teachers using movies	60 percent of teachers use inspirational movie clips
Stories	The percentage of teachers using stories	60 percent of teachers use inspirational stories
Quotations	The percentage of teachers using inspirational quotations	60 percent of teachers use inspirational quotes
Growth mindset thinking	The percentage of teachers directly teaching growth mindset	90 percent of teachers directly teach growth mindset
Perceptions of students, teachers, and parents	The percentage of students, teachers, and parents who perceive the school as fostering inspiration	90 percent of students believe the school fosters inspiration 90 percent of teachers believe the school fosters inspiration 70 percent of parents perceive the school fosters inspiration

Source: © 2021 by Robert J. Marzano.

FIGURE 1.8: Potential lagging indicators for school-level indicator 3.

Figure 1.9 depicts a useful convention for establishing lagging indicators—namely the use of *or* connectors for criteria. Specifically, the first criterion statement at the 3.0 level states that 100 percent of teachers will use inspirational movie clips *or* stories *or* quotations. This convention allows for flexibility on the design of lagging indicators for the various school-level indicators.

School-Level Indicator 4: Personal Projects

Personal projects create opportunities for every learner to complete a project focused on his or her personal interests and desires. They are one of the signature activities in the Marzano Academies model because they provide students with maximum latitude in the selection of the focus of their projects.

Evidence	
4 **Sustaining** **(quick data)**	Quick data like the following are systematically collected and reviewed. • Classroom walkthrough data • Focus-group data with students and parents • Quick conversations with students and parents
3 **Applying** **(lagging)**	Performance goals with clear criteria for success like the following are in place. • 100 percent of teachers use inspirational movie clips or stories or quotations • 90 percent of teachers directly teach growth mindset • 90 percent of students report that they like the inspirational events and activities • 80 percent of students report that the school in general gives them a more positive attitude about their lives
2 **Developing** **(leading)**	• The school implements schoolwide events and activities designed to inspire students • Individual teachers systematically implement brief activities designed to inspire students
1 **Beginning**	• The school has written plans for inspirational events and activities but there is little implementation • A few teachers independently employ inspirational activities and events but there is no schoolwide emphasis
0 **Not Using**	• The school has no written plans for the implementation of inspirational events and activities • There is no implementation of inspirational events and activities at the classroom level

Source: © 2020 by Marzano Academies, Inc. Adapted with permission.

FIGURE 1.9: Customized high reliability scale for school-level indicator 3.

Since one of the tacit goals of the academy model is to develop students' understanding of themselves and allow them to explore various interests, personal projects are the most flexible means to this end.

A common misconception about personal projects is that they are simply project-based learning activities by another name. Although there are similarities between project-based learning activities and personal projects, there are significant differences. Project-based learning can be entirely designed by the classroom teacher with little to no input from students. Even though personal projects are facilitated and guided by teachers, their focus is on student design and implementation, and when tied to solving a community problem, can allow students to not only experience self-actualization, but also transcendence. The following sections describe personal projects and several related topics.

The Process for Personal Projects

The academy model for personal projects involves seven phases.

Phase I: Identifying a personal goal to pursue

Phase II: Eliciting support

Phase III: Gathering information about the goal

Phase IV: Discerning discrepancies between current and future self

Phase V: Creating a plan

Phase VI: Moving into action

Phase VII: Evaluating the effectiveness of your actions

The specifics of these phases, including a total of twenty subcomponents, are described in more detail in the book *Motivating and Inspiring Students* (Marzano, Scott, et al., 2017). Briefly, though, the working dynamic of a personal project is that each year, each student selects a project to work on and progresses through these seven phases. A student might select a different topic each year. For example, one year a fourth-grade student might select the goal of learning how to swim. The next year, that same student as a fifth grader might select the goal of getting better at chess. Alternatively, a student might select a long-term goal that represents a dream he or she has about him- or herself in the future. For example, a student might select the long-term goal of visiting specific countries by the time he or she is twenty-one. Another student might set the long-term goal of a military career, and so on. While personal projects are a systematic part of the curriculum, much of the actual work on those projects is conducted outside of school due to the nature of the goals.

Each of the seven phases is designed to teach students something about their goal and about themselves. Phase I (identifying a personal goal) teaches students about the specifics of goal setting and how to articulate goals. To illustrate, consider the example of a fifth grader named Jacob. One of the activities in the first phase of the personal-project process is to respond to the prompt "What would you do if you knew you wouldn't fail?" Jacob's response is to declare that he would like to be a professional soccer player someday. A teacher then provides him with guidance about setting an effective long-term goal. In Jacob's case, such guidance might be, "Your goal should involve a concrete outcome, it should have specific timelines, and it should have concrete components."

Phase II (eliciting support) helps Jacob realize he will need support to accomplish such a lofty goal, and that it can come from a variety of sources. As part of this phase, Jacob identifies people he will ask to support him. He selects his father, who is a professional tennis player, as his coach regarding how to develop professional-level skills. He selects his mother as his coach regarding how to live a disciplined yet balanced life. If students don't know anyone with domain-specific knowledge related to their goal, it is perfectly legitimate for them to select someone who will simply encourage them as they move through their projects.

Phase III (gathering information about the goal) helps Jacob understand key steps along the path to playing professional soccer, including playing on club teams and attending specific types of camps. In the modern information-rich environment, it is easy for students to begin their search for information on the internet and then add resources as needed. The goal in this phase is simply for students to increase their knowledge about what might be involved in accomplishing their goals.

Phase IV (discerning discrepancies between current and future self) has Jacob compare skills and knowledge he has now with those he will need to fully realize his goal. During this phase, Jacob sees that there are some habits he will have to acquire and some current habits he will have to get rid of. For example, he sees that he will have to get up much earlier than he typically does to find the time to engage in certain training routines. He also realizes that he should stop being so critical of himself when he has a bad game.

During phase V (creating a plan), Jacob writes a detailed plan that gets him from where he is now to where he wants to be in the future. He does this by starting with his current point in life. He identifies things he should be doing right now in elementary school, which include a specific workout routine. Next, he thinks of things that he should do when he is in middle school, such as joining a specific club team. He continues with plans for high school, college, and so on, all the way up to making a professional soccer team.

Phase VI (moving into action) has Jacob identify those things he can do right now that might be small steps to his ultimate goal. He initiates a specific exercise routine and he studies the habits of his role model, the great Brazilian soccer star Neymar da Silva Santos.

Finally, during phase VII (evaluating the effectiveness of your actions), Jacob continually assesses how well he is doing, identifying and celebrating those things that are going well and those things he can improve on. To do this, he considers his plan developed during phase V. He examines whether he is actually doing what his plan specifies and how much effort he is putting into these actions.

The Logistics of Personal Projects

Personal projects can extend over the entire year or for half of the year. Many leaders select a half-year approach because it is easier to keep students engaged for a half-year activity than it is for a full-year activity. Assuming that a school has a thirty-six-week calendar, eighteen of those weeks represents one-half of the year. The seven phases of the process involve twenty specific components or activities. This roughly amounts to a little more than one component per week, although some components will take more time than others. Consequently, a teacher might address two or more components in a single week, and then provide two weeks for students to work on those components.

Homeroom periods (or their equivalents) are probably the best venue in which to house personal projects. In that way, students will have the same teacher throughout the duration of their projects. It is highly recommended that teachers engage in their own personal projects during this time and progress through the phases with the students. Teachers should complete the various components with their students and share their accomplishments and what they have learned about themselves along with students. For example, a teacher might set the goal of running a marathon during the summer and use the phases of the personal project model to plan and prepare for this endeavor.

The old adage of "practice makes perfect" is true, and the seven phases to the personal projects are no exception. A school using the Marzano Academies model must guarantee that every student will work on a personal project every year. When implementing personal projects as a schoolwide program, uniformity across all classrooms and grade levels in relation to the process of completing the personal project becomes important. When students embark on the same seven-phase process each year, they will begin to internalize the skills, as well as deepen their abilities in each phase.

Metacognitive Skills

The seven phases of personal projects are excellent vehicles to teach and reinforce virtually any of the metacognitive skills. Again, we address metacognitive skills in depth in the discussion of school-level indicator 10 (page 91). The metacognitive skills in the academy model are as follows.

1. Staying focused when answers and solutions are not immediately apparent

2. Pushing the limits of one's knowledge and skills

3. Generating and pursuing one's own standards for performance

4. Seeking incremental steps

5. Seeking accuracy

6. Seeking clarity

7. Resisting impulsivity

8. Seeking cohesion and coherence

9. Setting goals and making plans

10. Growth mindset

When executed well, personal projects inherently help students utilize many of these skills. For example, students are asked to push the limits of their knowledge and skills and set their own standards for excellence as they create possible futures for themselves. They must seek accuracy and clarity as they research the requirements of their goals, and so on.

In addition to relying on the inherent reinforcement of the metacognitive skills, teachers can use personal projects to directly teach and reinforce selected skills. For example, a teacher might select one or two specific metacognitive skills he or she wants students to demonstrate as they engage in their personal projects. Assume a fourth-grade teacher selects the skill of staying focused when answers and solutions are not immediately apparent. The teacher would introduce this skill to students using the appropriate proficiency scale, as depicted in figure 1.10. Some academy schools like to translate these scales into student-friendly "I can" versions that give students a first-person tool to periodically assess their own progress. Figure 1.11 (page 46) depicts such a scale. Teachers would take time to explicitly explain and exemplify the knowledge and skills stated at the score 2.0, 3.0, and 4.0 levels.

Most if not all of these metacognitive skills can be taught, reinforced, and practiced within the context of personal projects. Individual teachers might select specific metacognitive skills they will emphasize during personal projects. Conversely, leaders might assign specific metacognitive skills for certain grade levels or teams to emphasize during personal projects to ensure that as many of these skills as possible are used in some fashion within the context of personal projects.

The Accomplishment Fair

We encourage academy leaders to hold some type of accomplishment fair where students can showcase their personal projects. These might be modeled after the traditional science fair, in which students develop exhibits to share the designs and results of their science projects. Accomplishment fairs would follow the same format but focus on students' personal goals. Exhibits in this type of fair would display information and artifacts related to each student's personal project. For example, Jacob's exhibit might include his specific exercise routines and pictures of him practicing specific skills. It also might contain pictures of and information about the professional team he hopes to be on someday. During the fair Jacob would stand next to his exhibit and describe his project to individuals or small groups as they pass by.

If possible, all students from the school, along with their families and friends, should be invited to participate in these celebrations. Accomplishment fairs might be held after school. Schools with a larger student population might hold separate fairs for each grade level. On a Monday night, for example, the fair would be for first-grade students, on Tuesday night the fair would be for second-grade students, and so on. Teachers and school leaders should develop the plans and protocols for the various aspects and different nights of the fair with input and help from students.

High Reliability Leadership for School-Level Indicator 4

Personal projects have many functions within the Marzano Academies model. They provide students the opportunity to work on goals of their own choosing and explore interests about which they are passionate. At the same time, personal projects provide a vehicle for students to learn about and practice metacognitive skills. Students work on many aspects of these projects outside of school,

4.0	The student will: • When cued by the teacher, explain how well he or she stayed focused when answers or solutions were not immediately apparent
3.5	In addition to score 3.0 performance, partial success at score 4.0 content
3.0	The student will: SF1—When cued by the teacher, execute a simple teacher-provided strategy for staying focused when answers or solutions are not immediately apparent (for example, [1] remind yourself of what you are trying to accomplish, [2] try to state what it is you can't find or solve, [3] give it at least one more try)
2.5	No major errors or omissions regarding score 2.0 content, and partial success at score 3.0 content
2.0	SF1—The student will recognize or recall advanced vocabulary associated with staying focused when answers and solutions are not immediately apparent (for example, *alternatives, ambiguity, obstacle, perseverance, persistence, problem solving, re-engage*) and perform basic processes such as: • When asked by the teacher, accurately recognize when he or she is staying focused when answers or solutions are not immediately apparent (for example, stating that he or she got the wrong answer but tried again) • Recognize common mistakes or pitfalls associated with staying focused when answers or solutions are not immediately apparent (for example, trying the same ineffective approach repeatedly instead of trying a new solution)
1.5	Partial success at score 2.0 content, and major errors or omissions regarding score 3.0 content
1.0	With help, partial success at score 2.0 content and score 3.0 content
0.5	With help, partial success at score 2.0 content but not at score 3.0 content
0.0	Even with help, no success

Source: © 2017 by Marzano Resources. Used with permission.

FIGURE 1.10: Proficiency scale for staying focused when answers and solutions are not immediately apparent for grades 3–5.

but they receive guidance and support in school on a systematic basis. At the end of the year, families of students and interested community members have opportunities to hear about and observe what students have learned and what they have accomplished.

The previous discussion of school-level indicator 4 emphasizes the following aspects of personal projects.

- The process for personal projects
- The logistics of personal projects
- Metacognitive skills
- The accomplishment fair

Figure 1.12 (page 46) depicts the potential lagging indicators for personal projects. Figure 1.13 (page 47) depicts a customized high reliability scale for personal projects in which the school leader has used some, but not all, of the possible lagging indicators identified in figure 1.12.

4.0	When the teacher reminds me, I can explain how well I have stayed focused when answers and solutions were not immediately apparent.
3.0	When the teacher asks, I can use the following process.
	I remind myself of what I am trying to accomplish.
	I try to state what it is that I can't find or solve.
	I tell myself to try at least one more time.
2.0	I understand the following vocabulary terms: *alternatives, ambiguity, obstacle, perseverance, persistence, problem solving,* and *re-engage.*
	When my teacher asks me, I can recognize when I am staying focused when answers and solutions are not immediately apparent.
	I can recognize common mistakes people make when they are trying to stay focused when answers and solutions are not immediately apparent, like trying the same ineffective approach repeatedly instead of trying a new solution.
1.0	With help, I can do some of the things at score 2.0 level and 3.0.
0.0	Even with help, I can't do any of this.

Source: © 2017 by Marzano Resources. Adapted with permission.

FIGURE 1.11: Student-friendly version of proficiency scale for staying focused when answers and solutions are not immediately apparent for grades 3–5.

Programs and Practices	Lagging Indicator Data	Potential Standard for High Reliability Status
Personal project process	The extent to which the personal project process is followed	90 percent of students complete the personal project process
Logistics	Personal projects have concrete written protocols for their logistics	90 percent of teachers follow the written protocols for personal projects
Metacognitive skills	Specific metacognitive skills embedded in personal projects	90 percent of teachers embed specific metacognitive skills in personal projects
Accomplishment fairs	The accomplishment fair is a formal part of the school schedule	100 percent of students who have completed projects have the opportunity to present their accomplishments in an accomplishment fair
Perceptions of students, teachers, and parents	Surveys to students, teachers, and parents	90 percent of students say they enjoy and value their personal projects
		80 percent of teachers say they see positive effects from personal projects
		70 percent of parents say they value and respect the personal projects

Source: © 2021 by Robert J. Marzano.

FIGURE 1.12: Potential lagging indicators for school-level indicator 4.

Evidence	
4 **Sustaining** **(quick data)**	Quick data like the following are systematically collected and reviewed. • Quick conversations with students, teachers, and parents • Artifacts from personal projects
3 **Applying** **(lagging)**	Performance goals with clear criteria for success like the following are in place. • 90 percent of students complete the personal project process • 90 percent of teachers embed specific metacognitive skills in personal projects • 100 percent of students who have completed projects have the opportunity to present their accomplishments in an accomplishment fair • 90 percent of teachers follow the written protocols for personal projects • 90 percent of students say they enjoy and value their personal projects
2 **Developing** **(leading)**	• Personal projects are in place that provide students opportunities to work on projects of their own design that allow demonstration of multiple types of skills • Personal projects have well-defined phases • Teachers identify metacognitive skills to be used in personal projects • The school designs and schedules accomplishment fairs
1 **Beginning**	• The school has written plans for the use of personal projects but there is no implementation at the school level • Some teachers implement their own versions of personal projects but there is no schoolwide approach
0 **Not Using**	• The school has no written plans for the use of personal projects • There is no implementation of personal projects at the classroom level

Source: © 2020 by Marzano Academies, Inc. Adapted with permission.

FIGURE 1.13: Customized high reliability scale for school-level indicator 4.

Summary

This chapter addressed four school-level indicators of the academy model that help create an effective psychological, social, and emotional context for learning. Those indicators are:

School-level indicator 1: Safe, orderly, and supportive environment

School-level indicator 2: Student efficacy and agency

School-level indicator 3: Inspiration

School-level indicator 4: Personal projects

These indicators work together to create a context that not only aids students' academic learning but also stimulates introspection and personal growth in nonacademic areas. Student efficacy and agency might be considered the fulcrum for such endeavors since they deal with beliefs and actions that propel personal growth. The chapter also described how a school leader would approach these indicators from a high reliability perspective. When considered as a set, these four indicators address all six levels of the hierarchy of needs and goals.

CHAPTER 2

Indicators That Address Competency-Based Instruction

Instruction within the Marzano Academies model involves many facets that one might call best practice in traditional classrooms, but it also involves many aspects that are specific to competency-based systems. At its most basic level, a competency-based system is one in which students must demonstrate mastery of the content at one level before they move on to the next level. For example, students would have to demonstrate that they have learned the content for fourth-grade mathematics before they move on to fifth-grade mathematics. Another important aspect of competency-based education is that students can begin working on content at the next level as soon as they have mastered the content at the preceding level. For example, as soon as students have mastered the fourth-grade content, they can begin working on the fifth-grade content, regardless of their chronological age.

It is important to note that there are many terms educators use to describe this type of education, including *personalized competency-based education, standards-based education, standards-based learning,* and *mastery learning* to name a few. It is also important to note that these terms are not used in a uniform manner. For example, sometimes educators refer to the systems they use as *standards-based* but do not require students to master all the content at one level before moving up to the next. Rather, those systems simply report how students perform relative to the standards at each level using a scale like *below standard, meets standard,* and *exceeds standard.* This type of system is more properly referred to as *standards-referenced* since students' status is reported in *reference* to specific standards but students are not required to master all standards at one level before moving up to the next level.

There are four school-level indicators that deal directly with effective instruction in the academy's competency-based model. The first deals with an explicit model of instruction intended to be used for teacher development and evaluation. The other three deal with specific emphases of competency-based instruction: blended instruction, cumulative review, and knowledge maps. Each of these school-level indicators is designed specifically to maximize the impact of competency-based instruction.

School-Level Indicator 5: Instruction and Teacher Development

The leader of an elementary academy should ensure that the school has an instructional model focused on competency-based education and uses it to provide feedback to teachers regarding their status and growth on specific pedagogical skills. A school's instructional model should not be tacit or simply a general set of principles that are informally referenced within the culture of the school. Rather, a school's instructional model should be written in a detailed document and formally adopted by the school, creating a common language for educators to reference during self-assessment, professional development, goal setting, observations, and feedback. Many of our suggestions relative to this school-level indicator are explained further in the book *Improving Teacher Development and Evaluation* (Marzano, Rains, & Warrick, 2021).

Four Domains
Ten Design Areas
Forty-Nine Elements
Over Three Hundred Specific Strategies

Source: Adapted from Marzano et al., 2021.

FIGURE 2.1: Complete academy model of instruction.

Feedback

    I. Proficiency scales

    II. Assessment

Content

    III. Proficiency scale instruction

    IV. General instruction

Context

    V. Grouping and regrouping

    VI. Engagement

    VII. Comfort, safety, and order

Self-Regulation

    VIII. Belonging and esteem

    IX. Efficacy and agency

    X. Metacognitive and life skills

Source: © 2021 by Marzano Academies, Inc.
Used with permission.

FIGURE 2.2: The Marzano Academies model of instruction.

An Explicit Model of Instruction for CBE

Our preferred model of instruction is based on research and theory that spans decades (Marzano, 1992, 2007, 2017; Marzano et al., 1988, 2021; Marzano, Pickering, & Pollock, 2001). The Marzano Academies model specifically adapts the instructional elements in these previous works for competency-based education. At a very general level, the Marzano Academies instructional model has four tiers. This is depicted in figure 2.1. At the highest level, the model is comprised of four domains. Those four domains have ten embedded design areas. The ten embedded design areas involve forty-nine elements, and the forty-nine elements involve some three hundred specific instructional strategies.

Figure 2.2 depicts the four overarching domains and the ten design areas. As their name implies, design areas are primarily used when teachers are designing units and lessons. These ten design areas are embedded in four overarching domains: feedback, content, context, and self-regulation. These design areas and domains are explained in depth in the book *Teaching in a Competency-Based Elementary School: The Marzano Academies Model* (Marzano & Abbott, 2022). Briefly, though, *feedback* refers to design areas that provide students with continual updates regarding the topics they are expected to learn and are in the process of learning. *Content* refers to design areas that teachers use when addressing the content within the academy curriculum. *Context* refers to those design areas that optimize the learning environment for students. *Self-regulation* refers to design areas that develop students' independence as learners who take responsibility for their own learning.

Finally, each design area includes elements and each element includes a number of specific strategies. The elements of the instructional model, sorted into their design areas and domains, are depicted in figure 2.3. Again, all components of the model are described and discussed in detail in the book *Teaching in a Competency-Based Elementary School: The Marzano Academies Model* (Marzano & Abbott, 2022). Briefly, though, day-to-day classroom activities are most influenced by

Feedback	Content	Context	Self-Regulation
I. Proficiency Scales Ia. Providing Proficiency Scales Ib. Tracking Student Progress Ic. Celebrating Success **II. Assessment** IIa. Using Obtrusive Assessments IIb. Using Student-Centered Assessments IIc. Using Unobtrusive Assessments IId. Generating Current Summative Scores	**III. Proficiency Scale Instruction** IIIa. Chunking Content IIIb. Processing Content IIIc. Recording and Representing Content IIId. Using Structured Practice IIIe. Examining Similarities and Differences IIIf. Engaging Students in Cognitively Complex Tasks IIIg. Generating and Defending Claims **IV. General Instruction** IVa. Reviewing Content IVb. Revising Knowledge IVc. Examining and Correcting Errors IVd. Highlighting Critical Information IVe. Previewing Content IVf. Stimulating Elaborative Inferences IVg. Extending Learning Through Homework	**V. Grouping and Regrouping** Va. Supporting Group Interactions Vb. Supporting Group Transitions Vc. Providing Support **VI. Engagement** VIa. Noticing and Reacting When Students Are Not Engaged VIb. Increasing Response Rates VIc. Using Physical Movement VId. Maintaining a Lively Pace VIe. Demonstrating Intensity and Enthusiasm VIf. Presenting Unusual Information VIg. Using Friendly Controversy VIh. Using Academic Games **VII. Comfort, Safety, and Order** VIIa. Organizing the Physical Layout of the Classroom VIIb. Demonstrating Withitness VIIc. Acknowledging Adherence to Rules and Procedures VIId. Acknowledging Lack of Adherence to Rules and Procedures VIIe. Establishing and Adapting Rules and Procedures VIIf. Displaying Objectivity and Control	**VIII. Belonging and Esteem** VIIIa. Using Verbal and Nonverbal Behaviors That Indicate Affection VIIIb. Demonstrating Value and Respect for Reluctant Learners VIIIc. Understanding Students' Backgrounds and Interests VIIId. Providing Opportunities for Students to Talk About Themselves **IX. Efficacy and Agency** IXa. Inspiring Students IXb. Enhancing Student Agency IXc. Asking In-Depth Questions of Reluctant Learners IXd. Probing Incorrect Answers With Reluctant Learners **X. Metacognitive and Life Skills** Xa. Reflecting on Learning Xb. Using Long-Term Projects Xc. Focusing on Specific Metacognitive and Life Skills

Source: © 2020 by Marzano Academies, Inc. Used with permission.

FIGURE 2.3: The Marzano Academies instructional model.

decisions teachers make at the element level and the specific strategies within those elements. The ten design areas provide guidance when teachers design units of instruction (hence the term *design areas*), and the four domains remind teachers that the goals of the academy model of instruction certainly include teaching and assessing academic content, but they also encompass attending to students' needs (context) and developing them as effective learners (self-regulation).

Teacher Reflection on Design Areas

When first presenting the instructional model, it is useful to start at the design-area level in terms of asking teachers to reflect on their own performance. To this end, reflection tools like the statements of expectations for teachers and students in figure 2.4 are available to academy teachers.

I. Proficiency Scales (Feedback)

Teacher is

Communicating scales:

- Communicating the scope of domains
- Communicating proficiency scales for each topic
- Creating student-friendly proficiency scales

Tracking progress:

- Helping students track their progress on specific proficiency scales
- Implementing student use of data notebooks

Celebrating:

- Celebrating students' status on specific proficiency scales
- Celebrating students' growth on specific proficiency scales

When asked, the teacher can

- Describe the domain on which he or she is currently focused and how he or she makes proficiency scales user friendly for students
- Describe how he or she ensures students are tracking their progress
- Describe how he or she celebrates students' status and growth

Students are

- Tracking their progress on proficiency scales and referencing proficiency scales to determine what they must do to progress
- Seeking or providing help on working through specific proficiency scales
- Celebrating their status and growth

When asked, students can

- Identify the proficiency scale on which they are working
- Describe what they need to do to improve their status on proficiency scales
- Say they are proud of their status or growth

Source: © 2021 by Robert J. Marzano. Adapted with permission.

FIGURE 2.4: Expectations for design area I.

Figure 2.4 contains expectations for teachers regarding design area I: to engage in activities that involve communicating proficiency scales to students, tracking students' progress on proficiency scales, and celebrating success on proficiency scales. Teachers are also expected to be able to describe the nature and function of these activities and what they typically do relative to these activities. The expectations in figure 2.4 also include the behaviors students should exhibit as a result of the teacher's actions. For design area I, students should be doing things like tracking their own progress and explaining how well they are doing on a specific proficiency scale. Teachers should be encouraged to review these expectations at the design-area level and compare their answers with colleagues to provide them with an overview of the model as it relates to their current practice. Leaders should present one or two design-area expectations charts to teachers at a time. In this way, teachers can obtain a viable overview of the model within a few weeks.

Teacher Self-Evaluations

As part of the teacher development aspect of school-level indicator 5, teachers should reflect on their instructional practices and evaluate themselves on a regular basis. This should occur at the element level. While it is a good idea to introduce teachers to the instructional model at the design-area level, teacher development takes place at the element level. To this end, academy teachers can rate themselves on each element in the instructional model using specific teacher scales. As depicted in figure 2.3 (page 51), each design area in the model includes a number of elements. For example, consider the design area II, assessment. It involves four elements.

IIa. Using obtrusive assessments

IIb. Using student-centered assessments

IIc. Using unobtrusive assessments

IId. Generating current summative scores

Each of these elements is an important component of the way a teacher assesses students' status and growth on academic content. Briefly, using obtrusive assessments refers to assessments that interrupt instruction, such as presentations and pencil-and-paper tests. Student-generated assessments occur when students themselves take the initiative to devise a way to show what they know. Unobtrusive assessments include observations and discussions with students—the teacher gains information about student knowledge, but the student may not realize he or she is being assessed. The fourth element in this domain involves the process of using the evidence collected through various assessments to determine a score that accurately represents a student's current level of knowledge. Taken together, these four elements add up to sound classroom assessment practice.

On a yearly basis, school leaders ask academy teachers to rate themselves on the various elements in the model. To illustrate, consider figure 2.5 (page 54). Figure 2.5 is a teacher self-reflection scale relative to element IIa, using obtrusive assessments, which is one of the forty-nine elements in the model. Each self-rating scale is accompanied by a teacher evidence chart like that in figure 2.6 (page 54).

Academy teachers use evidence charts to help them analyze their level of performance on each element. Initially, teachers can use hard-copy self-reflection scales and their associated evidence charts to perform a thorough and thoughtful analysis of their areas of strength and areas of possible improvement. Teachers' self-reflection scores can also be digitally recorded using a simple online survey instrument such as Google Forms (figure 2.7, page 55).

School leaders should request that every teacher respond to the self-reflection survey. This serves several purposes. First, it acts as a communication tool for the principal regarding the school's adopted instructional model. Most often, high-quality instructional models are too complex to go over in a staff meeting, or even break down over several meetings. When each teacher is expected to digest every scale for self-assessment, the learning model itself is clearly communicated with tangible evidence provided. And, using this measurable evidence, the principal communicates his or her ability to monitor the model's implementation across every classroom. This communication tactic is especially important for those elements in the model that are not commonly found in traditional

	4 Innovating	3 Applying	2 Developing	1 Beginning	0 Not Using
Using Obtrusive Assessments	I engage in all behaviors at the applying (3) level. In addition, I identify those students who do not exhibit the desired effects and develop strategies and activities to meet their specific needs.	I design, administer, and score obtrusive assessments that relate to specific proficiency scales and the majority of students exhibit the desired effects.	I design, administer, and score obtrusive assessments that relate to specific proficiency scales without significant errors or omissions.	I design, administer, and score obtrusive assessments that relate to specific proficiency scales but do so with errors or omissions (for example, lacking clear relationships between specific items and specific levels of a proficiency scale).	I do not design, administer, and score obtrusive assessments that relate to specific proficiency scales.

Source: © 2021 by Robert J. Marzano. Adapted with permission.

FIGURE 2.5: Teacher self-reflection scale for element IIa, using obtrusive assessments.

Teacher Evidence	Student Evidence
Behaviors I systematically design, administer, and score selected-response and short-answer assessments that relate to specific proficiency scales. I systematically design, administer, and score essay assessments that relate to specific proficiency scales. I systematically design, execute, and score demonstration assessments that relate to a specific proficiency scale. I systematically design, execute, and score probing discussions that relate to specific proficiency scales. I systematically enter scores into the gradebook as evidence of student performance on specific proficiency scales. **Understandings** I thoroughly understand the nature and function of obtrusive assessments. I thoroughly understand the various ways I can use obtrusive assessments in the classroom.	**Behaviors** Students commonly use the feedback from obtrusive assessments to make judgments about what they know and don't know. Students commonly talk to me about the meaning of their test scores on obtrusive assessments and how they relate to specific proficiency scales. **Understandings** Students can explain what the score they received on an obtrusive assessment means relative to a specific progression of knowledge. Students can explain what their scores on obtrusive assessments mean in terms of their status on specific proficiency scales.

Source: © 2021 by Robert J. Marzano.

FIGURE 2.6: Evidence chart for element IIa, using obtrusive assessments.

II. Assessment and Feedback

The teacher designs and administers assessments that accurately measure students' status on proficiency scales and helps students understand the relationships between scores on assessments and overall status on a proficiency scale.

	Not Using	Beginning	Developing	Applying	Innovating
IIa. Obtrusive Assessments	○	○	○	○	○
IIb. Student-Centered Assessments	○	○	○	○	○
IIc. Unobtrusive Assessments	○	○	○	○	○
IId. Summative Scores	○	○	○	○	○

Source: © 2018 by Westminster Public Schools. Used with permission.

FIGURE 2.7: Teacher self-reflection survey.

instructional models, such as metacognitive skills or the development of student agency. Using teacher self-evaluation as a communication tool helps the principal clearly define the exact expectations teachers will be held to.

When completed with intentionality, the self-reflection process can help generate teacher realizations about the model itself. When combined with the numerical data the survey yields, it can produce meaningful opportunities for teachers to create professional goals.

Teacher Goal Setting

Although every element of the instructional model is important, it can be overwhelming when considered in its totality. Teachers should only focus on three to four elements they self-assessed at score 1 or 2 on the self-reflection scale and write professional goals on these alone. Then, using the specificity in the evidence charts, school leaders or instructional coaches can create detailed coaching plans that are tailored to each teacher's abilities and needs. In addition, all progress made toward professional goals should be framed and measured by the evidence laid out in the scales themselves. We suggest each teacher have a professional development data notebook where he or she records goals, artifacts, and information regarding these goals.

Each teacher should write time-bound, measurable goals surrounding the growth he or she intends to achieve, as well as actions he or she intends to implement to improve. It is best if teachers include the selected self-reflection scale in their notebooks for easy reference to the specific instructional strategies their development goals are focused on. Being able to quickly see the teacher and student actions associated with each professional goal allows for more intentional planning, as well as easy identification of anecdotal and student-data evidence for the eventual tracking of progress. We also suggest creating a template, as shown in figure 2.8 (page 56), for teachers to formally record

Name: _____

Instructional strategy: _____

My initial score: _____ My goal is to be at _____ by _____.

Specific things I am going to do to improve: _____

_____

_____

_____.

Instructional Strategy: _____

	a	b	c	d	e	f	g	h	i	S
Innovating 4										
Applying 3										
Developing 2										
Beginning 1										
Not Using 0										

a. _____   f. _____

b. _____   g. _____

c. _____   h. _____

d. _____   i. _____

e. _____   Summative Score: _____

FIGURE 2.8: Teacher progress chart.

their goals and track their progress. In addition, the data notebooks should house all instructional coaching artifacts and any other pertinent resources or materials.

The complexity of a comprehensive instructional model, particularly one that is competency-based, means it will be difficult for any teacher to master quickly. In fact, it might realistically take even the best teachers years to demonstrate a score 3 or 4 across all instructional elements. Toward this end, the principal should encourage teachers to embrace a continuous improvement perspective when setting their professional goals, and to always be working toward competency on about three elements at a time. If a teacher reaches score 3 competence on his or her first goal for the year in November, then he or she should identify a new instructional element, write a growth goal for that element, and begin work on that goal. This continuous improvement approach allows for teachers to master the instructional model quicker, while also reinforcing the school's (and principal's) belief that every member of the community must always strive for personal excellence.

The teachers' self-assessment surveys can also be used to set schoolwide goals, as well as identify formal professional development opportunities. After the faculty completes the electronic survey, the principal can calculate school average scores for each element of the instructional model, as shown in figure 2.9 (page 58). Next, the principal can identify four to five areas with low average scores and focus his or her schoolwide instructional goals and associated professional development on those areas. For example, in figure 2.9, the school average for tracking student progress is 1.89. This is clearly an area of growth for the school. The principal then writes a measurable schoolwide instructional goal such as, by February 1st of this academic year, the school's collective self-assessed score on tracking student progress will be at least 3.0. The principal would use the same templates and processes to formally record the schoolwide instructional goals, communicate the goals to all necessary stakeholders, and track the school's progress toward achieving them. Then, he or she would focus coaching and professional learning on the element of tracking student progress to help the whole faculty improve in this area. He or she would also adopt a continuous improvement model by ensuring new instructional goals are established as soon as an existing one receives a collective measure of score 3.

Coaching and Support for Teachers

With both individual teacher and schoolwide instructional goals set, it is important for school leaders to establish a coaching schedule and professional development calendar that will allow teachers to receive support and feedback on both their personal and schoolwide instructional goals. The principal should determine the frequency and timing of professional development in relation to individual teachers' instructional goals, as well as the schoolwide goals. Professional development might occur on a monthly basis for an hour or so after school. Coaching sessions should be established for individual teachers, with the frequency and duration dictated by individual teacher needs. The number of formal observations is usually set by the district or state but additional observations should be established for individual teachers again based on their needs.

The principal, assistant principal, instructional coach, or other members of the instructional leadership team should meet regularly with teachers to discuss instructional goals. These meetings should be preplanned and built into a protected coaching calendar. The instructional leadership team should strive to honor these meetings. This ensures these coaching sessions occur with regularity and helps communicate the importance of the instructional goals to teachers, as well as promote continuous improvement. During these meetings, teachers should discuss the challenges they are experiencing with achieving their goals, while instructional leaders should identify the gaps in teachers' professional knowledge and corresponding development opportunities to incorporate into future coaching sessions. In addition to personalizing training, these meetings will inform leaders about additional coaching supports they may need to implement.

The instructional leaders should also set up classroom observations specifically focused on teachers' instructional goals and follow-up meetings to discuss the observational findings. These classroom observations should employ a targeted observation tool that is focused on either the instructional goals of individual teachers or the school as a whole, as opposed to the entire instructional model. Figure 2.10 (page 59) gives an example of such a targeted observation tool. It lists five instructional elements that are current focus areas for improvement; some of these are schoolwide goals and some are the teacher's personal growth goals. Each teacher would have a similar form, which would include the elements that are being emphasized schoolwide but also the teacher's personal goals.

Instructional Model Element / School Average:

Instructional Model Element	School Average
I. Proficiency Scales [Ia. Providing Proficiency Scales]	1.95
I. Proficiency Scales [Ib. Tracking Student Progress]	1.89
I. Proficiency Scales [Ic. Celebrating Success]	2.10
II. Assessment and Feedback [IIa. Using Obtrusive Assessments]	1.74
II. Assessment and Feedback [IIb. Using Student-Centered Assessments]	1.84
II. Assessment and Feedback [IIc. Using Unobtrusive Assessments]	2.16
II. Assessment and Feedback [IId. Generating Current Summative Scores]	1.89
III. Proficiency Scale Instruction [IIIa. Chunking Content]	2.32
III. Proficiency Scale Instruction [IIIb. Processing Content]	2.16
III. Proficiency Scale Instruction [IIIc. Recording and Representing Content]	1.89
III. Proficiency Scale Instruction [IIId. Using Structured Practice]	2.32
III. Proficiency Scale Instruction [IIIe. Examining Similarities and Dissimilarities]	1.95
III. Proficiency Scale Instruction [IIIf. Engaging Students in Cognitively Complex Tasks]	1.95
III. Proficiency Scale Instruction [IIIg. Generating and Defending Claims]	1.68
IV. General Instruction [IVa. Reviewing Content]	2.05
IV. General Instruction [IVb. Revising Knowledge]	2.26
IV. General Instruction [IVc. Examining and Correcting Errors]	2.00
IV. General Instruction [IVd. Highlighting Critical Information]	2.00
IV. General Instruction [IVe. Previewing Content]	2.37
IV. General Instruction [IVf. Stimulating Elaborative Inferences]	1.95
IV. General Instruction [IVg. Extending Learning Through Homework]	1.68
V. Grouping and Regrouping [Va. Supporting Group Interactions]	2.42
V. Grouping and Regrouping [Vb. Supporting Group Transitions]	2.37
V. Grouping and Regrouping [Vc. Providing Support]	2.37
VI. Engagement [VIa. Noticing and Reacting When Students Are Not Engaged]	2.37
VI. Engagement [VIb. Increasing Response Rates]	1.95
VI. Engagement [VIc. Using Physical Movement]	2.52
VI. Engagement [VId. Maintaining a Lively Pace]	2.21
VI. Engagement [VIe. Demonstrating Intensity and Enthusiasm]	2.47
VI. Engagement [VIf. Presenting Unusual Information]	1.79
VI. Engagement [VIg. Using Friendly Controversy]	2.37
VI. Engagement [VIh. Using Academic Games]	2.21
VII. Comfort, Safety, and Order [VIIa. Organizing the Physical Layout of the Classroom]	2.74
VII. Comfort, Safety, and Order [VIIb. Demonstrating Withitness]	2.58
VII. Comfort, Safety, and Order [VIIc. Acknowledging Adherence to Rules and Procedures]	2.68
VII. Comfort, Safety, and Order [VIId. Acknowledging Lack of Adherence to Rules and Procedures]	2.32
VII. Comfort, Safety, and Order [VIIe. Establishing and Adapting Rules and Procedures]	2.68
VII. Comfort, Safety, and Order [VIIf. Displaying Objectivity and Control]	2.53
VIII. Belonging and Esteem [VIIIa. Using Verbal and Nonverbal Behaviors That Indicate Affection]	2.63
VIII. Belonging and Esteem [VIIIb. Demonstrating Value and Respect for Reluctant Learners]	2.63
VIII. Belonging and Esteem [VIIIc. Understanding Students' Backgrounds and Interests]	2.53
VIII. Belonging and Esteem [VIIId. Providing Opportunities for Students to Talk About Themselves]	2.32
IX. Efficacy and Agency [IXa. Inspiring Students]	2.00
XI. Efficacy and Agency [IXb. Enhancing Student Agency]	2.16
IX. Efficacy and Agency [IXc. Asking In-Depth Questions of Reluctant Learners]	1.95
IX. Efficacy and Agency [IXd. Probing Incorrect Answers With Reluctant Learners]	1.79
X. Metacognitive and Life Skills [Xa. Reflecting on Learning]	2.52
X. Metacognitive and Life Skills [Xb. Using Long-Term Projects]	2.37
X. Metacognitive and Life Skills [Xc. Focusing on Specific Metacognitive and Life Skills]	2.32

FIGURE 2.9: Teacher coaching chart.

Instructional Model Strategy Tracker

I. Proficiency Scales The teacher designs and communicates proficiency scales that help students understand the progression of knowledge they are expected to master for specific domains.	FEEDBACK
Tracking Progress	
Ib. Tracking Progress	
II. Assessment and Feedback The teacher designs and administers assessments that accurately measure students' status on proficiency scales and helps students understand the relationships between scores on assessments and overall status on a proficiency scale.	FEEDBACK
Using Obtrusive Assessments	
IIa. Using Obtrusive Assessments	
III. Proficiency Scale Instruction The teacher designs and executes instructional activities in real time and virtually that help students progress through the levels of specific proficiency scales.	CONTENT
Supporting Claims	
IIIg. Generating and Defending Claims	
VI. Engagement The teacher engages students in activities designed to help them pay attention and feel energized and intrigued.	CONTEXT
Interest and Intrigue	
VIf. Presenting Unusual Information	
IX. Efficacy and Agency The teacher engages students in activities that help develop a sense of agency and efficacy.	AGENCY
The Reluctant Learner	
IXc. Asking In-Depth Questions of Reluctant Learners	

Source: © 2018 by Westminster Public Schools. Used with permission.

FIGURE 2.10: Personalized observation form.

The teacher being observed and the instructional leader conducting the observation should pre-determine the exact instructional strategies to focus on during the observation and communicate those focal areas to the teacher. Using the example in figure 2.10, the leader might communicate that he or she will be focusing on elements IIa (using obtrusive assessments) and IIIg (generating and defending claims). This communication provides the teacher an opportunity to specifically plan a lesson that will highlight emerging abilities with his or her goals, as well as focus the instructional leader's attention during the observation to only the selected strategies.

When a dedicated coaching schedule is in place, it communicates the importance of the instructional model and allows the instructional leadership team to identify individual teacher needs, organize targeted classroom observations, and provide a team approach to teacher development. The next step for the instructional leadership team is to implement guided instructional rounds.

Instructional Rounds

Because witnessing an effective teaching strategy firsthand is a powerful professional development activity, an effective way for teachers to acquire new skills is through guided instructional rounds. This strategy involves a small group of teachers, guided by a leader or instructional coach, observing another teacher's lesson for the purpose of learning from that teacher's instructional practice. After the observation, the leader or instructional coach facilitates a discussion about what the teachers observed. This practice begins with an individual teacher's specific professional growth goal. After identifying the goal, the instructional leader schedules the instructional round in the classroom of a colleague who is particularly strong in that targeted instructional strategy. For example, if teacher A's goal concerns the instructional element of previewing (that is, activating students' prior knowledge by letting them know what content is coming up), and the school's leadership team knows teacher B is strong in this area, teacher A would observe teacher B's classroom during a lesson that employs previewing. This requires a relatively high degree of coordination but is beneficial because teacher A can observe highly effective practices on the exact instructional strategy he or she has selected.

In addition to benefiting individual teachers, guided instructional rounds enhance the professional culture of a school, helping to break down the traditional teaching silos that exist in many schools by providing opportunities for teachers to observe their colleagues and discuss instructional practice. Guided instructional rounds also leverage the strengths of existing faculty to improve the overall instructional capacity of the building. Since teachers only observe other teachers in only those areas they are strong in, guided instructional rounds provide opportunities for individual teachers' strengths to be highlighted. Guided instructional rounds are a win-win for a school and are highly recommended as part of any professional development model.

Finally, it is important that every teacher work in rounds with different members of the instructional leadership team throughout the year. Even when working under the same instructional model, different instructional leaders will inevitably provide unique insights as they support teachers' professional development goals. To structure this practice, the principal should create a rotational instructional coaching calendar for the instructional leadership team to follow throughout the year. We recommend breaking the school year into *hexters*, or six even blocks, as shown in figure 2.11, when planning instructional rounds. We have found that six-week blocks are long enough to provide teachers with concrete expectations regarding instructional rounds but short enough to make changes in the next hexter when the need for change becomes apparent.

	Hexter 1: August 26–October 4	Hexter 2: October 7–November 15	Hexter 3: November 18–January 17	Hexter 4: January 20–February 28	Hexter 5: March 2–April 17	Hexter 6: April 20–May 28
Group One: Primary Teacher 1, Primary Teacher 2, Intermediate Teacher 1, Intermediate Teacher 2, Intervention Teacher 1, Specials Teacher 1	Principal	Assistant Principal	Instructional Coach	Principal	Assistant Principal	Instructional Coach
Group Two: Primary Teacher 3, Primary Teacher 4, Intermediate Teacher 3, Intermediate Teacher 4, Intervention Teacher 2, Specials Teacher 2	Instructional Coach	Principal	Assistant Principal	Instructional Coach	Principal	Assistant Principal
Group Three: Primary Teacher 5, Primary Teacher 6, Intermediate Teacher 5, Intermediate Teacher 6, Intervention Teacher 3, Specials Teacher 3	Assistant Principal	Instructional Coach	Principal	Assistant Principal	Instructional Coach	Principal

FIGURE 2.11: Instructional rounds calendar.

High Reliability Leadership for School-Level Indicator 5

Ensuring the adoption and communication of a comprehensive instructional model, integrating both individual and schoolwide instructional goals based on the adopted model, and providing a detailed support system of coaching and observation protocols are some of the most important responsibilities of the principal in the Marzano Academies model.

This section's discussion of school-level indicator 5, instruction and teacher development, emphasizes the following leading indicators.

- An explicit model of instruction for CBE
- Teacher reflection on design areas
- Teacher self-evaluations
- Teacher goal setting
- Coaching and support for teachers
- Instructional rounds

Potential lagging indicators for this school-level indicator are presented in figure 2.12 (page 62). The customized high reliability scale that might result from the leader's selection of trim tab lagging indicators is depicted in figure 2.13 (page 63).

Programs and Practices	Lagging Indicator Data	Potential Standard for High Reliability Status
Articulating an explicit instructional model	A schoolwide instructional model specific to CBE is written and available to all faculty and staff	90 percent of faculty can describe the school's instructional model in depth
Learning targets for teachers	Specific scales and evidence charts are in place for all elements of the instructional model	90 percent of faculty can describe the content of the evidence charts in the instructional model
Teacher self-evaluation	All teachers are asked to engage in self-evaluation relative to the instructional model	90 percent of faculty complete self-evaluations regarding the instructional model
Teacher goal setting	All teachers are asked to set personal learning goals for specific instructional strategies	90 percent of teachers set specific learning goals based on their self-evaluations
Coaching and supporting teachers	Specific activities are established to provide coaching and support for teachers regarding their personal goals	90 percent of teachers actively engage in the coaching and support that is available to them
Instructional rounds	Protocols and practices for instructional rounds are in place such that all teachers can engage in them	90 percent of teachers actively engage in instructional rounds
Perceptions of teachers	Surveys are administered to teachers	90 percent of teachers report that they are increasing in competence as a result of the school's policies and practices

Source: © 2021 by Robert J. Marzano.

FIGURE 2.12: Potential lagging indicators for school-level indicator 5.

School-Level Indicator 6: Blended Instruction

Blended-learning environments integrate online resources with direct instruction to deliver personalized, self-paced, anytime learning. The essence of blended instruction is that students can interact face to face with teachers in real time, as in the traditional classroom setup, as well as virtually at a time of their own choosing. The leader of an elementary academy should procure digital devices and effective learning software and programs and help teachers develop online resources for the content in their proficiency scales.

Necessary Technology

To be sure, a blended-learning environment cannot be achieved if the classroom does not have student computers or devices available to access online platforms. School leaders should think

Evidence	
4 **Sustaining** **(quick data)**	Quick data like the following are systematically collected and reviewed. • Examination of teacher improvement plans • Progress charts depicting teacher growth in specific pedagogical skills • Quick conversations with teachers
3 **Applying** **(lagging)**	Performance goals with clear criteria for success like the following are in place. • 90 percent of faculty can describe the school's instructional model in depth and the general content of the evidence charts • 90 percent of teachers set specific learning goals based on their self-evaluations • 90 percent of teachers actively engage in the coaching and support that is available to them and engage in instructional rounds • 90 percent of teachers report that they are increasing in competence as a result of the school's policies and practices
2 **Developing** **(leading)**	• A written instructional model is in place that is understood by teachers • Self-reflection scales and evidence charts are in place for the instructional model • Systems and routines are in place for teachers to set personal learning goals • Systems and routines are in place to support teachers and help them learn from their peers
1 **Beginning**	• The school has written plans to create an instructional model but little progress has been made on a written model • Teachers are aware of a few strategies they use in common but these strategies do not constitute a model of instruction
0 **Not Using**	• The school does not have plans to create a written model of instruction • There is no implementation of common instructional strategies among teachers

Source: © 2020 by Marzano Academies, Inc. Adapted with permission.

FIGURE 2.13: Customized high reliability scale for school-level indicator 5.

carefully about the devices that will be an essential part of their CBE system. Rather than buying devices in an impulsive fashion, leaders should create an initial list of necessary devices that they add to on a yearly basis as resources allow. In this way, school leaders can keep an inventory of what they currently have and what they still need to acquire. *One-to-one technology* is a term used to describe learning environments where every teacher and student has a dedicated computer, tablet, or device. There is no doubt providing one-to-one equipped classrooms is expensive, and most likely will require years to build up to. As the budget manager, the principal will need to consider this and make appropriate short- and long-term decisions to ensure his or her school provides technology to students and teachers. In addition to the initial purchasing of devices, the principal will need to account for the ongoing expenses of servicing the devices, as well as replacement cycles. We recognize that schools operate under different budgetary constraints, but if a principal is not able to provide one-to-one devices in his or her school, many of the goals laid out in this section can still be achieved with only five to ten devices per classroom. Teachers can always create blended-learning stations, which still ensure every student has access to online learning tools, even if not simultaneously.

In addition to school-based resources, the principal will also need to understand the home-based resources of the families attending his or her school. Especially when considering cell phones, it is true most households have some degree of access to technology. However, it is a false assumption to think all students can equally participate in online learning from home. The principal should survey his or her families to determine what percentage of households have a device for students to access online learning, as well as the percentage of households with internet access. Utilizing a needs-based approach, the principal can use survey results to determine which families require school assistance to access the school's blended-learning resources. Checking out school technology to students, fundraising to provide hotspots for homes without internet connections, and applying for grants to purchase home-based technology for families in need are just a few examples of actions the principal can take to ensure every student can participate in the blended-learning opportunities being offered by the school.

After ensuring he or she has addressed access to technology, the principal can begin the challenging work of creating blended-learning activities and environments.

A Learning Management System for Blended Instruction

An effective blended-learning environment begins with the adoption of a high-powered learning management system (LMS). No shortages of LMS platforms exist, but the Marzano Academies model is best implemented with one that is designed to incorporate the school's proficiency scales (curriculum) and corresponding recording and reporting tools (such as gradebooks and report cards). This kind of system architecture allows teachers to input class learning targets, activities, and assessments as they integrate their classrooms with online tools, while also providing a single comprehensive resource for students as they navigate their blended-learning environment.

Critical to the academy model is the ability of the LMS to build proficiency scales into the course framework, enabling teachers to directly link online resources and instruction to learning targets within each scale. In addition, when the LMS includes recording and reporting functionality, teachers are able to connect all online work back to specific learning targets in specific proficiency scales. This creates opportunity for both students and teachers to easily track learning progress, and allows for robust student and teacher goal setting. The examples we describe in this section represent specific ways that an LMS might provide for the use of proficiency scales, links to online resources, and the like. Other systems might not have exactly the same features but should have similar functions.

To help with differentiation, the teacher should have access to a target browser to easily create ability-based small groupings. A target browser is a feature that allows teachers to obtain a quick overview of how entire groups of students are performing on particular learning targets. For example, figure 2.14 depicts the target browser found in the Empower Learning system. This display is for a specific group of students relative to the English language arts (ELA) topics on which they are working. Notice that at the top of the target browser there is a row of boxes that are labeled PK (prekindergarten) up through HS (high school). There are two boxes that are checked in this row, 04 and 05. This means that the LMS is currently displaying the status of students on the ELA content at grades 4 and 5.

Each row in figure 2.14 represents a group of related topics. Such groups are referred to as *domains*. Within each domain are specific topics, each of which has its own proficiency scale. For example, consider the second row, which represents the domain of vocabulary acquisition and use. That domain includes three proficiency scales—two at the fourth-grade level (labeled LI.04. L3.05.05 and LI.04.L3.07.05) and one at the fifth-grade level (LI.05.L3.02.05). The most powerful

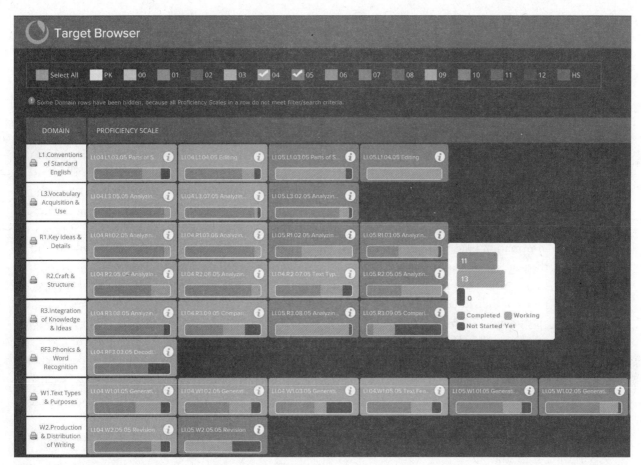

Source: © 2021 by Empower Learning. Used with permission.

FIGURE 2.14: Target browser.

part of this display is that it shows the overall progress on each proficiency scale for the selected group of students. This list of students is represented in each box for each proficiency scale by a bar that is shaded in three different ways. The shaded portion on the left of the bar represents the proportion of students who have completed the proficiency scale by demonstrating proficiency. The center portion represents the proportion of students who are working on the proficiency scale but have not completed it yet, and the portion on the right represents the proportion of students who have not yet started working on the proficiency scale.

Teachers can use this tool to strategically group students based on previous demonstrations of competency. For example, if the teacher is beginning his or her planning for the day's lesson, he or she can use the target browser to determine his or her students' existing competencies on the lesson's selected learning target and strategically create small groups for the day.

Playlists

The playlist feature of an LMS allows teachers to create specific, differentiated lessons for each group of students depending on their need. In general terms, a playlist is a progression of learning activities students can engage in virtually. Just as digital music apps allow users to pick songs from different artists and albums to create a playlist around a theme or mood, an LMS allows teachers to select and sequence various activities from different sources related to a given learning topic.

Teachers build these virtual learning progressions into their online classroom inside the LMS, and provide a sequenced set of tasks, activities, resources, and assessments for students to follow, as shown in figure 2.15. The power of the playlist resides in the fact that the teacher can draw on a host of online applications and learning programs to create the sequence of activities. He or she is not limited to a single curriculum resource or existing online courses. Furthermore, teachers can link all student learning activities embedded in the playlist back to the related proficiency scale, allowing all of students' work to be a measure of their competence.

The playlist in figure 2.15 is for the topic of text structures. There are twelve activities in this playlist, represented by the twelve tiles visible on the screen. For example, the first tile leads to information about text structures that deal with the big idea of the text; the third tile contains information about cause-effect structures; the fourth tile contains information about sequence structure; and so on. Students click on each tile to access the related information and activities. Some of the information might be in written form, some might be in the form of a video recording created by the teacher, and some might be in the form of a video recording downloaded from a website. With these resources, teachers can construct a series of online activities for the entire class or the specific needs of individual students. For example, for this topic of text structures, a teacher might require all students to complete the activities in four of the tiles, but also require some students to complete additional tiles that will help them with problems they might have regarding the topic of text structures. Alternatively or additionally, the teacher might designate some tiles as open to students' choice.

Playlists are a unique way to leverage the power of a blended classroom to differentiate instruction and personalize the learning experience. Utilizing tools like a target browser, the teacher can create

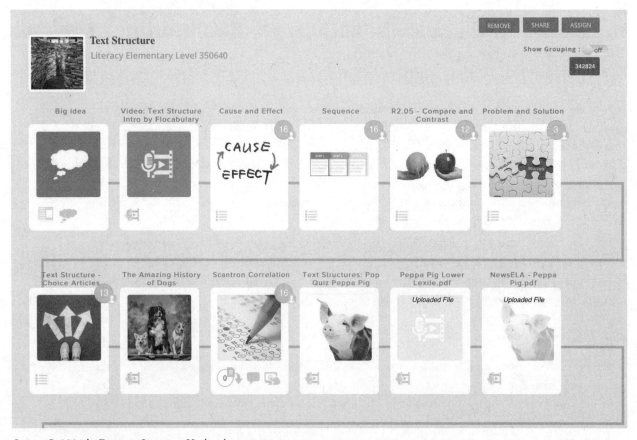

Source: © 2021 by Empower Learning. Used with permission.

FIGURE 2.15: Playlist.

and assign learning activities to different groups of students. This differentiation provides personalized instruction for students to move through content at their own pace, and since it is online, from anywhere and at any time.

Online Resources

In addition to an LMS with playlist capability, the principal must also identify other online resources for teachers to incorporate into instruction. Of course, there are a wide variety of online resources available to teachers with more developed each year. The Khan Academy website is the quintessential example of such resources containing free videos and assessments for various subject areas organized sequentially and in grade-level blocks. Similar resources can be found for a wide range of subject areas. Many schools utilize a patchwork of online programs, often dictated by individual teachers' preferences. We advocate for the principal to identify a limited number of high-quality programs to implement across the entire school. This provides several advantages. First, it is easier to research and vet a limited number of programs versus every online resource teachers might request. Second, high-quality programs most often require a subscription for licensed use, bringing budgetary considerations into the selection process. Third, the school must adhere to student privacy protections. Many online learning programs do not have stringent student data-protection clauses built into their user agreements, leaving the school at risk for personal privacy infractions. The principal must ensure any program used by his or her teachers is properly vetted.

Finally, it is important to consider the value that consistency brings to student learning. If all teachers use the same small set of online learning programs, as opposed to selecting their own, students will be familiar with the programs' platforms and know how to navigate their features. This will reduce the time a student spends learning the program architecture and increase the time he or she spends interacting with the content. Additionally, selecting a few online resources allows the principal to provide teachers with meaningful professional development on those programs, versus attempting to train faculty on a wide variety of programs with varying degrees of implementation across the whole school.

Effective Professional Development

Relative to professional development, the principal must recognize not all faculty are equally adept with technology, making some teachers more comfortable with the demands of a blended classroom than others. To support all teachers in delivering blended instruction, the principal must provide a wide array of training opportunities and platforms for teachers. To be sure, principals must provide dedicated face-to-face, all-staff professional development, especially on the learning management system and any vetted online programs the school adopts systemwide. If the principal requires blended instruction using a predetermined set of tools in every classroom, then that principal must provide the same training to every faculty member, regardless of his or her existing technological ability. Beyond this, however, the principal will want to make available additional training opportunities, both in person and virtual, for teachers to access on an on-demand basis.

Just as teachers are expected to differentiate instruction for students, principals should assume a differentiated professional development approach with teachers. Not all faculty will need the same degree of support. Principals should provide these differentiated trainings across both physical and virtual spaces. Using an online survey tool such as Google Forms, the principal should poll his or her staff to determine their professional competencies on the blended learning tools adopted by the school. Using these results, the principal can determine what trainings are necessary, and for which teachers. We recommend designing a suite of professional development opportunities for teachers. The principal can hold a monthly lunch and learn, where teachers can participate in training during their lunch hour, or after school. Face-to-face learning might be the only way some faculty can process and internalize technology-based capabilities. However, if possible, the principal should also model the blended instruction he or she expects by including an online component to the training.

One powerful training method the principal should consider is to provide his or her own trainings online. The principal can create playlists inside the LMS for teachers to access and move through. He or she can also model other learning tools for teachers to help solidify their facility with the technology before using it with students. For example, the principal can create screencast tutorials for online learning programs that teachers can access anytime, anywhere. This type of training demonstrates the power of online learning and can help teachers begin to envision using the same instructional techniques in their own classrooms. Perhaps most powerfully, the principal should utilize the expertise of his or her faculty. Every school has at least one teacher, if not many, who naturally gravitates toward blended instruction. The principal should leverage this expertise by asking these educators to share their resources, screencasts, or lesson plans. The old adage of many hands making light work is especially true when a school adopts a blended learning platform, and high levels of teacher collaboration will expedite the school's professional capacity for blended instruction.

After the principal has adopted a high-powered LMS, selected the online programs both subscription-based and free to build into playlists, and provided teachers with professional development, the next step is to ensure these tools are formally written into lesson plans and unit design. Teachers should be expected to explicitly state which online programs they will use, at what point in the instructional process, and for which learning targets. Although teachers can identify their use of online programs through a paper-based lesson design, this is best accomplished by requiring teachers to design their lesson plans as playlists for their units of instruction inside of the LMS. This practice of a playlists lesson design requires teachers to articulate a step-by-step progression of learning, with dedicated online tools, and with all learning activities tagged to proficiency scales. No matter what lesson plan format the principal determines his or her teachers will use, that format must account for blended instruction and provide teacher evidence of implementation.

Finally, the principal will need to conduct both physical and virtual walkthroughs of classrooms to support the blended-instruction requirements and determine next steps for professional development. The principal, along with the school's instructional leadership team, should incorporate a blended-learning checklist for classroom observations. The checklist should include both teacher and student actions and focus on classroom use of the LMS and other school-adopted online learning resources. Such a checklist might include the following.

- The frequency of teacher use of online resources
- Students' independent use of online resources
- The clear relationship between the online resources and the explicit topics in the curriculum

The walkthrough process should also include questions to ask students regarding their use of blended learning tools, or the teacher's expectations. The answers students provide can provide vital information as to the degree of implementation of blended instruction, as well as highlight strengths and weaknesses of the blended instruction in a particular classroom. The principal should also conduct virtual classroom observations inside the LMS, paying specific attention to the playlists and ensuring the natural sequence of learning steps is intuitive. The observation should also check that student work is attached to a learning target within a proficiency scale and that classes are using only preapproved online resources.

High Reliability Leadership for School-Level Indicator 6

This school-level indicator addresses blended instruction. Much more than simply purchasing a program for online instruction, leaders in the Marzano Academies model must procure an LMS that is designed to support CBE, along with online resources that allow teachers to create sequences of instructional activities that give students clear direction and flexibility in terms of the pace at which they learn.

The previous discussion on school-level indicator 6, blended instruction, emphasizes the following leading elements.

- Necessary technology
- An LMS for blended instruction
- Playlists
- Online resources
- Effective professional development

Figure 2.16 depicts potential lagging indicators for these elements. Figure 2.17 (page 70) depicts the customized high reliability scale for this school-level indicator.

Programs and Practices	Lagging Indicator Data	Potential Standard for High Reliability Status
Making sure teachers know how to use the technology	An inventory of necessary technology for blended learning	80 percent of necessary inventory is procured
Having the right LMS	Procuring an LMS that allows for basic requirements of a CBE system	100 percent of teachers use the blended-learning features of the LMS
Playlists	Design of playlists for the various proficiency scales in the curriculum	100 percent of teachers use the playlist feature in the LMS
Effective professional development	Professional development activities in place regarding how to use the LMS and various online resources teachers are expected to use	100 percent of teachers engage in the professional development activities for blended learning
Perceptions of students, teachers, and parents	Surveys administered to students, teachers, and parents	90 percent of students report that they feel confident using the LMS 90 percent of teachers report that they feel confident using the school's blended learning process 80 percent of parents report satisfaction with the blended learning process

Source: © 2021 by Robert J. Marzano.

FIGURE 2.16: Potential lagging indicators for school-level indicator 6.

Evidence	
4 **Sustaining** **(quick data)**	Quick data like the following are systematically collected and reviewed. • Examination of the online resources in the LMS • Reviews of teachers' lesson plans and unit plans • Walkthrough observational data • Quick conversations with teachers and students
3 **Applying** **(lagging)**	Performance goals with clear criteria for success like the following are in place. • 80 percent of necessary inventory is procured • 100 percent of teachers use the playlist feature in the LMS • 100 percent of teachers engage in the professional development activities for blended learning • 90 percent of teachers report that they feel confident about using the school's blended learning process
2 **Developing** **(leading)**	• An inventory process for necessary technology is in place • An LMS that adequately supports CBE is identified • Adequate professional development for blended learning is in place
1 **Beginning**	• The school has written plans for the design and use of online resources for score 2.0, 3.0, and 4.0 content but there is no implementation at the school level • Only a few teachers use online resources for content in proficiency scales
0 **Not Using**	• The school has no written plans for the design and use of online resources • There is no use of online resources for proficiency scales at the classroom level

Source: © 2020 by Marzano Academies, Inc. Adapted with permission.

FIGURE 2.17: Customized high reliability scale for school-level indicator 6.

School-Level Indicator 7: Cumulative Review

The leader of an elementary academy should ensure that the school has programs and practices in place that help students continually review and revise important academic content. Students will not master the critical content if teachers only provide a single point of instruction. Instead, high-quality learning must include opportunities for students to review and revise their understandings as they progress through the curriculum.

As with so many other elements of school leadership, the principal must begin the implementation of cumulative review with ensuring his or her teachers understand the rationale behind this practice. Many teachers feel overwhelmed by the amount of content they are expected to teach and their students are expected to learn in a school year. Therefore, it is especially important to establish a clear purpose for any activity that consumes instructional time. Simply put, the purpose of cumulative review is to reinforce and advance students' knowledge and skills and prevent newly learned information from fading away over time.

Since most states administer their high-stakes accountability assessments in the spring, students often demonstrate low proficiency on content that was adequately taught earlier in the year. An easy way to determine if this is true for a school is for the principal to analyze his or her school's test scores with an eye toward when content was taught. Many principals will find their students score well on topics that were taught in the weeks or month leading up to the exam date. Conversely, those standards taught in the beginning or first half of the year often produce lower scores on the high-stakes test. When a principal conducts this type of analysis, he or she can use these findings as part of the underlying rationale for teachers to implement a cumulative review process into their instruction.

Although performance on state assessments is important, test performance is decidedly not the main reason a school should implement a systemic review process. Particularly in a CBE system, by definition, the main reason is students' mastery of critical content. Expecting a student to demonstrate proficiency at a given point in time is different from expecting a student to obtain true mastery of content. Cumulative review is integral to real, long-term mastery because of the process of recall.

The cognitive process of recall has been much maligned in K–12 education, most likely because of the popularization of Bloom's taxonomy in 1956 (Bloom, 1956) and its revision in 2001 (Anderson & Krathwohl, 2001). In the 1956 version, the lowest order of cognition was recall of knowledge; in the 2001 version, the lowest order of cognition was referred to as *remembering*. This low ranking notwithstanding, in the neuroscience literature the act of recall or remembering is generally thought of as one of the most powerful tools in learning, as described in the book *Uncommon Sense Teaching* (Oakley, Rogowsky, & Sejnowski, 2021). This is because during recall, students don't just pull up stored information in a verbatim fashion. Instead, recall involves reassembling information from permanent memory into working memory. Each time students do this reassembling, it provides an opportunity for them to reshape and improve their understanding of the content recalled. This is the essence of a cumulative review. In effect, if students are not asked to recall content, that content will fade relatively quickly and they will not be able to use it.

The Process of Cumulative Review

In the academy model, the cumulative review process involves three phases: (1) recording, (2) reviewing, and (3) revising. Each phase is intentional and requires students to do something different with the content. The process typically starts relatively soon after a teacher has provided direct instruction on content at least parts of which are novel to students.

In the first phase of cumulative review, students record what they have newly learned about a topic the teacher has introduced to them. This can be through the use of serially recorded notes, informal outlines, summaries, graphic organizers, or pictorial notes and pictographs. Regardless of which structure is used, students are expected to represent what they understand about the content using their own words or their own representations.

The school leader should be prepared to articulate the recording structures he or she expects teachers to utilize, taking into account variations in grade levels. He or she may require fifth-grade teachers to provide student review journals, or three-ring binders tabbed with each learning target throughout the year. At the same time, he or she may require kindergarten teachers to provide their students with pictographic recording activities to be completed during centers. These expectations should be discussed and agreed on through a collective decision-making process where the teachers are given voice in how their students will record information. After these decisions are made, the principal should provide teachers with the necessary materials (for example, three-ring binders with tabs), as well as a shared library of cumulative review resources. An easy way to do this is through a shared cloud drive for cumulative review. Providing easy-to-use templates for serial notetaking, summarizing activities, combination written and graphic notes, or graphic organizers for teachers to quickly access will reduce the need for faculty to individually create or find their own materials. Access to shared templates also will ensure consistency for students across the school and eliminate the need to teach a new recording tool every time a student starts with a different teacher.

The review phase of the cumulative review process requires students to examine and test their understandings of the content they are reviewing. This can be achieved in a variety of ways. For example, providing practice assessments is a good way for students to test their comprehension. However, the principal must ensure these practice assessments require students to recall and explain specific details, or describe and exemplify generalizations and principles, or generate and defend claims about specific review topics. The key here is to ensure students are required to do something with the reviewed content, not simply describe it in a verbatim fashion. As with the recording phase, it is important for the principal to foster acceptance of the process through collective decision making and allowance of grade-level variations. It is equally important for the principal to create and house shared templates and processes for teachers to utilize to guarantee consistency across all classrooms.

After recording and reviewing, perhaps the most critical step of cumulative review occurs: revising. The real power of the cumulative review process is realized when students revise their knowledge. Revision involves such steps as (1) review your knowledge, (2) identify any mistakes, (3) fill any gaps, (4) add new information, and (5) explain your reasons. It is this final step that allows for cumulative review to help students enhance their knowledge of the topics they are reviewing. It is also the step of review that is most often skipped by teachers when designing content review activities. Thus, it is essential for the principal to ensure every teacher is building revising into his or her direct instruction. This can be done using sentence stems, quick writes, or peer feedback activities, all of which include the basic steps of revision. Once again, the principal should provide the necessary structures, such as sentence stem templates or collaborative learning processes for peer feedback, for teachers to use and follow. Many examples of graphic organizers and review processes can be found in *The Handbook for the New Art and Science of Teaching* (Marzano, 2019).

Test Items as Review Tools

One adaptation of cumulative review is to integrate assessment items into the process. This process is described in depth in the book *Ethical Test Preparation in the Classroom* (Marzano, Dodson, Simms, & Wipf, 2022). Briefly, items from large-scale external tests (for example, state exams, aptitude tests, and so on) have unique structures and require certain ways of thinking. If students are unfamiliar with these features, they may answer an item incorrectly even though they have mastered the skills that the item was designed to assess. To illustrate, consider the third-grade mathematics item in figure 2.18.

This sample assessment item is representative of the types of third-grade mathematics items students commonly encounter on such tests. On the surface, this item seems quite straightforward. Students simply read and interpret the two-way table and then answer questions about it. However, some third-grade students who understand the nature of two-way tables might be thrown off by the fact that there are four different questions asked about the information in the table, and the fourth question (part D) goes beyond what is typically required of reading such tables. In effect, there are a number of cognitive operations students must employ to correctly answer the questions in this item.

The book *Ethical Test Preparation in the Classroom* (Marzano et al., 2022) summarizes the findings from an analysis of over 8,800 test items from national, international, and state tests and catalogues the different item formats students are likely to encounter throughout their academic lives. Using

Two apartment complexes each have two buildings full of residents. The table displays the number of residents in each building.

	Building 1	Building 2	Total
Stony Brook Apartments	56	77	
Rocky Creek Apartments	84	93	

Part A

What is the total number of residents in the Stony Brook Apartments?

A. 133   B. 140   C. 170   D. 177

Part B

What is the total number of residents in the Rocky Creek Apartments?

A. 133   B. 140   C. 170   D. 177

Part C

What is the difference between the number of residents in Building 1 of the Rocky Creek Apartments and the number of residents in Building 1 of the Stony Brook Apartments?

Fill in your answer in the box.

Part D

One unit in the Stony Brook Apartments has 5 residents. Another unit has 7 residents. How many residents are in the rest of the Stony Brook Apartments?

Show the steps you used to solve the problem. Fill in your answer and your work.

Source: Marzano et al., 2022, pp. 189–190.

FIGURE 2.18: Typical third-grade mathematics item.

this source, teachers can identify the types of items that will be used to assess their students. They can then incorporate similar items into the cumulative review process. Teachers should introduce item types to students along with the related academic content from proficiency scales. Teachers should also supply students with strategies for discerning the unique requirements of the various item types they encounter on tests and navigating those requirements to accurately demonstrate their knowledge. For example, to navigate the item in figure 2.18, students should be aware of expectations like certain questions focusing on specific parts of the two-way table, and some questions requiring them to make new calculations based on what is presented in the table.

Systematic Use of Cumulative Review

Ideally, cumulative review should be included into weekly, if not daily, lesson planning. The principal will have to decide how frequently he or she wants cumulative review to occur and communicate this expectation to teachers. Next, he or she will need to design processes for systematic implementation and monitoring of implementation. For example, the principal can ask that every teacher write into his or her lesson plans specific times to conduct cumulative review. This could be as simple as a daily bell-ringer activity, or a weekly forty-five-minute review block built into the class schedule. Another approach is for the principal to require that cumulative review be included in unit plan designs. Regardless, the principal must ensure every teacher communicates when and how cumulative review will occur in his or her classroom, and the principal must observe classrooms to monitor the implementation.

If every teacher includes cumulative review into his or her planning, and communicates this to the principal, it becomes easy to observe in classrooms. For example, if a teacher determines his or her bell-ringer activity every Monday, Wednesday, and Friday will be oriented to cumulative review, the principal should make a point to conduct observations during these times. When in classrooms, the principal should be looking for several things. For example, is the teacher providing clear instruction on key components of cumulative review? Another artifact of cumulative review is the student work samples or products associated with the recording, reviewing, and revising phases. When the principal conducts a cumulative review observation, he or she should ask a few students to share their review journals. Students in classrooms where cumulative review is occurring with fidelity will not struggle to communicate what each phase of the review process looks like, while also displaying a well-used review journal with plenty of work products.

High Reliability Leadership for School-Level Indicator 7

This school-level indicator addresses a particular instructional activity that all academy teachers are expected to use on a regular basis: cumulative review. While review is a process used by most if not all teachers, review that systematically helps students make connections between new content and what they learned previously is relatively rare. The cumulative review process, when used frequently and systematically, keeps information fresh in students' memories and helps them continually update and shape their knowledge.

Cumulative review is a classroom instructional technique that should be executed in every classroom at every grade level. The preceding sections discussed the following aspects of the process.

- A clear process for cumulative review

- Test items as review tools within the cumulative review process

- Systematic use of the cumulative review process

Figure 2.19 lists potential lagging indicators for this school-level indicator. Figure 2.20 depicts the customized high reliability scale for this school-level indicator.

School-Level Indicator 8: Knowledge Maps

At one level, knowledge maps can be considered types of graphic organizers. This is certainly accurate to say in that graphic organizers provide students with ways to visually represent the content they are learning, as do knowledge maps. However, teachers typically use only a small set of graphic

Programs and Practices	Lagging Indicator Data	Potential Standard for High Reliability Status
A clear cumulative review process	Written protocols are in place for the cumulative review process	100 percent of teachers are familiar with the cumulative review process
Sample test items	Sample test items have been identified and tagged to the important content-area topics	100 percent of teachers use sample test items in the cumulative review process and can explain why they are important to that process
Systematic use	A walkthrough protocol for cumulative review is used on a systematic basis	Observational data are in place indicating that 90 percent of teachers systematically use the cumulative review process
Perceptions of students, teachers, and parents	Surveys of teachers and students	90 percent of teachers and 80 percent of students perceive cumulative review to be useful to their learning

Source: © 2021 by Robert J. Marzano.

FIGURE 2.19: Potential lagging indicators for school-level indicator 7.

Evidence	
4 **Sustaining** **(quick data)**	Quick data like the following are systematically collected and reviewed. • Reviews of teacher lesson plans and unit plans • Walkthrough observational data • Quick conversations with teachers and students
3 **Applying** **(lagging)**	Performance goals with clear criteria for success like the following are in place. • 100 percent of teachers are familiar with the cumulative review process • 100 percent of teachers use sample test items in the cumulative review process and can explain why they are important to that process • Observational data are in place indicating that 90 percent of teachers systematically use the cumulative review process • 90 percent of teachers and 80 percent of students perceive cumulative review to be useful to their learning
2 **Developing** **(leading)**	• Teachers follow specific protocols for systematically reviewing critical content • Cumulative review is executed on a systematic basis according to schedule • A walkthrough process is used to monitor the use of the cumulative review process in classrooms
1 **Beginning**	• The school has written plans for the use of cumulative review but there is no implementation at the school level • Only a few teachers utilize cumulative review
0 **Not Using**	• The school has no written plans for the use of cumulative review • There is no implementation of cumulative review at the classroom level

Source: © 2020 by Marzano Academies, Inc. Adapted with permission.

FIGURE 2.20: Customized high reliability scale for school-level indicator 7.

organizers with their students. In contrast, knowledge maps are designed in such a way as to represent a wide array of structures in which knowledge can be organized. To this extent, knowledge maps can provide students with a comprehensive set of tools to unpack the meaning of what they read and to organize their own thoughts when writing. Consequently, we recommend that teachers use knowledge maps in daily instruction as frameworks for reading comprehension and coherence in writing.

The leader of an elementary academy should ensure that the school employs knowledge maps as tools for students to comprehend and write various types of texts. Learning at all levels and for all content areas involves comprehending new content presented and continually reassembling that content in unique ways. Both of these activities are enhanced by the use of graphic organizers. It is certainly accurate to say that virtually all teachers are familiar with the concept of graphic organizers and probably accurate to say the majority of teachers use them in their classrooms. For the most part, teachers use their own versions of graphic organizers in ways that are specific to their content. For example, after students have read a passage, the teacher might ask them to create a graphic organizer depicting the content using a simple circle with spokes or some other ad hoc depiction. This, of course, is a legitimate way to employ graphic organizers. However, the power of graphic organizers increases when teachers use a specific, common set. This is the purpose of the system we refer to as *knowledge maps*: to provide a schoolwide common set of graphic organizers and a systematic approach to how they are used.

Vertical Alignment of Knowledge Maps

Knowledge maps, as used in the academy model, are a comprehensive system of graphic organizers. But not every knowledge map is appropriate for every learner at every grade level. Knowledge maps range from simple to quite complex. To illustrate the simpler end of the spectrum, consider figure 2.21, which depicts the knowledge map for simple sequences. The map works well for situations where one thing occurred, then another, and so on. For example, the story of Goldilocks could be depicted using this map: Goldilocks found the house of the three bears, then she entered the house, and so on. This knowledge map is appropriate even for preK students.

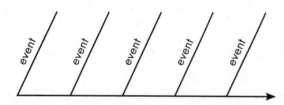

Source: © 2017 by Marzano Resources. Used with permission.

FIGURE 2.21: Simple sequence knowledge map.

To represent more complex information and relationships, knowledge maps become more and more complex. Figure 2.22 depicts a complex sequence map. This map can be used to represent a number of actions occurring simultaneously. For example, a passage describing a demonstration might detail the actions of three different people who were at the demonstration but did different things at different times. Each horizontal line would represent the actions of one person with each event listed at the relative point in time. This knowledge map would be appropriate to introduce at grades 3–5.

Finally, figure 2.23 depicts a knowledge map for nested lists, a complex type of collection. This knowledge map is appropriate at the high school level. To illustrate how the nested list knowledge map is used, consider figure 2.24.

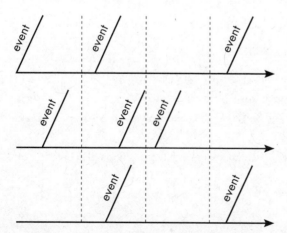

Source: © 2017 by Marzano Resources. Used with permission.

FIGURE 2.22: Complex sequence knowledge map.

		data A1			data A2		
		data B1	data B2	data B3	data B1	data B2	data B3
data C1	data D1	item	item	item	item	item	item
	data D2	item	item	item	item	item	item
data C2	data D3	item	item	item	item	item	item
	data D4	item	item	item	item	item	item
data C3	data D5	item	item	item	item	item	item

Source: © 2017 by Marzano Resources. Used with permission.

FIGURE 2.23: Collection—nested list knowledge map.

		Symphony			Marching Band		
		High Pitch	Medium Pitch	Low Pitch	High Pitch	Medium Pitch	Low Pitch
Bowing or Plucking	Strings	Violin	Viola Harp	Cello Bass			
	Reeds	Oboe	Clarinet Saxophone	Bassoon		Clarinet Saxophone	Bassoon
Blowing Through Mouthpiece	Brasses	Trumpet French horn	Trombone	Tuba	Trumpet Mellophone	Trombone	Tuba
	Woodwinds	Piccolo Flute			Piccolo Flute		
Striking a Surface	Percussion	Triangle	Piano	Bass drum	Triangle		Bass drum

Source: Marzano & Simms, 2019, p. 107.

FIGURE 2.24: Example of nested list knowledge map.

This type of knowledge map allows students to display complex classification systems that involve multiple facets and characteristics.

Because knowledge maps increase in complexity, leaders should develop a plan for the scope and manner in which students will use knowledge maps by creating a vertical implementation guide like that depicted in figure 2.25 (page 78). At the preK level, only three types of maps are appropriate: basic relationships, description, and simple sequence maps. There are twelve knowledge maps that are appropriate for primary students, and sixteen that upper elementary students can use effectively. A chart such as this defines which knowledge maps are appropriate and expected for use in each

Structure	PreK	K–2	3–5	6–8	9–12
1. Basic Relationships	x	x	x	x	x
2. Description	x	x	x	x	x
3. Sequence	simple	x	complex	x	x
4. Causation		simple	complex	x	x
5. Problem-Solution		simple	complex	advanced	x
6. Comparison		x	x	x	x
7. Collection		simple lists	combined lists	intersecting lists	nested lists
8. Classification		simple	complex	x	x
9. Argumentation		simple	complex	x	x
10. Reasoning				inductive	x
				deductive	x
11. Systems		process	x	x	x
		cycle	x	x	x
		flowchart	x	x	x
			system	x	x
12. Episode			x	x	x
13. Metaphor			x	x	x
14. Analogy			x	x	x
TOTALS	3	12	16	18	18

Source: © 2020 by Marzano Academies, Inc. Used with permission.

FIGURE 2.25: Vertical alignment of knowledge maps.

grade band. Teachers should feel free to use maps outside of the school's scope and sequence; however, the principal must ensure the selected maps are used in accordance with the schoolwide plan.

Professional Development for Knowledge Maps

As with any instructional mandate, the principal must provide professional development for knowledge maps to his or her faculty to ensure meaningful implementation across every classroom. However, in relation to knowledge maps, it is important that the training require teachers to use the maps as opposed to simply learn about them.

The principal should identify several maps to frame the training. For example, he or she can use the simple sequence map in figure 2.21 (page 76) to illustrate the steps of the training and eventual classroom implementation. Each event in the training would be recorded on the single horizontal line of the simple sequence knowledge map. The first event might be for teachers to read the section in the handout provided by the principal that introduces teachers to the knowledge maps. The second event listed might be for teachers to discuss the descriptions in the handout, and so on. Then, the principal might use the knowledge map for description (figure 2.26) to define the key characteristics of the knowledge maps themselves. Each teacher would write the phrase *knowledge maps* in the center of the figure, and then fill in characteristics of knowledge maps as they perceive them at this point in training. Teachers might record characteristics like the following.

- Knowledge maps become more complex across the grade levels.

- Knowledge maps provide more ways for students to organize information.

- Knowledge maps require students to think more deeply about content than simple graphic organizers do.

The final step in the training might be that each teacher plans a lesson or set of lessons that use one or more of the knowledge maps. Afterward, teachers compare their plans and discuss what they have learned about how they might use knowledge maps. Having teachers use knowledge maps during their professional development will help them see the purpose and power of visualized thinking and ensure a higher degree of implementation into daily lessons.

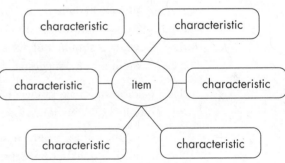

Source: © 2017 by Marzano Resources. Used with permission.

FIGURE 2.26: Description knowledge map.

Systematic Use of Knowledge Maps

The principal should expect that teachers explicitly incorporate knowledge maps into their lessons. This serves several purposes. First, it prompts teachers to consider the use and value of the knowledge maps by requiring them to write the tool into daily instruction. Second, the instructional leadership team can better support knowledge map implementation by reviewing submitted lesson plans. This will provide unique insights, such as which maps are utilized, how often, and in what capacities. These findings will provide valuable data for the school as it determines the best way to incorporate the maps into student learning. Finally, if teachers freely collaborate and use colleagues' lessons, the speed at which the faculty as a whole will adopt knowledge maps will be increased.

In order to support teachers' use of knowledge maps, the principal might ask teachers to determine the sequence of actions they will take when employing specific maps. For example, a lesson might require students to describe the structure of the text. Consequently, the teacher will want to consider which knowledge map will best aid students in this task. In any given situation, several different maps might be useable. For example, the teacher might instruct students to use the simple problem-solution map shown in figure 2.27, or the teacher might provide several maps for students to choose from and then experiment with imposing different structures on a particular text.

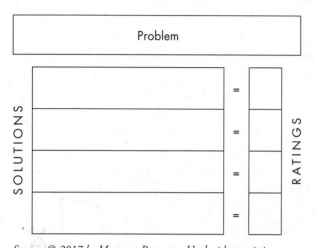

Source: © 2017 by Marzano Resources. Used with permission.

FIGURE 2.27: Simple problem-solution knowledge map.

To illustrate, assume a teacher has students watch a video regarding the various solutions scientists have proposed for slowing or reversing the negative effects of climate change. Students use the simple problem-solution map and record the term *climate change* in the top rectangle. Underneath that, they would record the various proposed solutions. Finally, in the box to the right of each proposed solution, students would rate the likelihood of each proposed solution working as high, medium, or low. On the following day, the teacher would have students use another knowledge map—perhaps causation or comparison—to reorganize the content they had read about the day before. Afterward, students would discuss how using a different organizational structure (that is, a different knowledge map) makes them see the content differently.

In addition to requiring teachers to incorporate knowledge maps into lesson design, the principal can incorporate knowledge maps into the instructional leadership team's walkthrough observation protocol. During walkthroughs, instructional leadership team members should look for evidence that maps are being used, if not daily, at least weekly in every classroom. Some suggested processes to include in classroom walkthroughs are as follows.

1. Look for identified knowledge maps from submitted lesson designs on classroom walls or in student learning journals.

2. Determine if the use of a knowledge map is formally included in the daily learning objective or students' daily action steps.

3. Ask students and teachers which knowledge map they are utilizing and why that particular map is useful for achieving the learning objective.

When the instructional leadership team incorporates knowledge maps into the classroom observation protocols, it provides critical information for the principal to determine the level of implementation of this instructional tool. It also communicates to the faculty the importance of using knowledge maps and provides observational data for improvement.

High Reliability Leadership for School-Level Indicator 8

While knowledge maps are similar to graphic organizers (which teachers have used for decades), their purpose in the Marzano Academies model is to serve as a common language of the structure of knowledge. This common language should be used by every teacher in every subject at every grade level, providing students with ways to see connections between content from seemingly disparate domains.

The previous discussion on school-level indicator 8 emphasizes the following activities relative to knowledge maps.

- Vertical alignment of knowledge maps

- Professional development for knowledge maps

- Systematic use of knowledge maps

Figure 2.28 depicts some potential lagging indicators for this school-level indicator. Figure 2.29 (page 82) depicts the customized high reliability scale for knowledge maps.

Programs and Practices	Lagging Indicator Data	Potential Standard for High Reliability Status
Vertical schoolwide alignment of knowledge maps	A document describing schoolwide vertical alignment of knowledge maps is in place	100 percent of teachers are aware of the guidance regarding vertical alignment of knowledge maps
Professional development for knowledge maps	Professional development activities are in place regarding knowledge maps	100 percent of teachers actively participate in the professional development activities
Systematic use of knowledge maps	Walkthrough protocols are employed that specifically include examination of the use of knowledge maps	100 percent of teachers demonstrate systematic use of knowledge maps in their classrooms
Perceptions of teachers and students	Surveys of teachers and students	100 percent of teachers respond that they understand how to use knowledge maps and employ them on a systematic basis 90 percent of students report that they understand knowledge maps and that the maps help their learning

Source: © 2021 by Robert J. Marzano.

FIGURE 2.28: Potential lagging indicators for school-level indicator 8.

Summary

This chapter addressed four school-level indicators of the academy model that, considered as a set, help create a comprehensive approach to competency-based instruction. Those indicators are:

School-level indicator 5: Instruction and teacher development

School-level indicator 6: Blended instruction

School-level indicator 7: Cumulative review

School-level indicator 8: Knowledge maps

While some of these school-level indicators can be found in traditional schools and classrooms, the four described in this chapter have been adapted specifically to competency-based instruction. Additionally, in the Marzano Academies model these indicators work together to not only enhance student learning but also improve teacher expertise. School-level indicator 5 deals directly with this latter goal in that teachers select instructional improvement goals for themselves, receive support from administrators and instructional coaches, and track their improvement throughout the year. Indicators 6, 7, and 8 represent schoolwide instructional strategies that ensure all students have similar powerful experiences from class to class and teacher to teacher.

Evidence	
4 **Sustaining** **(quick data)**	Quick data like the following are systematically collected and reviewed. • Reviews of teacher lesson plans and unit plans • Walkthrough observational data • Quick conversations with teachers and students
3 **Applying** **(lagging)**	Performance goals with clear criteria for success like the following are in place. • 100 percent of teachers are aware of the guidance regarding vertical alignment of knowledge maps • 100 percent of teachers actively participate in the professional development activities • 100 percent of teachers demonstrate systematic use of knowledge maps in their classrooms • 100 percent of teachers respond that they understand how to use knowledge maps and employ them on a systematic basis • 90 percent of students report that they understand knowledge maps and that the maps help their learning
2 **Developing** **(leading)**	• A vertical alignment document is in place for knowledge maps • Professional development is available for knowledge maps • Walkthrough protocols are used that include a focus on knowledge maps
1 **Beginning**	• The school has written plans for the use of knowledge maps but there is no implementation at the school level • Only a few teachers utilize knowledge maps as tools for reading and writing
0 **Not Using**	• The school has no written plans for the use of knowledge maps as tools for reading and writing • There is no implementation of knowledge maps at the classroom level

Source: © 2020 by Marzano Academies, Inc. Adapted with permission.

FIGURE 2.29: Customized high reliability scale for school-level indicator 8.

CHAPTER 3

Indicators That Address Curriculum

The Marzano Academies approach to curriculum focuses on traditional academic content in such a way that educators identify the individual needs of students and target instruction and assessment to meet those needs. In addition, the academy curriculum focuses on a wide range of other types of knowledge and skill that include highly transferrable cognitive and metacognitive skills, as well as essential vocabulary. The Marzano Academies perspective on curriculum is that the content of the curriculum should be transparent to students, parents and guardians, teachers, and any other interested constituents within the community. Proficiency scales provide this transparency. They are used to define content in traditional subject areas (that is, mathematics, science, social studies, and English language arts), nontraditional skills (that is, cognitive and metacognitive skills), and any other topic that is part of the curriculum. Each proficiency scale articulates a continuum of content that ranges from basic content to the application of more complex content for specific topics. This view of content translates into four school-level indicators that address curriculum in the academy model: measurement topics and proficiency scales, cognitive and metacognitive skills, vocabulary, and explicit goals for students' status and growth.

School-Level Indicator 9: Measurement Topics and Proficiency Scales

A *measurement topic* is a specific topic within a subject area that is defined by an explicit progression of knowledge referred to as a *proficiency scale*. These topics form the foundation of what is taught, measured, and reported in the academy model. The leader of an academy at the elementary school level should ensure that the school has well-articulated measurement topics with accompanying proficiency scales for all content. It is not an exaggeration to say that proficiency scales are the pillars of the academy model. Schools that are in the process of being officially certified as academies typically begin by examining the proficiency scales provided by Marzano Resources (MarzanoResources.com) and then adapting them to their specific needs and values. Other schools would simply create proficiency scales using the standards in their state or district. Since most states and school districts use high-stakes end-of-year standardized tests to measure student attainment of state-adopted academic standards, schools are wise to also consult their state's academic standards when designing their proficiency scales. Regardless of the academic standards used, a school must break down the standards into measurement topics. Then, a learning progression for each measurement topic must be defined by a proficiency scale. Academies employ a very specific format when designing proficiency scales.

A Specific Proficiency Scale Format

Proficiency scales within the academy model use a format that Marzano has employed since 1996 and continually improved since that time (Marzano & Kendall, 1996; Marzano, 2000, 2006, 2010). Figure 3.1 depicts a sample proficiency scale.

4.0	The student will: • Use mental computation and estimation strategies to assess the reasonableness of an answer at different stages of solving a problem (for example, when given that a boy has 374 more baseball cards than a friend who has 221 baseball cards, and when given that he then buys another 186 cards, use rounding to estimate that the number of baseball cards the boy started with would be close to 600 and the number of cards he ended up with would be close to 800)
3.5	In addition to score 3.0 performance, partial success at score 4.0 content
3.0	The student will: Round a given number to the nearest 10 or 100 (for example, round the numbers 23, 50, 95, 447, 283, 509, and 962 to the nearest 10 and the nearest 100)
2.5	No major errors or omissions regarding score 2.0 content, and partial success at score 3.0 content
2.0	The student will recognize or recall specific vocabulary (for example, *digit, estimate, hundreds, number line, ones, place, place value, round, round down, round up, tens, thousands*) and perform basic processes such as: • Identify multiples of 10 and 100 • Identify relationships between place values (for example, explain that ten 1s are equal to one 10 and that ten 10s are equal to one 100) • Explain that rounding a number to a given place estimates or approximates the value of the number to the nearest multiple of that place (for example, rounding a number to the nearest 10 approximates the value of that number to the nearest multiple of 10) • Explain that rounding a number to a given place will leave a value of 0 in each place that is smaller than (to the right of) the targeted place (for example, rounding a number to the nearest 100 will leave a value of 0 in the tens and ones places) • Use a number line to find the nearest multiple of a specified place for a given number (for example, when given the number 146 represented on a number line, identify 100 as the closest multiple of 100) • Explain that a number will be rounded up to a given place if the digit in the place immediately to the right is greater than or equal to 5, and will be rounded down if the digit is less than or equal to 4 • Identify situations in which rounding might be useful (for example, explain that rounding two addends and quickly calculating their sum can be useful for assessing whether or not the calculated sum of the unrounded addends is accurate)
1.5	Partial success at score 2.0 content, and major errors or omissions regarding score 3.0 content
1.0	With help, partial success at score 2.0 content and score 3.0 content
0.5	With help, partial success at score 2.0 content but not at score 3.0 content
0.0	Even with help, no success

Source: © 2016 by Marzano Resources. Adapted with permission.

FIGURE 3.1: Proficiency scale for third-grade mathematics measurement topic of estimation.

The fulcrum of a proficiency scale is score 3.0 content. Score 3.0 represents the desired state of knowledge or skill of a student being proficient at the focal content of the scale. In this case, that content involves rounding to the nearest 10 or 100. The score 3.0 level also provides specific examples of student actions that would demonstrate proficiency. Score 2.0 contains foundational content, including important vocabulary that the teacher will most probably teach directly. It also identifies basic skills that teachers will address, like identifying multiples of 10 and 100. The score 4.0 content involves an example of a specific task that, when executed correctly, demonstrates competency beyond the score 3.0 level. It might be thought of as advanced content for the particular measurement topic.

In addition to the three levels of content for a given measurement topic, proficiency scales also contain score values of 1.0 and 0.0, but these do not involve new content. Rather, a score value of 1.0 indicates that a student has partial success with score 2.0 and 3.0 content, if given help. The score value of 0.0 indicates that even with help, a student does not demonstrate even partial success with any of the content.

The proficiency scale also identifies student performances that rate half-point scores. The half-point values indicate partial movement to the next level up on the scale. For example, a score of 2.5 indicates that a student has competence at the 2.0 level but only partial competence with the score 3.0 content. In effect, the three levels of explicit content (score values 2.0, 3.0, and 4.0) can be translated into nine different score values representing increasing levels of competence regarding a specific measurement topic.

It's important to note that the third-grade mathematics scale in figure 3.1 has a single learning target at the score 3.0 level. However, scales may contain multiple targets at the 3.0 level, as depicted in figure 3.2 (page 86). Whether a proficiency scale has a single learning target at the 3.0 level or multiple targets is a function of how closely related the learning targets are and how focused the designers of a specific proficiency scale wish it to be. The book *Making Classroom Assessments Reliable and Valid* (Marzano, 2018) addresses this issue in depth.

Note that in this figure, score 3.0 includes three bullet points titled P1, P2, and P3. When there are multiple learning targets listed for score 3.0, those elements must be related such that if students are proficient with the content for one, they are most probably proficient with the others. Such a relationship is referred to as a *covarying relationship* (see Marzano, 2006; Marzano, 2018). In the example in figure 3.2, one of the elements deals with calculating the perimeter of irregular polygons, the second deals with finding and creating unknown side lengths of polygons, and the third deals with creating rectangles with the same perimeters and different areas or vice versa. These elements are closely related in terms of the underlying knowledge and skills required to demonstrate proficiency. For example, if a student's ability to calculate the perimeter of irregular polygons improves, he or she will also be more successful with finding unknown side lengths.

Figure 3.2 also depicts some conventions of well-designed proficiency scales. Each level is labeled with its score value on the left side of the scale, pointing to the nine half-point and whole-point score values. Each learning target at score 3.0 includes a standard reference code that identifies the state-level standard that the scale refers to (for example, target P1 relates to Common Core standard 3.MD.D.8). Every element listed for score 3.0 and score 2.0 also identifies the complexity level of the content as measured by the Depth of Knowledge index (Webb, 1997; for example, target P2 at score 3.0 is rated DOK 2). The scale also depicts the relationship between the three 3.0 elements and the 2.0 content that is foundational to each 3.0 element. The content listed under P1 at the score 2.0 level is fundamental to target P1 at the score 3.0 level, the 2.0 content under P2 correlates to P2 at the score 3.0 level, and so on. Each element of score 2.0 content highlights the terminology that is

Westminster Public Schools Proficiency Scale

Colorado Department of Education Strand: Data, Statistics, and Probability	
Common Core State Standards Strand: Statistics and Probability	

Proficiency Scale Theme: Perimeter

Empower	**Recorded Learning Target:** MA.03.MD.08.05	**CCSS Domain:** MD: Measurement and Data

Learning Target Breakdown

Score 4.0   In addition to exhibiting score 3.0 performance, in-depth inferences and applications that go beyond what was taught in class. (Score 4.0 does not equate to more work but rather a higher level of performance as articulated in this sample task.)

- Derive the formula for the perimeter of a rectangle (for example, reason about perimeter and the properties of rectangles to create the formula P = 2 [length + width] for calculating the perimeter of a rectangle) (DOK 3, AP)

Score 3.5   In addition to score 3.0 performance, in-depth inferences and applications with partial success

Score 3.0   The learner will . . .

P1—Calculate the perimeters of irregular polygons in real-world examples (for example, when given an irregular polygon with each side length labeled, a rectangle with height and width labeled, and a regular hexagon with one side length labeled, calculate the perimeter of each figure) (CAS: MA.3.MD.D.8) (CCSS: 3.MD.D.8) (DOK 2, AP)

P2—Find and create unknown side lengths of polygons (for example, when given a rectangle with its perimeter and one side length labeled, determine the lengths of the other sides) (CAS: MA.3.MD.D.8) (CCSS: 3.MD.D.8) (DOK 2, AP)

P3—Create rectangles with the same perimeter and different areas or the same area and different perimeters (for example, use grid paper or unit-square cutouts to create two or more rectangles with perimeters of 24 and different areas) (CAS: MA.3.MD.D.8) (CCSS: 3.MD.D.8) (DOK 2, AP)

The learner exhibits no major errors or omissions regarding any of the information and processes (simple or complex) that were explicitly taught.

Score 2.5   No major errors or omissions regarding the simpler details and processes (score 2.0 content) and partial knowledge of the more complex ideas and processes (score 3.0 content)

Score 2.0   **P1**—The learner will recognize or recall specific vocabulary (for example, *length, side length, unit, width*) and perform basic processes such as:

- Explain that the length of a figure's perimeter can be calculated as the sum of its side lengths (DOK 1, UN)
- Determine the length of a given figure's perimeter by counting unit lengths along its boundary (for example, when given a rectangle on a unit-square grid, determine its perimeter by counting the number of unit lengths necessary to travel around its boundary) (DOK 1, UN)

P2—The learner will recognize or recall specific vocabulary (for example, *equation, perimeter*) and perform basic processes such as:

- Represent a perimeter calculation as an equation (for example, when given a quadrilateral with side lengths 5, 9, 4, and 11, represent the perimeter of the quadrilateral as P = 5 + 9 + 4 + 11) (DOK 1, RE)
- Find unknown addends (for example, when given the problem 5 + 7 + 22 + __ = 55, identify the unknown addend as 21) (DOK 2, AP)

P3—The learner will recognize or recall specific vocabulary (for example, *area, boundary*) and perform basic processes such as:

- Explain that two rectangles can have the same perimeter and different areas, or the same area but different perimeters (DOK 2, UN)
- Compare rectangles with the same area and different perimeters, or the same perimeter and different areas (for example, when given two rectangles with the same area and with side lengths labeled, determine which rectangle has the greater perimeter) (DOK 2, UN)

The learner, however, exhibits major errors or omissions regarding the more complex ideas and processes.

Score 1.5   Partial knowledge of the simpler details and processes (score 2.0 content) but major errors or omissions regarding the more complex ideas and processes (score 3.0 content)

Score 1.0   With help, the learner exhibits a partial understanding of some of the simpler details and processes (score 2.0 content) and some of the more complex ideas and processes (score 3.0 content).

Score 0.5   With help, a partial understanding of some of the simpler details and processes (score 2.0 content) but not the more complex ideas and processes (score 3.0 content)

Score 0.0   Even with help, the learner demonstrates no understanding or skill.

Source: © 2020 by Westminster Public Schools. Adapted with permission.

FIGURE 3.2: Proficiency scale with multiple topics at the 3.0 level.

important for students' understanding. The vocabulary is shown in parentheses in each bullet point (for example, the vocabulary for P1 includes *length*, *side length*, *unit*, and *width*). Finally, the score 4.0 level includes a sample task that would demonstrate knowledge and skill above that required for proficiency at the 3.0 level. As this example illustrates, a well-constructed proficiency scale details the content for a specific topic (that is, a measurement topic) organized as a continuum of knowledge and coded in a way that it can be quantified to represent students' status on that continuum. As we explain in subsequent sections of this book, this allows teachers to use a variety of approaches to assess students' status and provide them with detailed feedback on what they can do to improve that status. The detail in a proficiency scale also provides teachers with guidance as to what should be the focus of instruction in upcoming lessons. In effect, proficiency scales not only define the curriculum; they also guide assessment and instruction. This is why they are pillars of the Marzano Academies model.

Teacher Involvement in Creating Proficiency Scales

Regardless of whether a school creates its own scales or customizes the proficiency scales developed by Marzano Resources, it is important that teachers be involved in the process. Their involvement will not only provide them with an understanding of the curriculum, but also serve to give them a sense of ownership over the curriculum. This is accomplished most efficiently when teacher teams collaborate during the authorship or revision of scales and have discussions about the exact determinants of student success relative to the content in the scale. To illustrate, consider the proficiency scale in figure 3.3 (page 88).

Figure 3.3 contains a proficiency scale from the Marzano Resources Critical Concepts. The school leader would ask teachers working in collaborative teams to make additions, deletions, and changes in this source. After the collaborative team examines the scale and discusses possible additions, deletions, and changes, the proficiency scale might look like that in figure 3.4 (page 89). In this example, teachers working in a collaborative team have modified the scale by deleting some elements, rewording some elements, and adding some elements. The books *Making Classroom Assessments Reliable and Valid* (Marzano, 2018) and *The New Art and Science of Classroom Assessment* (Marzano, Norford, & Ruyle, 2019) provide specific guidance as to how teachers might engage in deleting, rewording, and adding elements to proficiency scales. These changes, although fairly simple and straightforward, render the scale something about which teachers have a sense of ownership and pride in authorship.

A Guaranteed and Viable Set of Measurement Topics and Proficiency Scales

Ultimately, the purpose of designing proficiency scales is to identify clear learning progressions for a relatively small set of measurement topics that will be the subject of classroom assessment and instruction. Such a list should constitute what we refer to as a *guaranteed and viable curriculum* (Marzano, 2003). The curriculum in a school should be *guaranteed* in that the school can ensure every teacher addresses each measurement topic and proficiency scale for his or her content area or grade level. Thus, students are *guaranteed* to learn the same curriculum no matter which teacher they are assigned to. Such a curriculum is *viable* when it is focused and streamlined enough that teachers have sufficient time in the school year to adequately teach and reinforce the content.

Unfortunately, standards documents at the national level and the state level typically identify so much content that it's impossible for schools to adequately address those national or state standards. To illustrate, Robert J. Marzano, David C. Yanoski, Jan K. Hoegh, and Julia A. Simms (2013)

4.0	The student will:
	• Investigate ways in which an experiment might not be reliable (for example, after conducting an experiment, generate a list of ways in which human error or faulty experiment design might have affected the results)

| 3.5 | In addition to score 3.0 performance, partial success at score 4.0 content |

3.0	The student will:
	SM1—Use the scientific method to conduct an experiment (for example, after generating a simple hypothesis, develop an experiment to determine the accuracy of the hypothesis)

| 2.5 | No major errors or omissions regarding score 2.0 content, and partial success at score 3.0 content |

2.0	SM1—The student will recognize or recall specific vocabulary (for example, *analysis, conclusion, data, experiment, hypothesis, magnifier, observation, problem, question, repeat, ruler, scientific method, thermometer, tool*) and perform basic processes such as:
	• Describe each step of the scientific method (for example, observation, question, or problem; hypothesis; experiment; analysis; conclusion)
	• Generate a basic hypothesis based on an observation, question, or problem
	• Design an experiment to test a hypothesis generated from observation
	• Design an experiment that can be repeated multiple times
	• Identify multiple variables in an experiment
	• Isolate one variable to be tested by controlling for specific variables
	• Develop an experiment that can be replicated multiple times
	• Use tools to collect data (for example, thermometers, magnifiers, rulers)
	• Collect data from an experiment
	• Analyze data from an experiment to draw a conclusion about the experiment
	• Compare a conclusion about an experiment to an initial hypothesis

| 1.5 | Partial success at score 2.0 content, and major errors or omissions regarding score 3.0 content |

| 1.0 | With help, partial success at score 2.0 content and score 3.0 content |

| 0.5 | With help, partial success at score 2.0 content but not at score 3.0 content |

| 0.0 | Even with help, no success |

Source: © 2016 by Marzano Resources. Used with permission.

FIGURE 3.3: Proficiency scale from Marzano Resources Critical Concepts—scientific method.

analyzed national standards documents and identified seventy-three standards statements for eighth-grade English language arts. They also found an average of five topics embedded in each statement, making for a total of 365 topics teachers are expected to cover in a single academic year at the eighth-grade level. In contrast, Simms (2016) reported that removing the redundancy from standards and considering only those topics that are typically found on national assessments results in a list of essential measurement topics that is quite small. Table 3.1 (page 90) reports the number of

4.0	The student will:
	• Investigate ways in which an experiment might not be reliable (for example, after conducting an experiment, generate a list of ways in which human error or faulty experiment design might have affected the results; those errors should include issues like precisions of measurement and sampling)

3.5	In addition to score 3.0 performance, partial success at score 4.0 content

3.0	The student will:
	SM1—Use the scientific method to conduct an experiment (for example, after generating a simple hypothesis, develop an experiment to determine the accuracy of the hypothesis, carry out the experiment, compare the results with the original hypothesis, and make changes in the hypothesis as necessary based on the results)

2.5	No major errors or omissions regarding score 2.0 content, and partial success at score 3.0 content

2.0	SM1—The student will recognize or recall specific vocabulary (for example, *analysis, conclusion, data, experiment, hypothesis, question, observation, problem, scientific method, tool*) and perform basic processes such as:
	• Describe each step of the scientific method (for example, observation, question, or problem; hypothesis; experiment; analysis; conclusion)
	• Generate a basic hypothesis based on an observation, question, or problem
	• Identify multiple variables in an experiment
	• Isolate one variable to be tested by controlling for specific variables
	• Collect data from an experiment
	• Analyze data from an experiment to draw a conclusion about the experiment
	• Compare a conclusion about an experiment to an initial hypothesis

1.5	Partial success at score 2.0 content, and major errors or omissions regarding score 3.0 content

1.0	With help, partial success at score 2.0 content and score 3.0 content

0.5	With help, partial success at score 2.0 content but not at score 3.0 content

0.0	Even with help, no success

Source: © 2016 by Marzano Resources. Adapted with permission.

FIGURE 3.4: Proficiency scale customized by a collaborative team—scientific method.

topics considered essential in mathematics, science, and ELA. The complete list of essential measurement topics is found in the document titled *The Critical Concepts* (Simms, 2016). Educators can use these lists as a guiding framework as they translate their local or state standards into a guaranteed and viable set of measurement topics and proficiency scales.

High Reliability Leadership for School-Level Indicator 9

Proficiency scales provide a clear, transparent curriculum for each measurement topic within each subject area at each grade level. The Marzano Academies model uses a specific format for these scales, which provide teachers with guidance regarding assessment and instruction.

TABLE 3.1: Essential Topics in Mathematics, Science, and ELA

Subject	K	1	2	3	4	5	6	7	8	9	10	11	12	Total
Mathematics	10	9	14	14	15	14	16	15	16		64			187
Science	9	11	11	13	15	10		31			36			136
ELA	18	20	19	19	18	15	15	14	15		14		14	181

Source: Simms, 2016.

Involving teachers in the process of creating proficiency scales provides them with ownership of and pride in the curriculum.

The previous discussion on school-level indicator 9 emphasizes the following elements of measurement topics and proficiency scales.

- Using a specific type of proficiency scale format

- Involving teachers in the design of proficiency scales

- Ensuring a guaranteed and viable set of measurement topics and proficiency scales

Figure 3.5 depicts potential lagging indicators for these elements. Figure 3.6 depicts the customized high reliability scale for this school-level indicator.

Programs and Practices	Lagging Indicator Data	Potential Standard for High Reliability Status
A particular type of proficiency scale	A specific format for measurement topics and proficiency scales has been articulated	100 percent of measurement topics and proficiency scales follow the prescribed format
Involving teachers in the design and development process	A team representative of all teachers in the building is selected to be involved in the design and development process	100 percent of teachers selected for the design and development process actively participate
A guaranteed and viable set of topics and scales	Parameters for the defining features of a guaranteed and viable curriculum have been articulated	100 percent of measurement topics and proficiency scales adhere to the defining features of a guaranteed and viable curriculum
Perceptions of students, teachers, and parents	Surveys of teachers, students, and parents	90 percent of teachers perceive the measurement topics and proficiency scales as viable and useful 90 percent of students perceive the measurement topics and proficiency scales as viable and useful 70 percent of teachers perceive the measurement topics and proficiency scales as viable and useful

Source: © 2021 by Robert J. Marzano.

FIGURE 3.5: Potential lagging indicators for school-level indicator 9.

Evidence	
4 **Sustaining** **(quick data)**	Quick data like the following are systematically collected and reviewed. • Reviews of teacher lesson plans and unit plans • Quick conversations with teachers and students • Examination of evidence scores in the LMS
3 **Applying** **(lagging)**	Performance goals with clear criteria for success like the following are in place. • 100 percent of measurement topics and proficiency scales follow the prescribed format • 100 percent of teachers selected for the design and development process actively participate • 100 percent of measurement topics and proficiency scales adhere to the defining features of a guaranteed and viable curriculum • 90 percent of teachers perceive the measurement topics and proficiency scales as viable and useful
2 **Developing** **(leading)**	• The format for proficiency scales has been articulated • Representative groups of teachers are involved in the design of measurement topics and proficiency scales • Guidelines are in place for a guaranteed and viable curriculum based on measurement topics and proficiency scales
1 **Beginning**	• The school has written plans for the articulation and implementation of proficiency scales and measurement topics for the major subject areas but there is little execution of the plans at the classroom level • Relatively few teachers implement instruction and assessment based on measurement topics and proficiency scales
0 **Not Using**	• The school has no written plan for instruction and assessment of measurement topics for the major subject areas • There is no implementation at the classroom level of instruction and assessment based on measurement topics for the major subject areas

Source: © 2020 by Marzano Academies, Inc. Adapted with permission.

FIGURE 3.6: Customized high reliability scale for school-level indicator 9.

School-Level Indicator 10: Cognitive and Metacognitive Skills

In addition to measurement topics and proficiency scales to define specific academic content (school-level indicator 9, page 83), the curriculum in the Marzano Academies model also includes cognitive and metacognitive skills. Making these important thinking skills an explicit part of the curriculum ensures that students develop the ability to process information and "exert executive control" over their thinking (Marzano, 2017, p. 112). The leader of an elementary academy should ensure that the school has well-articulated measurement topics and accompanying proficiency scales for cognitive and metacognitive skills and these skills are systematically taught and assessed throughout the school.

Cognitive Skills

Generally speaking, cognitive skills are those involved in thinking, reasoning, and acquiring and using information. Cognitive skills fall into two types: cognitive analysis skills and knowledge application skills.

Cognitive Analysis Skills

Cognitive analysis skills are those that people use to analyze and dissect information so that they might understand it at deeper levels. There are eight cognitive analysis skills, as depicted in table 3.2.

TABLE 3.2: Cognitive Analysis Skills

Cognitive Analysis Skill	Description
Comparing	Comparing is the process of determining similarities and differences between elements or concepts.
Analogical reasoning	Analogical reasoning is the process of determining how one set of elements or concepts is related to another set of elements or concepts.
Classifying	Classifying is the process of using definable attributes to organize concepts or elements into categories or related subcategories.
Analyzing perspectives	Analyzing perspectives is the process of analyzing one's own perspective and the reasoning supporting it and contrasting that with a different perspective and the reasoning supporting it.
Constructing support	Constructing support is the process of formulating a claim and then developing a well-constructed argument that supports it.
Analyzing errors in reasoning	Analyzing errors is the process of recognizing logical fallacies or errors in information generated by others or oneself.
Analyzing inferences	Analyzing inferences is the process of identifying the inferences one makes automatically and unconsciously as well as the inferences one makes during conscious reasoning.
Generating mental images	Generating mental images is the process of creating images that represent information and procedures.

Source: © 2017 by Marzano Resources. Adapted with permission.

Knowledge Application Skills

Another type of cognitive skill involves the application of knowledge. These skills are typically employed when using knowledge in unique situations. There are six knowledge application skills in the Marzano Academies model, described in table 3.3.

TABLE 3.3: Knowledge Application Skills

Knowledge Application Skill	Description
Decision making	Decision making is the process of generating and applying criteria to select between alternatives that appear equal.
Problem solving	Problem solving is the process of overcoming obstacles or constraints to achieve a goal.
Invention	Invention is the act of creating a new process or product that meets a specific identified need. In a sense, it might be likened to problem solving in that it addresses a specific need. However, problem solving is limited in duration.
Experimental inquiry	Experimental inquiry is the process of generating a hypothesis about a physical or psychological phenomenon and then testing the hypothesis.
Investigation	Investigation is the process of identifying and then resolving differences of opinion or contradictory information about concepts, historical events, or future possible events.
Systems analysis	Systems analysis is the process of describing and analyzing the parts of a system with particular emphasis on the relationships among the parts.

Source: © 2017 by Marzano Resources. Adapted with permission.

Metacognitive Skills

Metacognition is most simply described as thinking about one's thinking. These skills come into play when one is planning, setting goals, making decisions, reflecting, and so on. Metacognition also involves two categories: traditional metacognitive skills and metacognitive life skills.

Traditional Metacognitive Skills

Traditional metacognitive skills (which we simply refer to hereafter as *metacognitive skills*) have been discussed in the literature since at least the 1980s. For example, the book *Dimensions of Thinking* (Marzano et al., 1988) was a joint effort of a number of professional organizations, including the Association for Supervision and Curriculum Development (ASCD), American Educational Research Association (AERA), and American Psychological Association (APA). The book highlighted metacognitive skills as the ultimate goal of a proposed "thinking skills" curriculum for K–12 schools.

In the Marzano Academies model, educators teach and reinforce ten traditional metacognitive skills. Table 3.4 (page 94) depicts these ten skills.

Metacognitive Life Skills

Life skills in the Marzano Academies model are focused on those actions and behaviors that help students become productive members of their school communities and create an environment that supports all learners. There are four life skills, described in table 3.5 (page 95).

TABLE 3.4: Traditional Metacognitive Skills

Metacognitive Skill	Description
Staying focused when answers and solutions are not immediately apparent	This skill helps students overcome obstacles and stay focused when challenges arise. It also helps students to recognize how much effort they are putting into accomplishing a specific task.
Pushing the limits of one's knowledge and skills	This skill helps students set goals and engage in tasks that are personally challenging. When using this skill, students will strive to learn more and accomplish more.
Generating and pursuing one's own standards for performance	This skill enables students to envision and articulate criteria for what a successful project will look like.
Seeking incremental steps	This skill helps students take on complex tasks using small incremental steps so they do not become overwhelmed by the task as a whole.
Seeking accuracy	This skill helps students vet sources of information for reliability and verify information by consulting multiple sources known to be reliable.
Seeking clarity	This skill helps students identify points of confusion when they are learning new information. This allows students to independently seek a deeper understanding.
Resisting impulsivity	When faced with a desire to form a quick conclusion, this skill helps students refrain from doing so until they can gather more relevant information prior to taking action.
Seeking cohesion and coherence	When students are creating something with a number of interacting parts, this skill helps them monitor the relationships between what they are currently doing and the overall intent of the project in which they are engaged.
Setting goals and making plans	This skill helps students set short- and long-term goals, create timelines or blueprints, monitor progress, and make necessary adjustments.
Growth mindset thinking	This skill helps students take on challenging tasks with an attitude that helps them succeed, even when confronted by major obstacles.

Source: © 2017 by Marzano Resources. Adapted with permission.

Cognitive and Metacognitive Skills as an Essential Part of the Curriculum

Simply asking teachers to incorporate cognitive and metacognitive skills into existing instruction will most likely not work well. The principal must establish a process whereby these skills are written into the curriculum. To this end, the first step is for the principal to form a committee to make curricular decisions about these skills. This committee should include teachers, instructional leaders, administrators, and school district officials (if applicable) to ensure a wide range of perspectives are represented. In relation to committee participation, the principal should invite at least one teacher from each grade-level or subject-area team, one interventionist or specialist, one instructional paraprofessional, a member of the instructional leadership team, and any appropriate administrative

TABLE 3.5: Life Skills

Life Skill	Description
Participation	Participation involves the set of decisions and actions that helps students add to group discussions and engage actively in questioning and answering questions.
Work completion	Work completion involves the set of decisions and actions that helps students manage their workload and complete tasks efficiently and effectively.
Behavior	Behavior involves the set of decisions and actions that helps students follow classroom rules and norms designed to create an efficient and orderly learning environment for all.
Working in groups	Working in groups involves the set of decisions and actions that helps students function as productive and supportive members of groups designed to enhance the learning of the students within those groups.

Source: © 2017 by Marzano Resources. Adapted with permission.

personnel. The primary job of the committee is to determine the scope and sequence of each cognitive and metacognitive skill delineated across grade levels or teaching teams.

It is important to note that not all cognitive and metacognitive skills can nor should be taught at every grade level. Instead, the skills should be strategically assigned to individual teams to ensure consistency across the vertical progression of learning. This strategic division of skills is depicted in table 3.6 (page 96). Some skills are listed for instruction at both the primary and upper elementary levels. This is because each of the skills has a vertical progression of learning, gaining in complexity as students age.

The primary job of the committee is to determine which cognitive and metacognitive skills are taught and reinforced at which levels. In table 3.6, the committee has made the distinction as to which skills are addressed at the primary level and which skills are addressed at the intermediate level. Note that life skills and many of the metacognitive skills appear at both levels, although skills are taught in more depth and detail at the intermediate level than they are when addressed at the primary level. This is evident in the differences in their respective proficiency scales. In our previous discussion of the metacognitive skill of growth mindset thinking (see school-level indicator 3, page 32), we presented the grades K–2 proficiency scale for this skill (figure 1.6, page 38) along with the grades 3–5 proficiency scale for this same skill (figure 1.7, page 39). An examination of these two scales for this one skill provides a sense of how the expectations for students increase in complexity as they move up through the grade levels.

The committee can also assign specific skills to specific grade levels and even specific subject areas within those grade levels. For example, the metacognitive skill of seeking clarity might be assigned to the second-grade English language arts class at the primary level, and the third-grade English language arts class at the intermediate level. The committee's reasoning might be that seeking clarity logically fits well with reading texts, which is a staple of English language arts instruction. This does not mean that the teachers at other grade levels and subject areas cannot use or reinforce this metacognitive skill. It simply means that this metacognitive skill will be a formal part of the curriculum in those designated classes. Armed with this knowledge, school leaders will be able to provide support to teachers for the specific skills they are tasked to address and monitor their progress.

TABLE 3.6: Vertical Alignment Chart

Cognitive and Metacognitive Skills Vertical Progression			
Cognitive Analysis Skills	Knowledge Application Skills	Metacognitive Skills	Metacognitive Life Skills
Primary			
Classifying		Growth mindset thinking	Behavior
Comparing		Resisting impulsivity	Participation
Constructing support		Seeking accuracy	Work completion
Generating mental images		Seeking clarity	Working in groups
		Seeking cohesion and coherence	
		Seeking incremental steps	
		Setting goals and making plans	
		Staying focused when answers and solutions are not immediately apparent	
Intermediate			
Analogical reasoning	Decision making	Generating and pursuing one's own standards for performance	Behavior
Analyzing errors in reasoning	Experimental inquiry	Growth mindset thinking	Participation
Analyzing perspectives	Invention	Pushing the limits of one's knowledge and skills	Work completion
Classifying	Investigation	Resisting impulsivity	Working in groups
Comparing	Problem solving	Seeking accuracy	
Constructing support	Systems analysis	Seeking clarity	
Generating mental images		Seeking cohesion and coherence	
Analyzing inferences		Seeking incremental steps	
		Setting goals and making plans	
		Staying focused when answers and solutions are not immediately apparent	

Source: © 2021 by Robert J. Marzano.

Proficiency Scales for Cognitive and Metacognitive Skills

Like academic content, the cognitive and metacognitive skills should be explicated in proficiency scales. To illustrate, figure 3.7 (page 98) depicts a customized version of the proficiency scale for the metacognitive skill of growth mindset at the primary level and figure 3.8 (page 99) depicts a customized version of the proficiency scale for the same skill at the upper elementary level. The original Marzano Resources proficiency scales appeared in our discussion of school-level indicator 3 (page 32). The versions here demonstrate how a particular school system made adaptations in the Marzano Resources scales to the needs and desires of their particular system.

Notice that the content of these two proficiency scales is basically identical to that in the original versions supplied by Marzano Resources. However, there are formatting changes that educators in the district find useful, such as indenting the half-point score values to emphasize the distinction between the whole-point score values and the half-point score values. They have also added some district-specific terminology. For example, at the top of the middle column in both scales they use the terminology *recorded learning target*. This is how the district refers to all topics for which students must demonstrate proficiency. The recorded learning target is defined by a detailed code. For the intermediate proficiency scale that code is COG.03.MC.05.01. While this doesn't mean much to those not familiar with the district's curriculum, to educators within the district it pinpoints the precise subject area, grade level, and standard to which the proficiency scale refers. Finally, in both scales there is a third column on the right side. In this column, teachers record specific examples of student success they have observed as well as sample tasks they have used or might use to determine student proficiency. In effect, even though the district made little if any change to the content of the proficiency scales, the changes they did make render both of these scales useful tools for which district teachers and administrators feel pride and ownership.

Schools should develop proficiency scales for each of the cognitive and metacognitive skills at different grade bands (typically, K–2, 3–5, 6–8, and 9–12). As is the case with academic knowledge and skills, schools seeking to become certified Marzano Academies typically customize the cognitive and metacognitive scales developed by Marzano Resources. As illustrated in figures 3.7 and 3.8, they should make changes to those scales to meet the specific needs of their administrators, teachers, and students. Of course, schools not seeking to become official Marzano Academies can create their own lists of cognitive and metacognitive skills and the proficiency scales that accompany them. A simple internet search for life skills, cognitive skills, or metacognitive skills will provide a vast array of possibilities to this end.

As with all proficiency scale design, skill development is scaffolded by the progression of learning, with the score 2.0 targets being prerequisites for score 3.0 competency. For example, in figure 3.7, the score 2.0 learning targets focus on necessary vocabulary, as well as basic processes on which students should demonstrate proficiency before attempting the more complex score 3.0 learning targets. When the proficiency scales are completed, they become the official cognitive and metacognitive curriculum for the school, and the better the design, the better the eventual implementation.

Professional Development for Cognitive and Metacognitive Skills

After a school has adapted or authored the proficiency scales for each cognitive and metacognitive skill, the principal should ensure quality professional development for faculty and staff. The leader would start by listing and explaining the ten metacognitive skills within the model. While their names will most probably be familiar to teachers, thinking of them as teachable skills might not be. One way to explain these skills is to walk teachers through the proficiency scales for specific skills. This would

Westminster Public Schools Proficiency Scale

Strand: Cognitive Systems	
Proficiency Scale Theme: Growth Mindset Thinking	

Recorded Learning Target: COG.01.MC.05.01	**Domain:** Metacognitive

Learning Target Breakdown	Success Criteria or Sample Tasks
Score 4.0 **In addition to exhibiting score 3.0 performance, in-depth inferences and applications that go beyond what was taught in class** (score 4.0 does not equate to more work but rather a higher level of performance) • ④ Provide a rudimentary description of what it looks like when someone develops a growth mindset	
Score 3.5 In addition to score 3.0 performance, in-depth inferences and applications with partial success	
Score 3.0 **The learner will...** • ③ When asked by the teacher, accurately recognize when he or she is or is not operating from a positive mindset (for example, the teacher asks, "Are you thinking positively about what you can accomplish in this upcoming task?" and the student correctly evaluates him- or herself) **The learner exhibits no major errors or omissions regarding any of the information and processes (simple or complex) that were explicitly taught.**	**Sample Tasks** Student evaluations Data binders Behavior and content evaluations
Score 2.5 No major errors or omissions regarding the simpler details and processes (score 2.0 content) and partial knowledge of the more complex ideas and processes (score 3.0 content)	

Score 2.0   **There are no major errors or omissions regarding the simpler details and processes as the learner...**
 	
   • Recognizes or recalls specific terminology such as:
     ◦ *care, goal, accomplish, growth, plans, yet*
   • Performs basic processes such as:
     ◦ ② Understanding that a growth mindset is a positive way to think about what you can accomplish (for example, you can learn to do almost anything if you are willing to work hard)
     ◦ ① Recognizing situations in which growth mindset thinking might be useful (for example, when you are learning a new skill or when you have a goal that is not easy to accomplish)
 	
The learner, however, exhibits major errors or omissions regarding the more complex ideas and processes.	

Score 1.5 Partial knowledge of the simpler details and processes (score 2.0 content) but major errors or omissions regarding the more complex ideas and processes (score 3.0 content)	
Score 1.0 **With help, a partial understanding of some of the simpler details and processes (score 2.0 content) and some of the more complex ideas and processes (score 3.0 content)**	**Primary Resources:** • SS.01.CIV.01.03 • SS.01.CIV.02.03 • SS.01.EC.01.03 • MA.01.MD.04.04 • MA.01.PFL.01.04 • SC.01.ETS1.03.04 • SC.01.LS1.01.04
Score 0.5 With help, a partial understanding of some of the simpler details and processes (score 2.0 content) but not the more complex ideas and processes (score 3.0 content)	

Source: © 2014 by Westminster Public Schools. Used with permission.

FIGURE 3.7: Primary proficiency scale for growth mindset thinking.

Westminster Public Schools Proficiency Scale

Strand: Cognitive Systems		
Proficiency Scale Theme: Growth Mindset Thinking		
Recorded Learning Target: COG.03.MC.05.01		**Domain:** Metacognitive

	Learning Target Breakdown	Success Criteria or Sample Tasks
Score 4.0	**In addition to exhibiting score 3.0 performance, in-depth inferences and applications that go beyond what was taught in class** (score 4.0 does not equate to more work but rather a higher level of performance) • ④ When cued by the teacher, the student will explain how well he or she operated from a positive mindset	
Score 3.5	In addition to score 3.0 performance, in-depth inferences and applications with partial success	
Score 3.0	**The learner will...** • ③ When cued by the teacher, execute a simple teacher-provided strategy for growth mindset thinking (for example, [1] notice how you are thinking about your ability to accomplish the upcoming task, [2] try to change any negative thoughts to positive thoughts [for example, change "I can't do this" to "I can accomplish some good things, if I try"; change "This is going to be boring" to "I can make this fun"; change "This is useless" to "I can learn something valuable from this"], [3] promise yourself that you are going to try your best and not let yourself get discouraged) **The learner exhibits no major errors or omissions regarding any of the information and processes (simple or complex) that were explicitly taught.**	
Score 2.5	No major errors or omissions regarding the simpler details and processes (score 2.0 content) and partial knowledge of the more complex ideas and processes (score 3.0 content)	

Score 2.0	**There are no major errors or omissions regarding the simpler details and processes as the learner...**
	• Recognizes or recalls specific terminology such as:
	  ◦ *positive, growth mindset, fixed mindset*
	• Performs basic processes such as:
	  ◦ ② When asked by the teacher, accurately recognizes when he or she is operating from a positive mindset (for example, when asked "Are you thinking positively or negatively about your ability to do this?")
	  ◦ ① Recognizes common mistakes or pitfalls associated with growth mindset thinking (for example, having a growth mindset in one area but a fixed mindset in others; starting out with a positive attitude but getting discouraged easily)
	The learner, however, exhibits major errors or omissions regarding the more complex ideas and processes.	

Score 1.5	Partial knowledge of the simpler details and processes (score 2.0 content) but major errors or omissions regarding the more complex ideas and processes (score 3.0 content)	
Score 1.0	**With help, a partial understanding of some of the simpler details and processes (score 2.0 content) and some of the more complex ideas and processes (score 3.0 content)**	**Primary Resources:**
Score 0.5	With help, a partial understanding of some of the simpler details and processes (score 2.0 content) but not the more complex ideas and processes (score 3.0 content)	Reflection journal Character traits Theme LI.05.R1.03 LI.04.R1.03

Source: © 2014 by Westminster Public Schools. Used with permission.

FIGURE 3.8: Intermediate proficiency scale for growth mindset thinking.

demonstrate that each skill includes information that can be taught to students and actions they can take to execute the skill. For example, the grades 3–5 proficiency scale for growth mindset involves vocabulary terms such as *ability, developed, effort, failure, innate,* and *intelligence.* It also involves student awareness of the differences between the growth mindset and the fixed mindset. This information is at the 2.0 level of the scale. At the 3.0 level of the scale, there is a specific set of steps students can take to execute growth mindset thinking: (1) notice how you are thinking about your ability to accomplish the upcoming task; (2) try to change any negative thoughts to positive thoughts; and (3) promise yourself that you are going to try your best and not let yourself get discouraged.

Equally important, professional development would focus on not only how teachers can use cognitive and metacognitive skills to enhance students' understanding of the traditional content, but also how those skills can be used outside of school. For example, during professional development, the leader might ask teachers to identify how students could use each metacognitive skill outside of the academic environment. One teacher might note that students can use growth mindset thinking when they are trying to make a particular sports team. Another teacher might note that students can use it when they want to make new friends they aren't sure will like them. It is this real-life use of the cognitive and metacognitive skills that constitutes their unique importance in the curriculum and their value to students. Creating this awareness with teachers should be one of the primary goals of professional development.

We recommend beginning the faculty conversation about the importance of cognitive and metacognitive skills with a discussion about a student's first day after graduation. What knowledge or skills make adults successful? This conversation should not be limited to professional or workplace practices, but also include personal social skills adults use on a daily basis. The principal might pose questions that require faculty and staff to consider how they personally use a growth mindset, or resist impulsivity, or work in groups, or solve problems to be successful in life. The conversation can highlight the fact that cognitive and metacognitive skills are just as important in personal relationships as they are in professional settings. In fact, one could argue that these skills are *more* important for a student on his or her first day after graduation than many of the content-specific learning targets state academic standards primarily focus on.

Assessment of Cognitive and Metacognitive Skills

Educators must also design an appropriate assessment system for cognitive and metacognitive skills. To illustrate how this might be done, consider the score 3.0 learning targets for the metacognitive skill of seeking clarity at the primary and intermediate levels, as shown in figure 3.9.

Taken together, these targets demonstrate how cognitive and metacognitive skills become more complex over time. At the primary level, the student is only expected to recognize whether or not he or she is seeking clarity. At the intermediate level, the student is expected to enact a process for seeking clarity when the teacher prompts him or her to do so.

For assessment purposes, notice that the K–2 (primary) target begins with, "When asked by the teacher . . ." while the 3–5 (intermediate) target begins with, "When cued by the teacher . . . ." Thus, by simply asking students questions or conducting probing discussions with students, teachers can adequately assess this skill at both primary and intermediate levels. Teachers can utilize assessment protocols like these with individual students or groups of students. For example, consider the grade 3–5 strategy for seeking clarity that students are expected to execute when cued by the teacher. After the teacher has presented students with new information about the science concept of kinetic energy, for example, the teacher might then remind them to use the three-step process for seeking

Seeking Clarity (K–2 Metacognitive) Score 3

The student will:

SC1—When asked by the teacher, accurately recognize when he or she is or is not seeking clarity (for example, the teacher asks, "Are you thinking about whether you are clear or not about this information?" and the student correctly evaluates him- or herself)

Seeking Clarity (3–5 Metacognitive) Score 3

The student will:

SC1—When cued by the teacher, execute a simple teacher-provided strategy for seeking clarity (for example, [1] identify something about which you are unclear, [2] identify the question you would need to ask to become more clear, [3] ask your question)

Source: © 2017 by Marzano Resources. Used with permission.

FIGURE 3.9: Expectation for specific metacognitive skills.

clarity. First, the teacher would have students identify information related to kinetic energy about which they are unclear, and then write down their responses. The teacher would also ask students to rate how well they think they did on this step. The teacher would repeat this process for the second and third steps of the process. The teacher would collect the written records of this assessment from students and use it to gauge how well they are using the skill of seeking clarity, both individually and as a group. This example illustrates that many of the cognitive and metacognitive skills do not require a formal, summative assessment. Instead, they can be readily observed through daily class interaction or through miniconferences between teacher and student.

We recommend that teacher teams create simple checklists based on the score 3.0 target descriptions for cognitive and metacognitive skills, as shown in figure 3.10. Although checklists might be considered reductionist by some, they tend to provide teachers with a clear focus as to the information they should collect.

Seeking Clarity (3–5 Metacognitive) Score 3 Checklist

The student will:

SC1—When cued by the teacher, execute a simple teacher-provided strategy for seeking clarity:

✓ Identify something about which you are unclear

✓ Identify the question you would need to ask to become more clear

✓ Ask your clarifying question

Source: © 2017 by Marzano Resources. Used with permission.

FIGURE 3.10: Checklist for seeking clarity assessment.

Another approach to developing assessments for cognitive and metacognitive skills is to describe the specific questions or prompts teachers might use to determine if students understand and can execute specific skills. For example, figure 3.11 (page 102) depicts assessment guidance at the K–2 level for the metacognitive skill of persevering when answers and solutions are not immediately apparent. For each level of the proficiency scale, this rubric suggests a task or a question that the teacher can pose to students, as well as indications of how students should respond if they are performing the skill at that level. Note that figure 3.11 only describes the whole-point score values of 2.0, 3.0, and 4.0. This is because half-point score values all use the whole-point score values as their reference points.

Score Level	Assessment Task
4.0	Ask students to describe what it looks like when one stays focused if answers and solutions are not immediately apparent. Students' answers should include things like, *you know when you are giving up but then decide to keep trying.*
3.0	Provide students with a task that requires them to stay focused when answers and solutions are not immediately apparent. Such tasks should have no obvious solution when initially addressed (for example, brain-teaser tasks). When asked, students should be able to accurately determine if they are trying to use this skill.
2.0	Ask students to explain the following terms: *challenge, effort, giving up, problem, quit, refocus, trying again.* Their answers should be generally accurate but not necessarily detailed or complete. Ask students to explain why it is not a good idea to give up when they can't immediately find answers and solutions. Their answers should include reasons like, *giving up prevents you from successfully solving complex problems.* Ask students to describe situations where perseverance would be useful. Their answers should include situations like, *when completing a project where your initial ideas are not working or solving a problem that is very difficult.*

Source: © 2017 by Marzano Resources. Adapted with permission.

FIGURE 3.11: Assessment guidance for persevering when answers and solutions are not immediately apparent (K–2).

Cognitive and metacognitive skills should be considered essential components of student learning. There is no doubt that such skills are critical for students' success after graduation, and they therefore need to be directly instructed and assessed. Formally incorporating these skills into the school's curriculum is necessary, as is ensuring the skills are integrated into teachers' daily lesson design.

High Reliability Leadership for School-Level Indicator 10

School-level indicator 10 addresses cognitive and metacognitive skills. Cognitive skills can be divided into two types: cognitive analysis skills and knowledge application skills. Metacognitive skills can also be divided into two types: traditional metacognitive skills and metacognitive life skills. In the Marzano Academies model, these skills represent a viable curriculum that should be explicitly taught to students and reinforced throughout the grade levels. Cognitive and metacognitive skills can enhance student learning of traditional academic content. Perhaps more importantly, students can use them outside of school and throughout life to support the achievement of virtually any goals students set for themselves.

The previous discussion on school-level indicator 10 emphasizes the following elements of cognitive and metacognitive skills.

- Cognitive analysis skills
- Knowledge application skills
- Traditional metacognitive skills
- Metacognitive life skills

- Vertical alignment of cognitive and metacognitive skills

- Proficiency scales for cognitive and metacognitive skills

- Professional development for cognitive and metacognitive skills

- Assessment of cognitive and metacognitive skills

Figure 3.12 lists potential lagging indicators for this school-level indicator. Figure 3.13 (page 104) depicts the customized high reliability scale for this indicator.

Programs and Practices	Lagging Indicator Data	Potential Standard for High Reliability Status
A specific set of cognitive analysis skills with accompanying proficiency scales and assessment practices	Written documents are in place with proficiency scales and assessment practices for cognitive analysis skills	90 percent of teachers understand the school's cognitive analysis skills
A specific set of knowledge application skills with accompanying proficiency scales and assessment practices	Written documents are in place with proficiency scales and assessment practices for knowledge application skills	90 percent of teachers understand the school's knowledge application skills
A specific set of traditional metacognitive skills with accompanying proficiency scales and assessment practices	Written documents are in place with proficiency scales and assessment practices for traditional metacognitive skills	90 percent of teachers understand the school's traditional metacognitive skills
A specific set of metacognitive life skills with accompanying proficiency scales and assessment practices	Written documents are in place with proficiency scales and assessment practices for metacognitive life skills	90 percent of teachers understand the school's metacognitive life skills
Professional development for cognitive and metacognitive skills	Professional development is in place for cognitive and metacognitive skills	100 percent of teachers actively engage in the professional development for cognitive and metacognitive skills
Cognitive and metacognitive skills embedded in the curriculum at specific grade levels and subject areas	Written documents are in place for embedding cognitive and metacognitive skills at specific grade levels	100 percent of teachers embed cognitive and metacognitive skills in the curriculum skills as prescribed
Perceptions of students, teachers, and parents	Surveys to students, teachers, and parents	90 percent of teachers report success at teaching cognitive and metacognitive skills 80 percent of students report that they are getting better at the metacognitive skills they are taught in school 70 percent of parents report that they see evidence of improvement in their children relative to cognitive and metacognitive skills

Source: © 2021 by Robert J. Marzano.

FIGURE 3.12: Potential lagging indicators for school-level indicator 10.

Evidence	
4 **Sustaining** **(quick data)**	Quick data like the following are systematically collected and reviewed. • Reviews of teacher lesson plans and unit plans • Quick conversations with teachers and students • Examination of evidence scores in the LMS
3 **Applying** **(lagging)**	Performance goals with clear criteria for success like the following are in place. • 90 percent of teachers understand the school's cognitive analysis skills • 90 percent of teachers understand the school's knowledge application skills • 90 percent of teachers understand the school's traditional metacognitive skills • 90 percent of teachers understand the school's metacognitive life skills • 100 percent of teachers actively engage in the professional development for cognitive and metacognitive skills • 100 percent of teachers embed the cognitive and metacognitive skills in the curriculum skills as prescribed • 90 percent of teachers report success at teaching cognitive and metacognitive skills • 80 percent of students report that they are getting better at the metacognitive skills they are taught in school
2 **Developing** **(leading)**	• Cognitive and metacognitive skills with accompanying proficiency scales are in place • Cognitive and metacognitive skills are embedded in the curriculum in a logical and organized fashion
1 **Beginning**	• The school has written plans for the integration of cognitive and metacognitive skills but there is little execution of the plans at the classroom level • Relatively few teachers implement instruction and assessment of cognitive and metacognitive skills
0 **Not Using**	• The school has no written plans for instruction and assessment of cognitive and metacognitive skills • There is no implementation of instruction and assessment of cognitive and metacognitive skills at the classroom level

Source: © 2020 by Marzano Academies, Inc. Adapted with permission.

FIGURE 3.13: Customized high reliability scale for leading indicator 10.

School-Level Indicator 11: Vocabulary

Within the Marzano Academies model, vocabulary development is a revered concept. Fundamentally, our perspective is that developing students' vocabularies is akin to developing their background knowledge, and well-developed background knowledge provides a sound foundation for academic learning of all types. The research behind this concept is detailed in the book *Building Background Knowledge for Academic Achievement* (Marzano, 2004). At an operational level, this means that the leader of an elementary academy should ensure that the school has programs and practices in place to ensure that all students have a working knowledge of tier one, tier two, and tier three vocabulary. To fully understand this indicator, one must address the nature of this tiered vocabulary model.

Three Tiers of Terms

As described in the book *Teaching Basic, Advanced, and Academic Vocabulary* (Marzano, 2020), the concept of a three-tiered vocabulary system was popularized in the mid-1980s (Beck & McKeown, 1985). Up until that point, educators considered direct instruction in vocabulary important in K–12 classrooms but there was little if any how-to guidance about prioritizing which terms were most essential to students' literacy development. The tiered approach provides this guidance simply by making a distinction between three different categories of words, primarily based on their frequency in the English language.

Tier one terms like *big*, *clock*, *walk*, and *baby* are very frequent in the English language and might not actually require instruction for most students who speak English as a first language. Regarding tier one vocabulary, scholars Isabel L. Beck, Margaret G. McKeown, and Linda Kucan (2002) explained, "Words in this tier rarely require instructional attention to their meaning in school" (p. 8). This is because students frequently encounter these terms outside of school. Consequently, by the time they enter school, tier one words are already very familiar to them. This notwithstanding, if students are English learners or come from family backgrounds that offer limited access to literacy experiences, then it is critical they receive instruction in tier one terms because without them, their literacy development will be impaired.

Tier two terms are words that may not be encountered frequently enough for teachers to assume that students know them. Consequently, tier two terms are often the focus of classroom instruction, specifically in language arts classes. Words such as *nimble*, *scrawny*, and *dexterity* exemplify tier two vocabulary.

Tier three terms represent the largest category, encompassing all those terms that are not tier one or tier two terms. By definition, tier three terms are all those that are relatively infrequent in the English language. A logical question relative to tier three terms is, Which ones should be the subject of direct instruction? Highly infrequent terms like *frippery* should probably not be the subject of direct instruction, simply because they are so rarely used in the language. However, tier three terms that are critical to subject-matter knowledge and academic content, even if infrequent in general language usage, should be the subject of direct instruction. Words like *meiosis* and *mitosis* in science would fall into this category. While a person will probably not encounter these terms in general interactions with others or in general reading, such terms are critically important to understanding some aspects of science.

The three-tiered system of vocabulary terms provides a framework that teachers can use to design a comprehensive and viable approach to vocabulary instruction. For the Marzano Academies model in elementary schools, we utilize resources that explicitly identify the tier one, tier two, and tier three terms, along with an instructional approach to ensure that students have a working knowledge of those terms by the time they enter middle school. Specifically, elementary academy schools use a list of tier one, tier two, and tier three terms articulated in the book *Teaching Basic, Advanced, and Academic Vocabulary* (Marzano, 2020).

Researchers working in tandem with classroom teachers identified which terms correspond to tier one and tier two in a series of related efforts that spanned three decades. The result of these efforts is a list of 2,845 tier one terms and 5,160 tier two terms. These terms are organized into

420 semantic clusters—groups of words with related meanings. To illustrate, consider cluster 102, titled Bodies of Water.

- Tier one terms: *lake, ocean, puddle, river, sea, stream, bay, creek, pond*
- Tier two terms: *brook, cove, current, delta, gulf, inlet, marsh, outlet, rapids, strait, surf, swamp, tide, tributary, waterfall, waterline, bog, eddy, estuary, fjord, geyser, headwaters, lagoon, marshland, reef*

Clusters provide a rich semantic context for students to obtain an initial understanding of unknown words. Students who know the meaning of some or most of the tier one terms will have a semantic context with which to understand less common terms like *inlet, eddy,* and *estuary.* Simply stated, teaching vocabulary in semantic clusters aids student learning of those terms (Graves, 2006; Marzano, 2004; Marzano & Marzano, 1988).

In this vocabulary model, the semantic clusters are organized by the frequency of their tier one words. Cluster 1 includes tier one terms that are the most frequent tier one terms in the English language; cluster 420 includes terms that are the least frequent tier one terms. Finally, the clusters themselves can be organized into larger groups, referred to as superclusters. The superclusters can be thought of as clusters of clusters. There are sixty superclusters. To illustrate the nature of a supercluster, consider the supercluster titled *vehicles and transportation.* It involves the following clusters.

Cluster 93: Things You Travel On

Cluster 97: Vehicles (Actions/Characteristics)

Cluster 120: Vehicles (Air Transportation)

Cluster 128: Transportation (Types)

Cluster 159: Vehicles (Sea Transportation)

Cluster 234: Parts of Vehicles

Cluster 318: Vehicles (Snow)

Cluster 331: Vehicles (Work Related)

Superclusters provide teachers a way to organize a wide variety of vocabulary terms around a single theme. A teacher planning a unit on a topic for which the topic of vehicles and transportation plays a significant role could draw vocabulary from any or all of the constituent clusters that comprise this supercluster.

Tier three terms in the academy model focus on academic vocabulary. Within the academy model, teachers should teach tier three terms in the context of specific units of instruction. For example, the term *campaign* should be addressed in a unit that deals with the topic of participating in government. Elementary schools that partner with Marzano Academies are provided with tier three vocabulary for English language arts, mathematics, science, and social studies for grades K–5. These terms, identified by analysts at Marzano Resources, were taken from the proficiency scales designed in these areas (see Dodson, 2019; Simms, 2016). For an illustration, consider table 3.7. In all, there are 2,141 tier three vocabulary terms for these four subject areas across grades K–5, as depicted in table 3.8. However, note that elementary academies can and should supplement or replace the tier three terms suggested by Marzano Resources with tier three terms taken from their local proficiency scales.

TABLE 3.7: Tier Three Topics

Subject	Critical Concepts Topic	Related Vocabulary
English Language Arts	Analyzing Text Organization and Structure	*introduce, section, link, transition, main idea*
Mathematics	Measurement Conversion	*kiloliter, kilometer, mile, millimeter, pint, quart, ton, yard, liquid volume, mass*
Science	Waves	*amplitude, frequency, mass, midline, period, wave, wave cycle, wavelength, crest, energy, longitudinal wave, matter, medium, oscillate, transverse wave, trough*
Social Studies	Participating in Government	*campaign, candidate, demonstration, elected official, monitor, petition, political party, public official, vote*

TABLE 3.8: Distribution of Tier Three Terms and Topics

Subject Area			K	1	2	3	4	5	Total
ELA		**Number of Words**	66	68	63	57	62	66	382
		Number of Topics	17	20	19	19	18	15	108
Mathematics		**Number of Words**	85	40	60	63	85	59	392
		Number of Topics	10	9	14	14	15	14	76
Science	Content Knowledge	**Number of Words**	76	63	89	75	97	65	465
		Number of Topics	6	8	8	10	12	7	51
	Engineering Design	**Number of Words**		11			15		26
		Number of Topics		2			2		4
	Scientific Method	**Number of Words**			7				7
		Number of Topics			1				1
Social Studies		**Number of Words**	67	127	145	205	172	153	869
		Number of Topics	5	14	12	21	17	19	88

In effect, the terms in the Marzano Academies model represent a comprehensive treatment of the tier one, two, and three terms at the elementary level. If students have a working knowledge of these terms by the end of elementary school, then secondary teachers need only be concerned with the tier three subject-matter terms from grade 6 on up and selected tier two terms. Quite obviously, this would relieve middle school and high school teachers from a great burden of addressing basic terms that are foundational to the more complex concepts students will encounter in the higher grade levels.

Planning for Vocabulary

One responsibility of the principal is to help teachers determine which clusters they should assign with which instructional units. To this end, the principal should establish committees that comb through each of the semantic clusters from the vocabulary framework and determine which particular clusters best align with which existing units of instruction. The final product of this work should be an easy-to-use tool that teachers can reference as they plan unit instruction, as shown in figure 3.14. Specific vocabulary clusters are mapped to units of instruction for each grade level, including cluster number and name, proficiency scale, unit or lesson title, content area, and identified weeks of instruction.

After collaborative teams have mapped vocabulary clusters to specific units, the principal will easily be able to observe the efficacy of implementation. This begins with unit-plan review. The principal should require teachers to follow the vocabulary cluster-alignment tool and determine when the unit plan will be executed. This provides time-specific opportunities for the principal, or instructional coach, to observe and determine the efficacy of the vocabulary instruction occurring across each classroom, as well as provide additional supports to the teacher when concerns arise. Even when mapped to a unit design, simply handing students a list of vocabulary clusters to learn does not suffice as adequate vocabulary instruction. Instead, the principal should ensure each teacher is providing systemic, in-context learning opportunities for students to develop vocabulary acquisition. For example, if the unit of instruction is focused on weather patterns, the associated vocabulary clusters should be weather related, such as seasonality or temperature. Finally, scheduling classroom walkthroughs targeted specifically at vocabulary instruction communicates that the school values vocabulary acquisition and expects teachers to teach clusters within the context of existing lesson designs.

Vocabulary Notebooks

As part of robust vocabulary instruction, student vocabulary notebooks are a powerful tool. This resource should clearly and sequentially list the vocabulary clusters, as well as provide a scoring method for student self-evaluation on each cluster. For example, each cluster could have a four-point scale, with the score levels indicating the following levels of understanding.

1. I'm very uncertain about the term. I really don't understand what it means.

2. I'm a little uncertain about what the term means, but I have a general idea.

3. I understand the term, and I'm not confused about any part of what it means.

4. I understand even more about the term than I was taught.

Using the scale, students would systematically self-evaluate their level of understanding of the words in a cluster. Figure 3.15 (page 110) presents a sample page from a student vocabulary notebook.

Grade	Date	Content Area	Unit or Lesson Title	Proficiency Scale	Vocabulary Cluster
Kindergarten English Learners	Week 3	Language Acquisition	At School	Vocabulary—LI.00.03.06.04	60. Places Related to Learning and Experimentation
Grade 1 English Learners	Week 3	Language Acquisition	School Days	Vocabulary—LI.01.03.06.04	60. Places Related to Learning and Experimentation
Grade 2 English Learners	Week 3	Language Acquisition	Proud to Be Me	Vocabulary—LI.02.03.06.04	94. Family Relationships
Kindergarten	Week 3	Literacy—Level 00	Understanding Text	Text Types—LI.00.R2.07.05	3. Primary Auxiliary Verbs
Kindergarten	Weeks 3–4	Mathematics—Level 00	Count and Graph and Interpret Data	Measurement—MA.00.MD.02.04	27. Relationship Markers (Contrast)
Kindergarten	Week 3	Social Studies—Level 00	Wants and Needs	Personal Financial Literacy—SS.00.EC.02.03	55. Caring and Trust
Kindergarten	Week 3	Science—Level 00	Weather Components	Weather—SC.00.ESS3.02.05	78. Temperature
Grade 1	Week 3	Literacy—Level 01	Writing	Text Features—LI.01.R3.07.05	16. Relationship Markers
Grade 1	Weeks 3–5	Mathematics—Level 01	Subtraction	Properties of Operations—MA.01.OA.04.04	166. Mathematical Operations
Grade 1	Week 3	Social Studies—Level 01	Citizenship	Civic Responsibility—SS.01.CIV.02.03	265. Public Officials
Grade 1	Weeks 2–4	Science—Level 01	Seasonality	Seasons—SC.01.ESS1.02.05	29. Days and Months
Grade 2	Weeks 2–4	Literacy—Level 02	Informational Writing	Informative-Explanatory—LI.02.W1.02.04	238. Words, Phrases, and Sentences
Grade 2	Week 3	Mathematics—Level 02	Geometric Figures	Geometric Figures—MA.02.G.01.05	270. Curved and Circular Shapes
Grade 2	Weeks 2–4	Social Studies—Level 02	Societal Structures	Historical Interconnectedness—SS.02.HIS.02.03	200. Social and Political Groups
Grade 2	Week 3	Science—Level 02	Material Magic	Structure and Properties of Matter—SC.02.PS1.02.04	202. Texture

FIGURE 3.14: Unit planning chart.

Tier One: Basic Words								
Buy	4	3	2	1	Pay	4	3	2	1
Sale	4	3	2	1	Sell	4	3	2	1
Spend	4	3	2	1	Bet	4	3	2	1
Earn	4	3	2	1	Owe	4	3	2	1
Purchase	4	3	2	1					
Tier Two: Challenge Words								
Afford	4	3	2	1	Bargain	4	3	2	1
Budget	4	3	2	1					

Source: Marzano, 2020, p. 76.

FIGURE 3.15: Sample vocabulary notebook page for cluster 122—Actions Related to Money and Goods.

The pages of the notebook contain the tier one and tier two terms in each cluster. As depicted in figure 3.15, the tier one terms for cluster 122 are *buy, sale, spend, earn, purchase, pay, sell, bet,* and *owe.* Tier two terms for cluster 122 are *afford, budget,* and *bargain.* Along with the four-point self-evaluation scale, the student vocabulary notebook contains space for students to record notes that help them recall the meaning of words that are new to them. Much like student data notebooks (see school-level indicator 2, page 25), each student should be provided his or her own vocabulary cluster notebook. One unique feature of the cluster approach to vocabulary instruction used in the Marzano Academies model is that students can work on the clusters outside of school (for example, at home) on their own or with the aid of their parents. There is a set of resources for each cluster that includes a video illustrating and explaining each term, written definitions of each term, and activities that allow students to judge their understanding of each term. As students move through these resources, they use their vocabulary notebooks to record information that helps them remember the meaning of words and update their level of knowledge for words using the self-assessment scale. The book *Teaching Basic, Advanced, and Academic Vocabulary* (Marzano, 2020) provides a detailed description of these resources and how they might be used. In addition to providing student vocabulary notebooks and other resources, the principal must also create a schoolwide incentive system, such as a badging system, to be associated with these resources.

Badging Systems

Implementing a badging system is an easy way to increase student motivation for learning the vocabulary in an elementary academy. *Badging* simply refers to awarding physical symbols (that is, badges) to students as they accomplish specific goals. The term is a reference to the system of badges used in the Boy Scouts and Girl Scouts organizations. While there are many online resources and existing applications teachers can use for badging systems, we recommend that the principal create a unique badging system directly tied to the school's identified vocabulary clusters. For example, if there are a total of four hundred vocabulary clusters in the school's vocabulary notebooks, the principal might create a badging system with levels for every hundred clusters mastered.

We also recommend that this badging system be fun for students. Borrowing from the colored belt system of martial arts, the principal might create a colored vocabulary badging system, where students strive to become a "black badge," which indicates they have achieved competence with all the expected vocabulary. It is important that every classroom regardless of grade level uses the same vocabulary resource and badging system. To increase student buy-in, the principal should provide physical badges, like colored dog tags or belts, to signify a student's progression through the vocabulary resource.

Even though teaching specific vocabulary in the context of existing classroom content is preferable, the principal should also consider providing opportunities for students to also encounter an array of vocabulary words throughout the school day. This might manifest as a "word of the day" that is included in the morning announcements with an associated classroom challenge. Similarly, the principal might strategically post vocabulary words on hallway walls, in the cafeteria, or in the gym for students to find and write down in a scavenger hunt–type game. Another idea is to have the "principal's vocabulary challenge" where the principal selects a topic associated with a current event or school-spirit-based theme. Students then create their own vocabulary clusters around that topic. Or, students could select their own topics of interest and create related vocabulary clusters. Finally, vocabulary instruction is a great place to strengthen the school-home partnership. The principal can include a monthly vocabulary cluster in his or her newsletter for families to discuss and work with their students while at home. A principal might even identify grade-specific clusters and easy-to-follow, home-based vocabulary activities for families to do while having dinner or as weekend activities. As described previously, the Marzano Academies vocabulary approach includes activities for each cluster that allow students to test their knowledge of the terms, such as comparison activities and matching activities. These can serve as quick game-like contexts in which parents and students can compete.

High Reliability Leadership for School-Level Indicator 11

Elementary schools following the Marzano Academies model should pay particular attention to ensuring that all students have a working knowledge of tier one and tier two terms in the English language. To this end, the academy model uses a cluster approach to learning these terms that can be employed in school and at home.

The previous discussion on school-level indicator 11 addressed the following topics relative to vocabulary.

- Addressing tier one, tier two, and tier three terms
- Planning for vocabulary instruction, including tier one and tier two terms in clusters and tier three terms in proficiency scales
- Using student vocabulary notebooks
- Establishing a badging system or other incentives

Figure 3.16 (page 112) depicts possible lagging indicators for this school-level indicator. Figure 3.17 (page 113) depicts the customized high reliability scale.

Programs and Practices	Lagging Indicator Data	Potential Standard for High Reliability Status
Addressing tiers one, two, and three	Tier one, two, and three terms have been identified and listed	100 percent of teachers are adequately familiar with the nature and intent of the tier one, tier two, and tier three terms
Tier one and tier two clusters	Tier one and tier two terms are organized in clusters	100 percent of teachers are adequately familiar with the nature and intent of the cluster approach
Tier three terms in proficiency scales	Critical tier three terms are embedded in proficiency scales	100 percent of teachers are adequately familiar with the nature and intent of the tier three terms embedded in proficiency scales
Systematic planning	Explicit plans for instruction, assessment, and record keeping regarding tiers one, two, and three are in place	90 percent of teachers explicitly follow the plans for instruction, assessment, and record keeping regarding tier one, two, and three terms
Student notebooks and badging	Student notebooks are in place for tier one and tier two terms, along with badging systems	90 percent of teachers utilize student notebooks and badging with their students
Perceptions of students, teachers, and parents	Surveys for teachers, students, and parents	90 percent of teachers report success at teaching tier one, two, and three terms 80 percent of students report that their knowledge of tier one, two, and three terms is increasing 70 percent of parents report that they see evidence of improvement in their children's knowledge of tier one, two, and three terms

Source: © 2021 by Robert J. Marzano.

FIGURE 3.16: Potential lagging indicators for school-level indicator 11.

School-Level Indicator 12: Explicit Goals for Students' Status and Growth

Economists sometimes invoke the statement, "In God we trust, all others must bring data." Although its origins are not firmly established, its meaning rings true across a wide array of fields, including education. In effect, data allow educators to determine where they are and where they wish to go in concrete terms. Toward this end, every school principal must use data as the foundation for setting and monitoring achievement goals. In the academy model, the principal should actively set schoolwide goals, as well as expect teachers and students to set individual goals, to ensure achievement is objectively measured with data as the basis for continuous improvement.

It might not be immediately apparent why setting explicit goals for students' status and growth is an indicator associated with the curriculum. However, a school's curriculum dictates the type of goals that can be set within that school. In a traditional system that only keeps track of students'

Evidence	
4 **Sustaining** **(quick data)**	Quick data like the following are systematically collected and reviewed. • Examination of records indicating students' status on tier one, two, and three vocabulary • Quick conversations with students about their status on tier one, two, and three vocabulary
3 **Applying** **(lagging)**	Performance goals with clear criteria for success like the following are in place. • 100 percent of teachers are adequately familiar with the nature and intent of the tier one, two, and three terms • 90 percent of teachers explicitly follow the plans for instruction, assessment, and record keeping regarding tier one, two, and three terms • 90 percent of teachers utilize student notebooks and badging • 80 percent of students report that their knowledge of tier one, two, and three terms is increasing
2 **Developing** **(leading)**	• Tier one, two, and three terms have been identified and have explicit protocols for their use • Student notebooks and badging systems are in place for tier one and tier two terms • Critical tier three terms are embedded in proficiency scales
1 **Beginning**	• The school has written plans regarding instruction in tier one, two, and three vocabulary but there is no implementation of the plans • Instruction in tier one, two, and three vocabulary is available but relatively few students have access to it
0 **Not Using**	• The school has no written plans for instruction in tier one, two, and three vocabulary • There is no direct instruction in tier one, two, and three vocabulary at the classroom level

Source: © 2020 by Marzano Academies, Inc. Adapted with permission.

FIGURE 3.17: Customized high reliability scale for school-level indicator 11.

overall scores in each subject using some type of omnibus letter grade or percentage score, goals for an entire class or individual students are limited to these general metrics. In the Marzano Academies model, the school-level indicator that is the centerpiece of the curriculum is the development of proficiency scales (indicator 9, page 83). With proficiency scales in place, individual teachers can establish goals for individual students in terms of both their final status on specific scales at the end of a grading period and how much they have increased their knowledge throughout the grading period. Teachers and leaders can also set such goals for entire classes and the entire school. In addition to setting goals based on proficiency scales, the school leader and teachers should also set goals based on external tests like benchmark tests and end-of-year tests. Given the attention typically paid to external test scores, administrators are well advised to consider them in their goal setting.

Schoolwide Goals Using External Assessments

Most schools are required to participate in annual state-administered assessments. At the beginning of a new school year, using the previous year's scores, the principal should write schoolwide goals for student achievement that aim for growth from the previous year. How his or her school performed the prior year will dictate the stretch or reach of these goals. By this we mean that every school should identify goals they know from the outset will be challenging for them to attain. We recommend that every school, even those already scoring high marks, strive to improve from the previous year. With that said, it is important for leaders to be realistic. Measured, steady growth year after year is preferred to a boom-bust cycle that often plagues schools with abnormal years of growth.

In the Marzano Academies model, we encourage principals to write goals to improve the school-wide achievement and growth scores by 5 percent to 10 percent per year. In addition to scores aggregated across all grade levels, the principal should dig deeper into the individual grade-level scores for particular standards. For example, if the school scored below the state or district average on one standard in fifth-grade mathematics, but then above the state or district average on another standard, the principal should take note. This is the case in figure 3.18. On topic 6, the school scored below both the state average and the district average. On topic 23, the school scored above the state average and the district average. These findings are of interest and the school leader should try to discern the root cause for both results—in one case to mitigate underperformance, and in the other case to emulate the cause of higher performance.

Most states only administer assessments once per year, with results typically not released until several months later. This end-of-year, single-point-in-time testing with delayed release of scores limits a principal's ability to meaningfully use this type of assessment data. To acquire more and better data, the principal should also use other types of assessments as the foundation for goal setting,

Mathematics, Grade 5

Purpose: This report represents the average percent of points earned by Evidence Statement for the school, district, and state.

Students With Valid Scores (29)

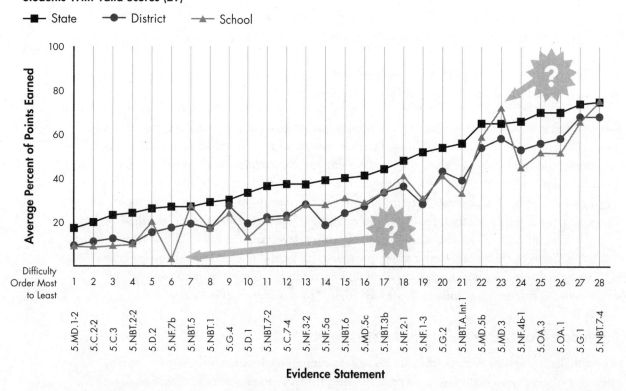

Source: © 2019 by Westminster Public Schools. Used with permission.

FIGURE 3.18: School performance.

preferably ones that can be administered multiple times throughout the year and provide immediate results. These are referred to as *benchmark assessments* or *interim assessments*.

There are many standardized interim or benchmark assessments available for schools, which provide national percentile ranking or grade-level equivalency composite scores to track student learning during the year. Typically, these assessments are externally designed and scored. That is, a third-party entity like a testing company designs the assessments, which are administered by the district or school but then scored by the third-party entity. This provides data schools and districts can use as indicators of student learning. After selecting which assessment tool the school will use, the principal should ensure administration occurs in the beginning of the year (BOY), the middle of the year (MOY), and the end of the year (EOY). Using the BOY results, he or she can set school-wide growth goals for the year, which are then measured by MOY and EOY testing. Similar to the state assessments, the principal can set a goal to increase school averages by 5 percent to 10 percent from the previous year's EOY results, or he or she can set growth goals based on the current year's BOY scores. For example, in figure 3.19 the principal uses BOY scores to set annual growth goals for the school's average scaled score. The progress monitoring that occurs during the MOY assessment window provides timely information that teachers can use to make midyear corrections. The EOY scores allow the principal to compare the school's actual results to goals.

Note that this chart includes goals and data not only for mathematics overall, but also for the specific mathematics topic strands. One advantage to setting goals at the strand or standard level is that doing so provides the school a more focused approach to improvement. The school might be overperforming in the numbers and operations strand, while underperforming in data analysis and probability. In this case, the principal would write different goals for these two strands, which will create different focal points for his or her school throughout the upcoming year.

Principals should follow these same processes to set annual growth goals for each grade level and in each subject area. Using a variety of assessment data, the principal can set annual growth goals at the school level, grade level, strand level, and individual standard level. It is also important that teachers and students are setting goals using these same assessment data.

Strands	BOY National Averaged Scaled Score	BOY School Scaled Score	Annual Goal Growth	MOY School Scaled Score	MOY School Scaled Score Growth	EOY Scaled Score Goal	EOY School Scaled Score	EOY School Growth	Difference Between Actual and Goal
Mathematics Mean Scaled Score	2244	2097	**299**	2167	70	2396	2371	274	–25
Numbers and Operations	2244	2342	**54**	2401	59	2396	2446	104	50
Algebra	2244	2134	**262**	2210	76	2396	2342	208	–54
Geometry	2244	2201	**195**	2301	100	2396	2404	203	8
Measurement	2244	2256	**140**	2341	85	2396	2415	159	19
Data Analysis and Probability	2244	2267	**129**	2321	54	2396	2387	120	–9

FIGURE 3.19: Goal-setting chart.

Teacher-Level Goals

Much like the principal sets goals for the school, teachers should be setting goals for their classrooms. Some of these teacher goals will correlate to the principal's schoolwide goals. For example, if the principal sets a school goal that students will achieve an average academic growth of 1.25 years, then each teacher should set his or her classroom's growth goal for at least 1.25 years as well. Teachers should also be aware of the principal's grade-level growth goals, as well as his or her individual standard and subject-strand goals where appropriate. For example, if the principal sets a goal to see a 10 percent increase in fifth-grade numbers and operations as measured by the EOY assessment, the fifth-grade teachers should all write classroom growth goals accordingly. In addition, teachers may have other goal areas they wish to focus on. Examples might be data specifically tied to professional-growth goals (see school-level indicator 5, page 49), or classwide goals developed with students, such as adherence to the code of collaboration. These goals will commonly employ the metric of proficiency scale scores. Since teachers enter these scores into an LMS, they are much easier to gather and analyze immediately. Because all proficiency scales employ the same score levels, educators can set comparable growth goals referencing that common metric. For example, a teacher might set a goal that his or her students exhibit an average gain of at least 1.5 levels on a specific set of proficiency scales. Much like the schoolwide goals, the classroom goals need to be time bound, measurable, and communicated with all stakeholders—specifically, in this case, the students.

Student-Level Goals

An important aspect of this school-level indicator is the alignment of student goal setting to the schoolwide goals. At the start of the school year, teachers should help students write personal growth goals based on their previous year's state assessment results, as well as their BOY local assessment results. Since most states release assessment results over the summer months, teachers should share each student's previous-year results with him or her early in the next school year, as well as give students time to reflect on how they did. Next, each student should set a goal for the upcoming year's state assessment. The same process should occur with BOY local assessment data. Once again, steady and measured growth should be the expectation. Setting unrealistic goals can lead to feelings of failure or inadequacy if or when the student doesn't achieve lofty marks.

Unless student goal setting has been integrated into the school design for years, most students will not know how to effectively set, write, or track goals. Thus, each teacher will need to devote instructional time to teach students the art of goal setting. As already mentioned a number of times in this book, we strongly recommend that each student use a data notebook to formally record and track his or her goals and monitor his or her progress on them. An example data notebook goal-setting page is shown in figure 3.20. Students' use of data notebooks has many benefits, including ownership of their learning, accountability, and increased motivation. Students can also use data notebooks to help themselves (and teachers) communicate to parents academic standing and progress made throughout the year.

Student data notebooks can contain a variety of tracking tools, including graphs and charts, rubrics, self-assessments, reflections, and data-driven dialogues. At the very least, they should include summative recordings of assessment scores and stated goals for improvement. Notice in figure 3.20 the spaces for the student to record his or her baseline data, as well as MOY and EOY goals in a single, easy-to-read sheet. This goal-setting page should be located at the front of the data notebook, with all progress-monitoring and reflection portions to follow. Depending on the grade level, students should employ different assessments and goal setting. A fifth grader might set composite growth scores on

Name: ______________________________

School Year: ______________________ My Grade Level: ______________________

MY PERFORMANCE LEVELS	**Literacy**	**Mathematics**	**Science**	**Social Studies**
Performance Level				

Reading Diagnostic	**BOY**	**MOY**	**EOY**
Scaled Score			
Color Code (Red/Yellow/Green)			

Local Assessment	**Fall**	**Winter**	**Spring**
Scaled Score			
GLE (Grade-Level Equivalent)			

My goals for the upcoming data cycles are:

1) ______________________________

2) ______________________________

3) ______________________________

My strategies for achieving my goals are:

1) ______________________________

2) ______________________________

3) ______________________________

Source: © *2016 by Westminster Public Schools. Used with permission.*

FIGURE 3.20: Data notebook goal setting.

state and local assessments, while kindergartners might set goals on specific skills like letter names and number recognition. What is most important is the school has a defined practice of student goal setting, as well as a resource (student data notebook) for students to record and track progress.

Transparency

Once the schoolwide, classroom, and student-level goals are established, it is important that these goals be communicated with the appropriate stakeholders. Goals are more likely to be achieved when they are written down, and even more likely when they are shared with others. Toward this end, the principal should determine how best to communicate his or her schoolwide goals, including explicit statements of measurement and expected timelines for progress updates, to students, teachers, and the larger school community. For example, the principal might share his or her schoolwide goal of increasing the literacy scores on the upcoming state assessment by 10 percent, or his or her goal of increasing the fifth-grade numbers and operations overall composite score on the local assessment by 5 percent during an annual beginning-of-the-year goal-setting assembly. He or she might also include the school's goals as part of the morning announcements. In relation to communicating school goals with the larger community, the principal should include schoolwide goals in his or her parent newsletters. The principal should share highlights of the school's baseline data, projected goals, and when parents can expect progress updates on those goals. Finally, he or she should have the goals written down and posted in the school hallways and on the cafeteria walls for students to see daily as they eat lunch and transition from classroom to classroom. Constant reminders like these will help keep the goals alive as the school year progresses.

Teachers should then mirror this process. Much like the principal's parent newsletter, each teacher should send home a parent letter at the start of the year describing what a data notebook is and what purpose it will serve. The teacher's letter should also solicit at-home parent support for the student goal-setting process and provide ways to solidify the school-home partnership. Figure 3.21 is an example parent letter sent home by a classroom teacher. The principal will want to ensure that every teacher in his or her school is sending home this type of letter, as well as sharing the contents of the student data notebooks at least monthly.

Dear Parents,

This year, your child will be monitoring his or her learning by using a data notebook. This is a learning tool that teaches students how to set goals and track their progress toward successful completion. It is also a great way for me to communicate with you about how your child is progressing in class. I hope it also provides you opportunities to ask questions and work with your child on possible areas of improvement.

I will be sending home your student's data notebook with Friday Folders once a month. I encourage you to review the data notebook and discuss with your child the progress he or she is making toward his or her personal goals. There will also be a blank "Note to My Child's Teacher" form where you can ask questions or request a phone call home regarding your child's progress. I hope your child's data notebook becomes a continuous progress monitoring tool, as well as a means for you to communicate with me along the way.

In addition to information on your child's academic progress, I will also include a parent guide to help you focus on your child's targeted areas for growth, as well as a parent-reflection page where you may make comments. We are a team in educating your child, and I appreciate all that you do to support the data notebooks and your child's learning.

Looking forward to a great school year!

Teacher's name

FIGURE 3.21: Letter to parents about data notebooks.

Progress Tracking

Beyond communicating the school, classroom, and student goals, the principal will need to determine how to track progress. A critical component of successful goal completion is monitoring relevant data and making necessary adjustments when appropriate. Principals need to build progress monitoring into the school's academic scheduling, including designated times to discuss the results. The principal needs to ensure each teacher is aware of, and actively utilizing, the assessment tools for progress monitoring, as well as recording the data in a central location. Principals can build data recording into each teacher's unit planning design, which the principal should also review.

In addition to ensuring systematic progress monitoring occurs, the principal must schedule specific meeting times to discuss the progress-monitoring data, as well as adjust instructional practices when necessary. Our recommended approach to regular progress-monitoring meetings is schoolwide implementation of data cycles.

Data Cycles

Data cycles are routine meetings where teachers, interventionists, and administrators discuss the results of the most recent progress-monitoring data, the instructional strategies teachers are using, and any adjustments deemed necessary. Data cycles should be held at minimum every six weeks, but even more frequently, if possible. The principal needs to build data cycles into each teacher's planning calendar, as well as his or her own. He or she needs to create a shared resource, like a Google Doc, where the progress-monitoring data for each student is housed, as well as instructional and intervention strategies being employed, and reflections from the teachers. Before the data cycle meeting, each teacher and interventionist should update progress-monitoring data and his or her reflections about each student. Then, during the data cycle meeting itself, the educator can discuss the progress-monitoring data, the instructional strategies, and reflections and determine next steps. Figure 3.22 (page 120) is an example of a shared tracking resource for a first-grade teacher. This chart includes a row for each student, where the teacher records information such as predicted status at the end of the year (using the school's color-coded system), progress-monitoring scores from various types of reading tests, and interventions. The teacher updates this tracking resource regularly and in preparation for data cycle meetings.

Data cycles act as a regular progress-monitoring device for student and classroom goals. Depending on what types of data staff monitor and discuss in these meetings, leaders can also measure the schoolwide goals. However, schoolwide goals are commonly more macro in nature, and therefore will need to be tracked differently. Figure 3.22 and figure 3.23 (page 121) are examples of how the principal can track his or her school's progress of assessment data based on macro goals. Both figures use the school's local assessment data, but figure 3.22 focuses on an individual grade-level subject content—in this case, grade 1 ELA. Figure 3.23, however, is a snapshot of the school's overall middle-of-year composite scores from year to year. Tracking the micro-level progress of grade-level strand data, as well as overall school-level achievement data, is critical to gaining a complete picture of goal completion.

In addition to tracking the data, the principal needs to share these data with his or her school community. At the very minimum, he or she should provide these progress-monitoring updates to faculty and staff. We recommend that the principal create these updates in a shared online resource, like Google Docs, and share with appropriate stakeholders. Since edits can be viewed in real time, every teacher can review the school's data from anywhere, at any time. Some principals may prefer to physically post these progress-monitoring data in the staff lounge or another place in the school.

Student	Grade	What is your EOY prediction for each student in your class? When making your predictions, indicate whether you think students will be blue, green, yellow, or red and include an explanation for each student prediction. (Completed before data meetings)	What are the most recent progress-monitoring scores or the scores from the recommended test for the student (for example, the student needs one more benchmark score for NWF)? (Completed before data meetings)	Based on the progress-monitoring data, recommended test, and classroom data, what are the areas of improvement for the student? (Completed before data meetings)	Check in on current interventions and classroom practices. What is working well and what needs to be adjusted or changed?	Based on MOY data, have interventions been adjusted?
Sunny	1	RED: Sunny has been declining. I have noticed changes in his behavior. This might be because of a new baby in his family. His dad asked for extra work to practice at home and I am not noticing any improvements. He really struggles, even one on one.	CLS: 25; WWR: 0; DORF: 14; Accuracy: 58; Retell: 4	final sounds, letter sounds and names, consonant-vowel-consonant words	Fay shared an idea about helping Sunny build better knowledge with letter names and sounds. Denise is going to add this.	
Clara	1	BLUE: Clara has been working so hard and I have noticed so much growth with her. She is no longer having behavior issues and she is constantly on task and doing her best. I have noticed she has been pushing herself to become a better reader.	CLS: 55; WWR: 19; DORF: 27; Accuracy: 77; Retell: 9	multisyllabic words		In a group with Cindi working on fluency and accuracy; this group is from 8:40–9:00
Leroy	1	GREEN: Leroy is capable of doing so well. I believe he does struggle with literacy but with more practice he can get there.	CLS: 46; WWR: 15; DORF: 14; Accuracy: 64; Retell: 13	sight words, vowel combinations, multisyllabic words, reading at a faster rate		
Zachary	1	GREEN: Zachary's reading skills have improved so much. I believe this growth is still happening.	CLS: 31; WWR: 0; DORF: 40; NWF: 0; Accuracy: 83; Retell: 16	multisyllabic words, comprehension		

NWF: nonsense-word fluency   WWR: whole words reading   DORF: DIBELS oral reading fluency   CLS: correct letter sound

Source: © 2019 by Westminster Public Schools. Used with permission.

FIGURE 3.22: Shared tracking resource.

Grade Level	Middle-of-Year Composite	Change From Previous Year	Middle-of-Year Growth	Change From Previous Year	Middle-of-Year Percent on Track	Change From Previous Year	Middle-of-Year Percent School Year Growth	Change From Previous Year	Percent at High or Above	Change From Previous Year
2017–2018 School Year (Baseline)										
K	1489	n/a	n/a	n/a	n/a	n/a	n/a	n/a	21	n/a
1	1703	n/a	208.5	n/a	56.8	n/a	56.8	n/a	16	n/a
2	1927	n/a	119.5	n/a	56.4	n/a	56.09	n/a	26	n/a
3	2194	n/a	159.5	n/a	60	n/a	77.37	n/a	26	n/a
4	2402	n/a	144.2	n/a	57	n/a	84.54	n/a	13	n/a
5	2599	n/a	141.2	n/a	61	n/a	95.05	n/a	23	n/a
Primary (K–2)	1815	n/a	164	n/a	56.6	n/a	56.445	n/a	18.5	n/a
Intermediate (3–5)	2398.333333	n/a	148.3	n/a	59.33333333	n/a	85.65333333	n/a	20.66666667	n/a
School (K–5)	2165	n/a	154.58	n/a	58.24	n/a	73.97	n/a	19.58333333	n/a
2018–2019 School Year										
K	1499	n/a	n/a	n/a	n/a	n/a	n/a	n/a	18	-3
1	1745	42	207	-1.5	60.9	4.1	60.9	4.1	27	11
2	1983	56	152	32.5	59.57	3.17	84.84	28.75	40	14
3	2250	56	195	35.5	75.75	15.75	84.95	7.58	26	0
4	2404	2	143	-1.2	65	8	66.66	-17.88	24	11
5	2601	2	59	-82.2	50	-11	59.7	-35.35	37	14
Primary (K–2)	1864	49	179.5	15.5	60.235	3.635	72.87	16.425	28.33333333	9.833333333
Intermediate (3–5)	2418.333333	20	132.3333333	-15.96666667	63.58333333	4.25	70.43666667	-15.21666667	29	8.333333333
School (K–5)	2196.6	31.6	151.2	-3.38	62.244	4.004	71.41	-2.56	28.66666667	9.083333333
2019–2020 School Year										
K	1530	n/a	n/a	n/a	n/a	n/a	n/a	n/a	29	11
1	1808	63	173	-34	53	-7.9	117.47	56.57	37	10
2	2034	51	121	-86	58	-1.57	128.7	43.86	47	7
3	2253	3	117	-78	56	-19.75	120.38	35.43	26	0
4	2429	25	65	66.2	39	-26	83.33	16.67	26	2
5	2549	-52	60	1	44	-6	88.13	28.43	26	-11
Primary (K–2)	1921	57	147	-32.5	55.5	-4.735	123.085	50.215	42	13.66666667
Intermediate (3–5)	2410.333333	-8	80.66666667	-51.66666667	46.33333333	-17.25	97.28	26.84333333	26	-3
School (K–5)	2214.6	18	107.2	-44	50	-12.244	107.602	36.192	32.4	3.733333333

Source: © 2020 by Westminster Public Schools. Used with permission.

FIGURE 3.23: Snapshot form of school year-to-year goal tracking.

Oh no. 2,
not interested!

Incentives

A final issue that leaders should entertain relative to goal setting is creating schoolwide incentive systems. Beyond the feeling of success generated by individual achievement, principals can enhance students' and teachers' motivation to accomplish their goals through friendly classroom competitions. For example, if the fifth-grade team has a goal of increasing the composite score on the numbers and operations strand by 10 percent, the principal might establish a pizza party challenge between the fifth-grade classrooms, where the classroom with the highest composite growth on that particular strand, as measured by MOY testing, wins a pizza party. Using a similar format, the principal can also create schoolwide incentive challenges, like a themed party day if the school achieves its annual goal of increasing student composite scores by 10 percent in mathematics, as measured by EOY assessments.

High Reliability Leadership for School-Level Indicator 12

In summary, goal setting is a critical component of the academy model. The principal should ensure he or she is setting schoolwide goals on all aspects of schooling he or she deems valuable. Teachers should set goals regarding their personal professional development, as well as their students' achievement, and students need to set individual goals focused on academic growth. After principals, teachers, and students all establish goals, they need to communicate those goals to all appropriate stakeholders—not just initially, but also with the progress-monitoring data collected throughout the year. Educators should routinely track progress on every goal throughout the year, hold data cycle meetings to discuss the results, and most importantly, make any needed adjustments. Finally, the principal should make all progress-monitoring data available for the school community, whether through an online tool or physically posting the data in a shared space within the school.

The previous discussion on school-level indicator 12 emphasizes the following elements of explicit goals for students' status and growth.

- Schoolwide goals using external assessments
- Teacher-level goals
- Student-level goals
- Transparency
- Progress tracking
- Data cycles
- Incentives

Figure 3.24 depicts possible lagging indicators for this school-level indicator. Figure 3.25 (page 124) depicts the customized high reliability scale for school-level indicator 12.

Programs and Practices	Lagging Indicator Data	Potential Standard for High Reliability Status
Schoolwide goals	Schoolwide goals for status and growth are established with clear criteria for meeting those goals	90 percent of schoolwide goals are met
Teacher-level goals	Individual teacher goals for status and growth are established with clear criteria for meeting those goals	90 percent of individual teacher goals are met
Student-level goals	Individual student goals for status and growth are established with clear criteria for meeting those goals	90 percent of individual student goals are met
Goal transparency	Specific activities have been employed to make schoolwide goals transparent to the community	70 percent of community members report that they are aware of the schoolwide goals and believe they are appropriate
Tracking goals	Specific protocols are executed for tracking progress of goals at the school level, teacher level, and individual level	100 percent of administrators are aware of the current status of schoolwide goals 90 percent of teachers are aware of the status of their individual goals 70 percent of students are aware of the status of their goals
Data cycles	Data cycles employed every six weeks	100 percent of administrators and teachers can describe the conclusions reached from data cycles
Incentives	Activities to provide incentives for teachers and students are executed	100 percent of teachers and 90 percent of students report that the incentive activities motivate them
Perceptions of students, teachers, and parents	Surveys of teachers, students, and parents	90 percent of teachers report that the goal-setting process has been beneficial and useful to them 80 percent of students report that the goal-setting process has been useful to them 70 percent of parents report that the goal-setting process has been useful to them

Source: © 2021 by Robert J. Marzano.

FIGURE 3.24: Potential lagging indicators for school-level indicator 12.

Evidence	
4 **Sustaining** **(quick data)**	Quick data like the following are systematically collected and reviewed. • Examination of growth scores and summative scores in the LMS • Examination of benchmark assessment scores • Examination of end-of-year assessment scores
3 **Applying** **(lagging)**	Performance goals with clear criteria for success like the following are in place. • 90 percent of schoolwide goals are met • 90 percent of individual teacher goals are met • 90 percent of individual student goals are met • 100 percent of administrators and teachers can describe the conclusions reached from data cycles
2 **Developing** **(leading)**	• Schoolwide goals using external assessments are in place and monitored • Teacher-level goals are in place and monitored • Individual student goals are in place and systematically monitored • Incentive activities are executed around specific types of goals
1 **Beginning**	• The school has written goals but those goals are not translated into quantifiable student outcomes • The school has written goals but they do not address both status and growth
0 **Not Using**	• The school has no written goals for students' status and growth • Data regarding student status and growth are not analyzed

Source: © 2020 by Marzano Academies, Inc. Adapted with permission.

FIGURE 3.25: Customized high reliability scale for school-level indicator 12.

Summary

This chapter addressed four school-level indicators of the academy model that, considered as a set, constitute the curriculum in the academy model. Those indicators are:

School-level indicator 9: Measurement topics and proficiency scales

School-level indicator 10: Cognitive and metacognitive skills

School-level indicator 11: Vocabulary

School-level indicator 12: Explicit goals for students' status and growth

Proficiency scales are the structure within which all content is articulated. Educators should develop these scales for traditional academic content as well as cognitive and metacognitive skills. The academy model also has a strong focus on ensuring that all students understand basic vocabulary foundational to literacy, as well as vocabulary critical to the academic content they are learning. Finally, with well-defined curricula in place, school leaders can set and monitor specific goals for student learning at multiple levels.

CHAPTER 4

Indicators That Address Structural Changes in the Way Schools Run

A competency-based approach to schooling requires some structural changes in the way schools run. These structural changes include assessment, reporting, collective responsibility, and flexible scheduling. While the first two of these (assessment and reporting) seem related in terms of the specific actions they encompass, the other two may not. The characteristic that binds this final group of school-level indicators together is the magnitude of change they require in a school. Each of these school-level indicators represents schoolwide changes that require leaders, teachers, and even students and parents to think and act in ways that are different from how they think and act within a traditional system.

School-Level Indicator 13: Classroom Assessment

The leader of an elementary academy should ensure that the school has an assessment system that uses reliable and valid classroom assessments as the primary tools to measure each student's status and growth on specific measurement topics. An assessment is considered reliable if educators can be relatively sure that students would receive the same scores if they were to retake the same test having forgotten about the first time they took it. An assessment is considered valid if educators can be relatively sure that what the assessment purports it is designed to measure is what the assessment actually measures.

The rationale for the academy model of assessment is outlined in two related books, *Making Classroom Assessments Reliable and Valid* (Marzano, 2018) and *The New Art and Science of Classroom Assessment* (Marzano et al., 2019). Briefly, the academy model of assessment is depicted in figure 4.1.

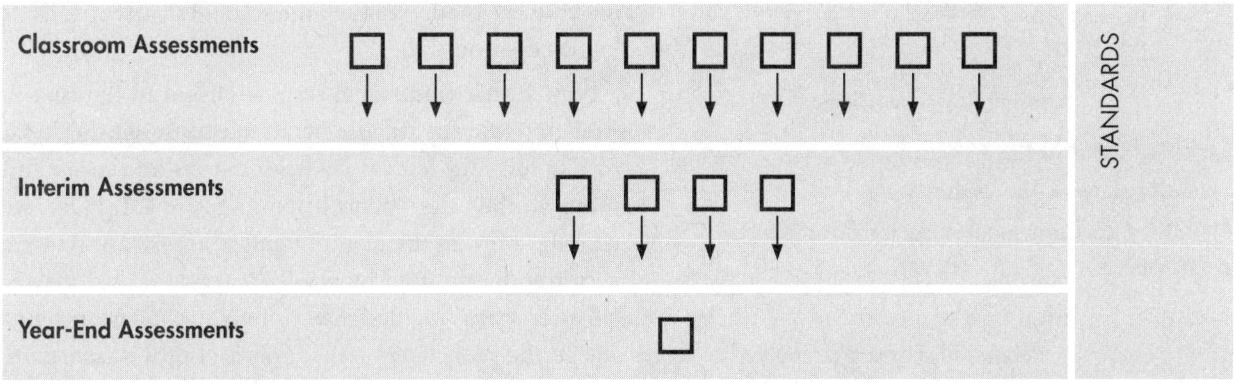

Source: Marzano, 2018, p. 6.

FIGURE 4.1: Marzano Academies assessment model.

As depicted in figure 4.1, the main source of data about student learning is classroom assessments. As the name implies, these are the assessments that teachers create and administer to students in their classrooms. In a traditional system, a teacher might only give end-of-unit exams to assign a score, but in a competency-based system, assessments are frequent and serve to inform learning going forward. They provide daily and ongoing evidence of students' status and growth. Given that classroom assessments are designed around measurement topics and proficiency scales, they assess students' knowledge at a very granular level of detail.

Next are interim assessments, sometimes referred to as *benchmark assessments*. As mentioned previously (see school-level indicator 12, page 112), they are typically designed and administered by organizations outside of the school or school system (that is, testing companies) and are used to gauge student growth but not at the level of granularity of classroom assessments.

The least frequent type of assessment employed in schools is the end-of-year assessment. Typically, states use year-end assessments to gauge how well schools and districts are performing with respect to state standards. These tests are broad in scope. They are designed to determine how well a school or district is performing as opposed to individual students within those systems.

As indicated in figure 4.1, classroom assessments are at the heart of the assessment process in the academy model. Employing frequent and formative classroom assessments is one of the most powerful structural changes a school can make. To be clear, academies still employ interim assessments and end-of-year assessments. However, they are used more for checks and balances at the school level. They are also used as validity criteria against which classroom assessments are judged.

Assessments

- Traditional tests
- Essays
- Performance tasks, demonstrations, and presentations
- Portfolios
- Probing discussions
- Student-centered assessments
- Voting techniques
- Observations

Score on Proficiency Scale

Source: Adapted from Marzano, 2018.

FIGURE 4.2: Conceptual model for classroom assessment.

Types of Classroom Assessments

The academy model for classroom assessment provides teachers with many options for classroom assessments not available in the traditional classroom. Figure 4.2 lists some of those options. Teachers can use these various types of assessments to gather information about a student's current status on a particular proficiency scale. This wide array of types of classroom assessment is possible only because the content within an academy is stated as measurement topics with accompanying proficiency scales. In effect, when proficiency scales are available, the types of activities that qualify as an assessment increase dramatically. Teachers can compare any evidence of student learning to the proficiency scale and determine which score best represents the student's current level of knowledge and skill.

Notice that traditional tests are listed in figure 4.2. Academy teachers still use traditional tests, but they tend to rely less and less on traditional tests and more and more on the other forms listed in figure 4.2. Here, we describe a few of these other types of assessment that are very frequently used by academy teachers. No matter what type of assessment the teacher uses, all assessments are designed using a specific proficiency scale and all scores are reported as scores on specific proficiency scales. This is critical to achieving the necessary structural changes in classroom assessment.

Probing Discussions

Perhaps the most flexible type of assessment within the academy model is a probing discussion. It involves the teacher sitting down with a student with a proficiency scale in hand and asking a series of questions. For example, assume students are working on a proficiency scale for the measurement topic of weather. This is depicted in figure 4.3.

4.0	In addition to score 3.0 performance, the student demonstrates in-depth inferences and applications that go beyond what was taught. For example, the student will: • Generate a hypothesis about how the continued rise in global temperatures could impact weather conditions in a particular region
3.5	In addition to score 3.0 performance, partial success at score 4.0 content
3.0	The student will: • Understand factors that change weather conditions • Understand factors that have contributed to the rise in global temperatures over the past century
2.5	No major errors or omissions regarding score 2.0 content, and partial success at score 3.0 content
2.0	The student will recognize or recall specific vocabulary (for example, *air mass, air pressure, atmosphere, cold front, continental air mass, front, humidity, maritime air mass, occluded front, polar air mass, precipitation, pressure, stationary front, tropical air mass, warm front*) and perform basic processes such as: • Explain how weather is a natural event that results from interactions among temperature, air pressure, wind, relative humidity, and precipitation • Identify characteristics of high-pressure and low-pressure areas • Explain the relationships between air pressure, gravity, the density of air molecules, and elevation • Identify characteristics of different types of air masses (maritime, continental, polar, tropical) • Explain how air masses and fronts interact to create different weather conditions The student will recognize or recall specific vocabulary (for example, *absorb, atmosphere, global temperature, greenhouse gas, orbit, radiate, reflect, solar activity, solar energy*) and perform basic processes such as: • Explain how global temperature is determined • Show how solar energy can be transmitted, reflected, or absorbed by the atmosphere, clouds, or Earth's surface • Identify greenhouse gases • Explain how greenhouse gases prevent heat from being radiated into space • Identify ways humans have contributed to greenhouse gases • Identify ways natural processes create greenhouse gases • Compare how global temperatures have changed over time
1.5	Partial success at score 2.0 content and major errors or omissions regarding score 3.0 content
1.0	With help, partial success at score 2.0 content and score 3.0 content
0.5	With help, partial success at score 2.0 content but not at score 3.0 content
0.0	Even with help, no success

Source: © 2016 by Marzano Resources. Adapted with permission.

FIGURE 4.3: Proficiency scale for weather, grade 6.

Using this proficiency scale, the teacher would structure questions to address the content at score 2.0, 3.0, and 4.0. For example, the teacher might design questions for each level like the following.

Score 2.0

- Can you explain what a weather front is?

- Why do you think it rains more in Hawaii than it does in Arizona?

- What are some ways that humans contribute to creating greenhouse gases?

Score 3.0

- Why do you think it's often so much cooler in a larger town fifty miles away from us?

- How could El Niño have an influence on our weather here at home?

- What are some reasons that global temperatures have increased over the past several decades?

Score 4.0

- The density of the trees in the Amazon rainforest absorbs a great deal of carbon dioxide. As much of the rainforest is destroyed by human activities, more greenhouse gases could be released into the atmosphere than are absorbed. How could this contribute to increased temperatures and impact the rainy season throughout the Western Hemisphere?

When engaged in the probing discussion, the teacher would use these preplanned questions, along with those that he or she thinks up on the spot, to verbally examine an individual student's knowledge of the content one level at a time. Once the teacher is convinced that the student understands the score 2.0 content, he or she would move to score 3.0 queries. If the student responds accurately to some of the 3.0 questions but not all, the teacher assigns a half-point score of 2.5 on the proficiency scale. Probably the most useful aspect of probing discussion as an assessment is that the teacher can ask the student to clarify his or her answers if the teacher needs more evidence to determine the student's current status on the proficiency scale.

Student-Centered Assessments

One of the more profound findings in education scholar John Hattie's research, in our opinion, is the value of student-centered assessment coupled with teacher judgment of student achievement. Specifically, Hattie (2009) ranked 138 variables identified from his research in terms of their correlation with student achievement. The variable ranked highest was what he referred to as *student self-reported grades*. In effect, Hattie reported that the activity schools could engage in that was most strongly associated with student achievement, as measured by external assessments, is students self-reporting their own achievement. While Hattie did not provide a specific example of how this plays out in classrooms, one can infer from his discussion that it can manifest in various ways such as students rating their understanding of a particular topic or suggesting the grade they believe they deserve on a particular assignment or in a specific course. In 2012, Hattie updated his research and added twelve variables, bringing the total to 150. The highest-ranked variable in this new list was *student self-reported grades/student expectations*. While student self-reported grades still held the highest position, Hattie amended his original description to include students' setting goals about their own learning. Hattie (2012) explained this dynamic in the following way: "Educating students to have challenging, appropriate expectations is among the most powerful influence in enhancing student achievement" (p. 60). In 2015, Hattie again expanded his list to 195 variables. This time, the top-ranked variable was *teacher estimates of achievement*, and the third-ranked variable was *student self-reported grades*. While we use the term *student-centered assessments*, both phrases refer to the fact that students have some control over the information that is used to assign a score or the actual score that is assigned. This implies that student-centered assessments, along with teacher judgments about those assessments, are at the top of the list in terms of what educators can do to enhance student achievement. In the academy model, there are two types of student-centered assessments: (1) student-generated assessments and (2) student self-assessments.

Student-generated assessments are those that students themselves design as evidence that they have reached a certain level of competence on a specific proficiency scale. For example, in mathematics, assume students are working on a proficiency scale focused on understanding tables, and level 3.0 of the scale states that students are required to interpret or construct a table that demonstrates the relationship between two variables. As a student-generated assessment, a student might video-record a verbal description of the relationship between two variables, along with data illustrating this relationship. The student would also create a two-way table inserting the appropriate data in each cell of the table, explaining how the data represent the relationship as he or she does so. All of this would be part of the video recording, so the teacher could examine the student's work at any time. The teacher would also archive the recording so that other students can view it at any time as an exemplar of what proficiency looks like for this particular measurement topic.

Student self-assessment involves students asserting that they have attained a specific score on a specific proficiency scale and providing concrete evidence for the assertion. This form of assessment works best if personal tracking matrices are used. As described by Marzano, Norford, and colleagues (2017), teachers can develop personal tracking matrices for students or work with students to help them develop the matrices. A personal tracking matrix resembles a proficiency scale in that content is organized in a learning progression, with the complex content at the top and the simpler content at the bottom. However, the personal tracking matrix uses student-friendly language to restate the learning targets within a proficiency scale as "I can" statements. To illustrate, figure 4.4 (page 130) shows a personal tracking matrix designed for a proficiency scale on the measurement topic of health and wellness at the intermediate level.

Personal tracking matrices typically have a row dedicated to each piece of content, whereas a proficiency scale will combine such pieces. For example, each vocabulary term has its own line in a personal tracking matrix, as shown in figure 4.4, while vocabulary is listed together as score 2.0 content in a proficiency scale. It's important to note that the personal tracking matrix includes columns for students to rate themselves on each learning target and a column to provide evidence of their learning. Specifically, when using a personal tracking matrix, students rate themselves using a scale with three values, as follows.

1. I'm still confused about this topic.

2. I've learned some but not all of the topic.

3. I've got this now.

The last column of the personal tracking matrix is titled My Evidence. Students' gathering and presenting their own evidence is critical to the validity of a personal tracking matrix as a form of assessment. In this column, students record the evidence on which they are basing their self-evaluation. Such evidence might include a paper-and-pencil assignment students have completed, a virtual assignment, a written explanation of content designed by students, and so on.

Level	Indicator	My Rating			My Evidence
		I'm still confused about this topic.	I've learned some but not all of the topic.	I've got this now.	
4	I can show examples of different types of diets and explain how they might affect a person's body.				
3	I can explain what eating different types of foods might do to my body.				
2	I can explain foods that are in a balanced diet.				
2	I can read and explain a food label.				
2	I can give examples of fad diets and explain why they are not always healthy choices.				
2	I can give examples of unhealthy foods using the Dietary Guidelines for Americans.				
2	I can give examples of healthy foods using the Dietary Guidelines for Americans.				
2	I can explain the term *dietary guidelines*.				
2	I can explain the term *fad*.				
2	I can explain the term *additive*.				
2	I can explain the term *nutrition*.				
2	I can explain the term *calorie*.				
2	I can explain the term *protein*.				
2	I can explain the term *carbohydrate*.				
2	I can explain the term *sodium*.				

Source: Adapted from Marzano, 2017.

FIGURE 4.4: Personal tracking matrix for health and wellness proficiency scale.

Current Summative Scores

Ultimately, within the Marzano Academies model, teachers must assign each student a current summative score for each measurement topic, which represents the student's level of knowledge at that time. It is important to note that we are using the term *current summative score*. This is an important distinction within the academy model. We explain that distinction and its purpose briefly here, but detailed discussions of current summative scores are presented in the books *Making Classroom Assessments Reliable and Valid* (Marzano, 2018) and *The New Art and Science of Classroom Assessment* (Marzano et al., 2019).

It is safe to say that in many schools, formative assessments are only considered practice for a summative test. Stated differently, some schools have adopted the position that students' scores on the summative assessment are the only scores that count. In fact, scores on summative tests might be the only ones teachers record in a gradebook. We believe this is one of the biggest and most consequential mistakes currently made in elementary schools, at least in terms of classroom assessment. There are many reasons for our belief, not the least of which is that precision or accuracy of an individual student's score on an individual test can be very low. To illustrate this, consider table 4.1.

TABLE 4.1: Errors in Assessment Scores—95 Percent Confidence Interval for Observed Score of 70

Reported Reliability Coefficient for the Test	The Score a Particular Student Receives on the Test	Lowest Probable Score	Highest Probable Score	Range
0.85	70	59	81	22
0.75	70	55	85	30
0.65	70	53	87	34
0.55	70	50	90	40
0.45	70	48	92	44

Note: The standard deviation of this test was 15 and the upper and lower limits have been rounded.

Source: Adapted from Marzano, 2017.

Table 4.1 depicts the amount of error one can expect in an individual student's score across five levels of test reliability: 0.45, 0.55, 0.65, 0.75, and 0.85. Most educators are familiar with the fact that they can compute a reliability coefficient for any test using formulas that have been in existence for decades. A reliability coefficient ranges from 0.00 to 1.00. The common belief among educators is that the larger the reliability coefficient on a specific test, the more precise a particular score is for a particular student. While there is some truth to this statement, it is also true that even when a test has a high reliability coefficient, an individual student's score on that test will contain a great deal of error.

Table 4.1 depicts a situation in which a specific student receives a score of 70 on a test. Additionally, the table shows how the precision of that student's score changes across different levels of test reliability. The best-case scenario is reported in the top row of the table, indicating that the test on which the student received a score of 70 has reliability of 0.85. We see in the third and fourth columns that there are two other scores: the lowest probable score and the highest probable score. To understand these scores, it is necessary to consider some underlying principles of test theory.

All tests are designed under the assumption that the score a student receives on a test, called the observed score, contains some error. Actually, the conceptual equation used to represent an individual student's score on a particular assessment is:

$$\text{Observed score} = \text{true score} + \text{error}$$

This equation states that the score a student receives on a test has a component called the *true score*. This is the score the student would have received under ideal conditions. It represents the precise measure of what the student knows relative to the content on the test. However, there is a second component on the right side of the equation. It is the error score (or simply *error*). Sometimes the error component artificially increases a student's observed score. This might occur if a student guesses an answer, or if a teacher inadvertently gives the student credit for an incorrect answer. Sometimes the error component artificially deflates a student's observed score. This might occur if a student knows an answer but simply doesn't record it correctly on the test, or if a teacher inadvertently does not give a student credit for a correct answer.

Using this foundational equation, test makers can compute the range of scores in which a student's true score might fall. In the case of table 4.1, when the test has a reliability of 0.85, the range of scores that would account for error working for or against the student is between 59 and 81. If the reliability of the test is 0.45 instead of 0.85, that range of probable true scores increases dramatically. It is now between 48 and 92. These facts have massive implications for how educators should design and interpret individual students' scores on assessments. They certainly call into question using a single summative test score to determine if a student is proficient regarding a specific topic, yet this is a common practice in elementary schools. More specifically, in many schools, if a student's observed score is equal to or greater than a set cut score, the student is considered to be proficient. If that student's score is below the cut score even by a single point, the student is considered not to be proficient. As is clear from table 4.1, this is a poor way to make decisions about the competence of an individual student on a specific topic.

Taken at face value, the situation illustrated in table 4.1 and the ensuing discussion call for an immediate change in how classroom assessments are designed, scored, and (most importantly) interpreted. Changes in traditional practices are needed immediately. Educators should use multiple assessments to judge student proficiency and should update students' reported scores as their knowledge and skills improve (as implied by the term *current summative score*).

The Marzano Academies model addresses this issue using a tool in the LMS it employs. One of the unique features of the Marzano Academies model is the use of mathematical models to aid in determining any student's current summative score on any topic. Formulas for these calculations are presented in the book *Making Classroom Assessments Reliable and Valid* (Marzano, 2018) and can be applied to any spreadsheet program, including Excel. The example we show here uses a tool embedded in the Empower LMS, which all official Marzano Academies employ. Within the Empower LMS, scores that teachers collect for students on a specific measurement topic are referred to as *evidence scores*. Once the teacher has compiled sufficient evidence for a particular proficiency scale for a particular student, a calculator embedded in the LMS is automatically activated, helping teachers interpret the pattern of evidence scores and assigning a current summative score to that student at that time. This is depicted in figure 4.5.

The scores in figure 4.5 represent about a five-week period of time. This figure is refreshed and the current summative score recomputed in the LMS each time a teacher enters a new evidence score

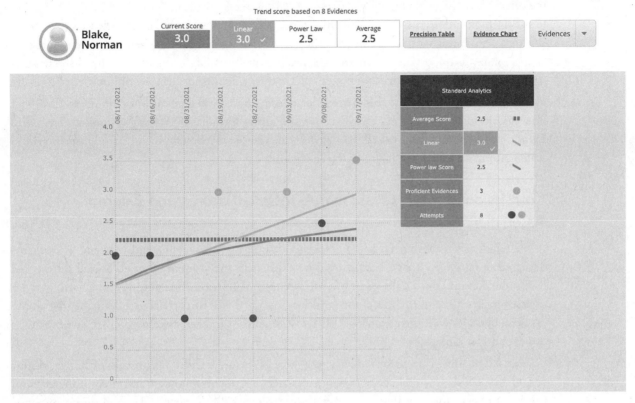

FIGURE 4.5: Current summative score calculator in the Empower LMS.

for this specific student on this specific proficiency scale. As depicted in figure 4.5, the first score the student received was 2.0. The last score was 3.5. Altogether, the teacher has entered eight evidence scores during the five-week period. These scores came from the various types of assessments previously described, such as traditional tests, probing discussions, student-centered assessments, and so on. The teacher must now report a summative score that represents the student's final status.

There are a number of ways teachers can arrive at a summative score by analyzing the pattern of scores. The Empower LMS makes this relatively easy since it uses three mathematical models to compute the most probable summative score. One model is the average. This model gives equal weight to each evidence score, in effect assuming that little if any learning has occurred over the time the teacher scored assessments and entered the resulting evidence scores into the LMS. The average is depicted by the horizontal dotted line. A second mathematical pattern is the linear trend. The linear trend is computed under the assumption that students learn at a constant rate. It is the line that moves from lower left to the upper right in a straight line. This means that students learn as much from week 1 to week 2 as they do from week 2 to week 3 and so on. The third mathematical pattern, the power law trend, is depicted by the curved line that flattens out over time. It is computed under the assumption that students learn quickly in the beginning, but when they get to the more complex content at the higher levels of a proficiency scale, their rate of learning slows down or flattens.

The LMS doesn't just compute these three analyses—it also identifies the mathematical model that has the least amount of error. In figure 4.5, this is indicated by the highlighted rectangle labeled *Linear* with the checkmark in it. This indicates that, in this case, the linear trend is the best model of the three. Thus, the mathematically recommended summative score of "best fit" is 3.00. The teacher uses this information to enter a summative score, which appears in the box labeled *Current Score*. In this case, the teacher has opted to use the summative score recommended by the mathematical analysis, but it is important to note that the teacher can override the calculator if he or she has reason to believe that a different score better reflects the student's current level of knowledge or skill.

Educators who wish to use this type of detailed mathematical analysis but employ an LMS that does not do so can create their own Excel version using formulas in *Making Classroom Assessments Reliable and Valid* (Marzano, 2018) or they can visit www.cbe.empowerlearning.net/marzano -calculator to access a free version of the calculator.

Correlation Between Classroom Assessment Scores and External Assessment Scores

The relationship among classroom assessments, interim assessments, and year-end assessments depicted in figure 4.1 (page 125) should be explicit in the academy model. Stated differently, the leader should continually examine the strength of relationships among these various types of assessments. One of the more powerful ways to do this is to correlate students' scores on the proficiency scales with their scores on EOY assessments or interim assessments. To see how this is done, consider table 4.2.

Table 4.2 provides correlational data across three grade levels: third, fourth, and fifth. Specifically, at each grade level, the table depicts the percentage of students who demonstrated proficiency on the measurement topics at that grade level, as measured by proficiency scales, and the corresponding proportion of students who achieved passing or higher scores, as measured by the end-of-year state assessment. To illustrate, the first column lists the number of proficiency scales for a given subject area. In ELA and mathematics at the third-grade level, there are twelve such proficiency scales. Fourth-grade ELA has eleven scales, and fourth-grade mathematics has fourteen scales. Fifth-grade ELA has ten scales and fifth-grade mathematics has eighteen scales.

Each cell in the table reports the percentage of students who demonstrated proficiency on a specific number of proficiency scales and also demonstrated proficiency on the EOY state test. For third-grade ELA, 98.84 percent of students who demonstrated proficiency on all twelve of the proficiency scales also demonstrated proficiency on the state test. For fifth-grade mathematics, 100 percent of students who demonstrated proficiency on all eighteen proficiency scales also demonstrated proficiency on the state test, and so on. By contrast, students who mastered only a small number of proficiency scales were unlikely to pass the state test—only 15 percent of students who were proficient on three fifth-grade mathematics scales passed, for example. The correlations between proficiency-scale competence and proficiency on the state test for each subject area and grade level are reported in the last row of the table. These correlations are extremely high, ranging from 0.929 to 0.977. These high correlations mean that teachers can confidently use students' performance on the proficiency scales measured using classroom assessments as valid indicators of student learning.

This type of yearly analysis is one of the most important leadership functions that principals can use relative to assessment. If correlations between student scores on end-of-year external tests and proficiency scales are high, then classroom assessment can be considered valid. If they are not, then changes should be made in the proficiency scales, the way they are scored, or both. For example, educators may need to align the proficiency scales more precisely to the content on the end-of-year test, or teachers might be scoring students too leniently or harshly on the proficiency scales.

TABLE 4.2: Percentage of Students Who Passed the 2016 State Test by Number of Proficiency Scales Mastered

Number of Proficiency Scales on Which Students Were Proficient	Third-Grade Language Arts Pass Percentage	Third-Grade Mathematics Pass Percentage	Fourth-Grade Language Arts Pass Percentage	Fourth-Grade Mathematics Pass Percentage	Fifth-Grade Language Arts Pass Percentage	Fifth-Grade Mathematics Pass Percentage
0	24	0	4.35	0	5.88	0
1	25	7.69	12	7.69	13.64	0
2	29.41	0	43.75	0	22.22	13.33
3	60	16.67	56.52	12.5	27.03	15
4	54.16	18.75	37.5	6.67	35.14	34.78
5	61.9	31.58	64.71	29.17	50	38.1
6	72	17.65	66.67	21.05	74.36	39.13
7	88.89	68.97	65.63	36	88.89	56.52
8	87.5	54.55	75	40	84.21	68.75
9	82.35	53.33	79.49	56.67	92.68	60
10	95.56	78.38	78	61.76	95.31	70
11	92.86	88.46	97.09	60.61		73.68
12	98.84	97.85		85.29		72.22
13				95.35		87.5
14				100		82.61
15						100
16						100
17						100
18						100
Correlation	0.952	0.948	0.929	0.959	0.976	0.977

Note: All correlations significant at 0.01.

Source: Adapted from Marzano et al., 2018.

High Reliability Leadership for School-Level Indicator 13

School-level indicator 13 deals with changes in how classroom assessments are designed, scored, and interpreted. These changes begin with an explicit reference to a proficiency scale when designing any assessment. All scores on all assessments use the metric of proficiency scales and are interpreted in terms of status on a proficiency scale. Additionally, the procedures employed when executing this school-level indicator help solve the problem of inherently low reliability associated with assigning summative scores to students based on a single assessment.

The previous discussion on school-level indicator 13 emphasizes the following components of assessment.

- Various types of classroom assessments
- Current summative scores
- Correlations between classroom assessment scores and external assessment scores

Figure 4.6 depicts potential lagging indicators for this school-level indicator. Figure 4.7 depicts the customized high reliability scale for this school-level indicator.

Programs and Practices	Lagging Indicator Data	Potential Standard for High Reliability Status
Classroom assessments	A classroom assessment model is in place that allows teachers to use a wide variety of assessment types, including student-centered assessment	100 percent of teachers implement the range of assessments in the classroom assessment model
Current summative scores	Teachers record multiple evidence scores for each student on each measurement topic	100 percent of teachers use multiple evidence scores to compute current summative scores for students on measurement topics
Correlations between classroom assessment scores and external assessment scores	The school regularly computes correlations between the percentage of students who demonstrate proficiency on proficiency scales and the percentage of those students who demonstrate proficiency on the state test	Computed correlations between the percentages of students who demonstrate proficiency on measurement topics and state tests are 0.80 or greater
Perceptions of students, teachers, and parents	Surveys of teachers, students, and parents	90 percent of teachers report that the classroom assessment process has been beneficial to them 80 percent of students report that the classroom assessment process has been useful to them 70 percent of parents report that the classroom assessment process has been useful to them

Source: © 2021 by Robert J. Marzano.

FIGURE 4.6: Potential lagging indicators for school-level indicator 13.

Evidence	
4 **Sustaining** **(quick data)**	Quick data like the following are systematically collected and reviewed. • Examination of reports in Empower showing the number of teachers entering evidence scores • Quick conversations with teachers about how they determine current summative scores using patterns of evidence scores
3 **Applying** **(lagging)**	Performance goals with clear criteria for success like the following are in place. • 100 percent of teachers use multiple evidence scores to compute current summative scores for students on measurement topics • Computed correlations between the percentages of students who demonstrate proficiency on measurement topics and state tests are 0.80 or greater
2 **Developing** **(leading)**	• A comprehensive model of classroom assessment is in place that calls for a wide variety of assessment types • An assessment system is in place that requires teachers to use evidence scores to compute current summative scores
1 **Beginning**	• The school has written plans for an assessment system that employs evidence scores to compute current summative scores but there is no implementation of the system • A system is in place but only a few teachers use it
0 **Not Using**	• The school has no written plans for an assessment system that employs evidence scores to compute current summative scores • There is no implementation of evidence scores to compute current summative scores

Source: © 2020 by Marzano Academies, Inc. Adapted with permission.

FIGURE 4.7: Customized high reliability scale for school-level indicator 13.

School-Level Indicator 14: Reporting and Grading

The leader of an elementary academy should ensure that the school has a reporting and grading system that depicts both status and growth for individual students and allows students to work at multiple levels across different subject areas.

To understand the rationale underlying this school-level indicator, it is useful to start with the inherent weaknesses of the traditional reporting and grading systems used widely across most school systems. Historically, schools have recorded and reported a student's academic status using a point-based letter grade. These letter grades are a compilation of student work submitted through class assignments and test scores. Since students can earn academic credit for things like class participation or on-time assignment completion, a student's final grade is partially determined by measures that are separate from academic competence and thus not always representative of what the student knows or is able to do. This is problematic. When students are allowed to advance to the next level of study (such as moving from third-grade mathematics to fourth-grade mathematics) without demonstrating proficiency at their current level, unforeseen consequences can result. This is readily seen in subjects like mathematics, where knowledge builds on itself. For example, if a student isn't proficient at multiplication but advances to the next level of mathematics without shoring up this deficiency, he or she will struggle when the curriculum requires the multiplication of fractions. Continual use of a point-based grading system can not only lead to premature advancement but also leave students with inaccurate perceptions of what they know and what they don't know. Point-based grading systems can also work against students' developing efficacy and agency, particularly when students struggle with topics in which they have previously received high grades. The academy model employs a different kind of reporting and grading system that mitigates these inherent weaknesses and allows students to develop a full and accurate understanding of both their academic strengths and their areas of need.

Reporting for Competency-Based Education

To achieve the highest degrees of reporting accuracy while still fostering student agency, an academy school should adopt a reporting and grading system that depicts students' status and growth and lets students work on multiple levels concurrently across different subject areas. This, of course, is the essence of a CBE system.

At its very core, a CBE reporting and grading system only advances students based on demonstrated competency. This is an important shift from traditional practice, as it removes the inherent weaknesses of assigning academic credit to nonacademic proficiencies such as class participation or mere attendance. This makes accurate reporting of student status and growth more likely. Since a CBE grading system preloads all academic standards into the gradebook, students can track exactly which standards they still need to complete in order to advance to the next level. Also, when academic matriculation is determined by competency only, students move through the levels of content at varying speeds, depending on natural strengths and prior knowledge. This allows for true personalized pacing. The CBE grading system provides opportunity for accelerated movement in subjects of strength and allots more time for subjects that are particularly challenging for specific students.

Figure 4.8 is an example of a student report card designed for a CBE system. Notice that point-based letter grades are absent; instead, there is only a simple accounting of a student's demonstrated competencies in each subject area. It is clear this sixth-grade student is accelerating in mathematics with seventeen of seventeen mathematics targets complete in level 6, and three of seventeen targets complete in level 7. However, at the same time, this student only has eight of fifteen literacy targets complete at level 6, showing a clear area for improvement. This snapshot is easy to read, but provides only an overview, so additional reporting tools are needed for detailed information regarding the student's progress on the individual academic standards.

A key of a CBE reporting and grading system is the ability for students to see precisely what is still required for advancement. In figure 4.8, the student has demonstrated competency on eight of the fifteen sixth-grade literacy standards. This leaves seven remaining to be mastered. Figure 4.9 depicts a deeper look into four of the academic standards for sixth-grade literacy: analyzing ideas and themes, analyzing narratives, analyzing text organization and structure, and analyzing points of view and purpose. As described previously, a score 3.0 equates to proficient, while a score 2.0 or lower indicates partially proficient. A student must earn a score 3.0 on every academic standard before advancing to the next level. In figure 4.9, it is easy to see that this particular student has already demonstrated competency, or earned a score 3.0, on analyzing narratives and analyzing text organization and structure. However, the student has scores of 1.5 for analyzing ideas and themes and analyzing points of view and purpose. This indicates that even with help, the student still

Student Snapshot

'●' marks active levels	Levels									
Areas	PK	00	01	02	03	04	05	06	07	08
Math	Promoted	3.0	3.0	3.0	3.0	3.0	3.0	17 of 17 ●	3 of 17	
Literacy	Promoted	3.0	Promoted	Promoted	Promoted	3.0	3.0	8 of 15 ●		
Science	Promoted	3.0				3.0	3.0	11 of 16 ●		
Social Studies	Promoted	3.0	Promoted	Promoted	Promoted	3.0	3.0	2 of 8 ●		
Technology							1 of 7 ●			
Visual Arts		3.0			3.0	3.0	3.0	4 of 10 ●		
Physical Education		3.0	0 of 8	0 of 6	3.0	3.0	5 of 7 ●	3 of 10	0 of 7	

Source: © 2021 by Empower Learning. Used with permission.

FIGURE 4.8: CBE reporting by level.

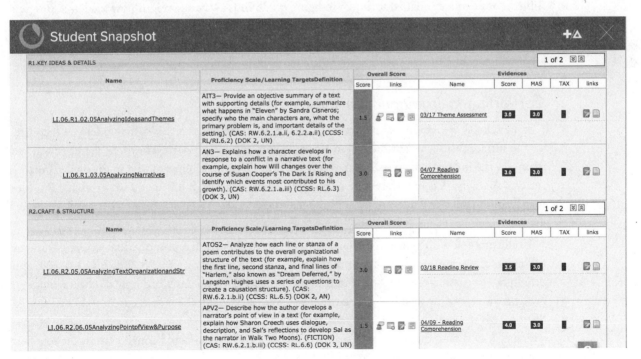

Source: © 2021 by Empower Learning. Used with permission.

FIGURE 4.9: CBE reporting by standard.

doesn't demonstrate full understanding of the simpler content at the 2.0 level. The student clearly needs more instruction and support with this topic. This detailed accounting within student records provides the necessary information for the student, and the teacher, to focus future learning on those standards on which the student still needs to reach 3.0 or higher.

Communicating the Tenets of a CBE System

Since most schools operate under a point-based grading system, many teachers may not inherently understand the tenets of a CBE reporting system, such as this one we have described, at the outset of implementing the Marzano Academies model. Moving away from point-based letter grades to a CBE reporting system can also be confusing to students and parents. To better help all stakeholders adjust to a CBE reporting system, the principal must ensure he or she provides a multitude of avenues for the school community to become well versed in this type of grading protocol.

Parents most often will initially direct questions or concerns about grading to their student's classroom teachers. Knowing this, the principal should ensure teachers understand the tenets of CBE grading and are able to explain them. At a basic level, the principal should create a list of talking points or easy-to-understand materials, as demonstrated in figure 4.10 and figure 4.11 (page 144), that help explain a CBE grading system for teachers to reference while interacting with students and parents. In addition to providing such resources to teachers, the principal might consider devoting a school newsletter leading up to the fall parent-teacher conferences to similar information.

When a school adopts a CBE reporting and grading system, parent-teacher conferences manifest in ways that are different from current practice. Whereas in traditional parent-teacher conferences, the teacher discusses a student's point-based grade and missing assignments, in a CBE system the parent-teacher conference highlights the student's performance on specific academic standards using the CBE grading system as the backdrop for the conversation. Walking a parent through his or her child's snapshot report, as shown in figure 4.8, as well as the student's performance on a particular subject's academic standards, as shown in figure 4.9, builds awareness about how academic progress is measured and reported in a CBE system. This awareness increases parents' and students' ability to read and understand a CBE report, and ultimately creates a deeper understanding of student ability, all of which contribute to strong student agency within a school.

Converting to Traditional Grades

Some schools are required to report traditional percentage or letter grades for students. Of course, on the surface this seems antithetical to a competency-based approach. However, there are ways to maintain the integrity of a CBE system but still fulfill the requirements of a traditional reporting system. Actually, it is relatively easy to translate the 0.0 through 4.0 scores on proficiency scales into traditional letter grades, or even into percentage scores. Table 4.3 (page 142) provides a conversion scale.

To illustrate how the conversion chart might be used, consider an individual student with the following seven summative scores at the end of a grading period: 1.5, 2.5, 2.5, 3.5, 3.0, 3.0, and 3.5. In the discussion of school-level indicator 13 (page 125), we described how teachers would use evidence to determine each student's current summative score on the measurement topics addressed during a given grading period. Suppose that the teacher chose to use the average of these scores, which is 2.79. Using the conversion scale in table 4.3, the teacher could convert that score to a percentage grade of 85 or a letter grade of B.

empower

Reading the Assignment Report

The assignment report tells you about your child's progress and performance in class. This report can be printed out by teachers at any time and may require parents to sign and return.

This is the class time, class name, and teacher.

These are the dates the assignments were given and when they were due.

These are the learning targets that the assignments hit.

Educate Assignment Report

Class and Teacher	Assignment Name	Assigned On	Due On	Score	Maximum Achievable Score	Standard	Content Area
Mathematics, Middle Level	Adding Decimals Homework	10/05 12:00 a.m.	10/12 12:00 a.m.		2.0	MA.05.NBT.07.04	Mathematics
Erica Raleman					2.0	MA.08.NS.04.04	Mathematics
Mathematics, Middle Level	Comparing and Ordering Decimals Homework	9/14 12:00a.m.	9/21 12:00 a.m.	2.0	2.0	MA.05.NBT.04.04	Mathematics
Erica Raleman							
Mathematics, Middle Level	Mathematician Research Project	8/28 12:00 a.m.	9/4 12:00 a.m.	1.5	2.0	LI.07.W4.07.04	Literacy
Erica Raleman				1.5	2.0	LI.07.W4.08.04	Literacy

These are the scores your child earned on the activities.

MAS stands for maximum achievable score, which is the highest score the student could earn on the activity. You can think of it as a goal score.

Score	MAS
M	2.0
	2.0
2.0	2.0
1.5	2.0
1.5	2.0

The designation M means the assignment is missing or incomplete.

The student score matches the MAS, which means the student met the goals of the assignment.

A blank space means the assignment has not been scored by the teacher yet.

The student completed the assignment, but the learning goal was not met. With more practice, the score could go up.

To see your child's progress throughout the year, you may log into Empower anytime at EmpowerWPS.org. Please contact the school's office to receive your username and password. Also, every student can log in with Google, using his or her district email address and password.

EmpowerWPS.org

FIGURE 4.10: Empower Learning summary.

TABLE 4.3: Converting Proficiency Scale Scores to Percentages and Letter Grades

Scale Score	Percentage	Grade	Scale Score	Percentage	Grade	Scale Score	Percentage	Grade	Scale Score	Percentage	Grade
4.00	100	A	2.30 to 2.34	76	C	1.30 to 1.31	50	F	0.73 to 0.75	25	F
3.90 to 3.99	99	A	2.25 to 2.29	75	C	1.28 to 1.29	49	F	0.70 to 0.72	24	F
3.80 to 3.89	98	A	2.20 to 2.24	74	C	1.26 to 1.27	48	F	0.67 to 0.69	23	F
3.70 to 3.79	97	A	2.15 to 2.19	73	C	1.24 to 1.25	47	F	0.64 to 0.66	22	F
3.60 to 3.69	96	A	2.10 to 2.14	72	C	1.22 to 1.23	46	F	0.61 to 0.63	21	F
3.50 to 3.59	95	A	2.05 to 2.09	71	C	1.20 to 1.21	45	F	0.58 to 0.60	20	F
3.40 to 3.49	94	A	2.00 to 2.04	70	C	1.18 to 1.19	44	F	0.55 to 0.57	19	F
3.30 to 3.39	93	A	1.95 to 1.99	69	D	1.16 to 1.17	43	F	0.52 to 0.54	18	F
3.20 to 3.29	92	A	1.90 to 1.94	68	D	1.14 to 1.15	42	F	0.49 to 0.51	17	F
3.10 to 3.19	91	A	1.85 to 1.89	67	D	1.12 to 1.13	41	F	0.46 to 0.48	16	F
3.00 to 3.09	90	A	1.80 to 1.84	66	D	1.10 to 1.11	40	F	0.43 to 0.45	15	F
2.95 to 2.99	89	B	1.75 to 1.79	65	D	1.08 to 1.09	39	F	0.40 to 0.42	14	F

Score	#	Grade
2.90 to 2.94	88	B
2.85 to 2.89	87	B
2.80 to 2.84	86	B
2.75 to 2.79	85	B
2.70 to 2.74	84	B
2.65 to 2.69	83	B
2.60 to 2.64	82	B
2.55 to 2.59	81	B
2.50 to 2.54	80	B
2.45 to 2.49	79	C
2.40 to 2.44	78	C
2.35 to 2.39	77	C

Score	#	Grade
1.70 to 1.74	64	D
1.65 to 1.69	63	D
1.60 to 1.64	62	D
1.55 to 1.59	61	D
1.50 to 1.54	60	D
1.48 to 1.49	59	F
1.46 to 1.47	58	F
1.44 to 1.45	57	F
1.42 to 1.43	56	F
1.40 to 1.41	55	F
1.38 to 1.39	54	F
1.36 to 1.37	53	F
1.34 to 1.35	52	F
1.32 to 1.33	51	F

Score	#	Grade
1.06 to 1.07	38	F
1.04 to 1.05	37	F
1.02 to 1.03	36	F
1.00 to 1.01	35	F
0.98 to 0.99	34	F
0.96 to 0.97	33	F
0.94 to 0.95	32	F
0.91 to 0.93	31	F
0.88 to 0.90	30	F
0.85 to 0.87	29	F
0.82 to 0.84	28	F
0.79 to 0.81	27	F
0.76 to 0.78	26	F

Score	#	Grade
0.37 to 0.39	13	F
0.34 to 0.36	12	F
0.31 to 0.33	11	F
0.28 to 0.30	10	F
0.25 to 0.27	9	F
0.22 to 0.24	8	F
0.19 to 0.21	7	F
0.16 to 0.18	6	F
0.13 to 0.15	5	F
0.10 to 0.12	4	F
0.07 to 0.09	3	F
0.04 to 0.06	2	F
0.01 to 0.03	1	F
0.00	0	

Source: Marzano, 2018, pp. 100–101.

Using Empower at Conferences

This handout is not meant to be distributed to parents and guardians. It is designed to ensure teachers know what data are easy for parents to access in Empower. Make sure parents know how to find missing and low-scored work in Empower. Make sure they understand that course completion (and credit) is based on successfully demonstrating proficiency on a set of standards, and that they can see how close their students are to completing courses in Empower.

Parent Log-Ins

In order to log into Empower, parents will have to receive their username and password from their child's school. They will have one username and password, which will allow them to view data for any of their children. Once logged in, clicking on their child's name will bring up a list of other students in their family.

Missing and Low-Scored Work

MISSING

- Any work that has been assigned to a student and marked by the teachers with an *M* in the gradebook will be identified on the Parent Homepage. When parents hover over this alert icon, the names of the missing assignments will appear.

LOW-SCORED WORK

- If a student receives a score for an assignment that is below the teacher's expectations (below the set MAS), that work will be identified on the Parent Homepage. Hovering over this alert icon will bring up a list of these low-scored assignments.

Completing Classes or Levels

TARGET BROWSER

- When a parent clicks the Target Browser link from their homepage, they can select a content area and a class (like teachers do) to see how their child is doing in the class overall. They can see all the standards that will be covered in the class and their child's current scores.

Source: © 2018 by Westminster Public Schools. Used with permission.

FIGURE 4.11: Parent-teacher conference suggestions.

Another perplexing problem that some CBE teachers face is that within a single class, they may have students who are the same chronological age but are working on topics at different grade levels. For example, in the snapshot report in figure 4.8 (page 139), the student is working on level 6 topics except for mathematics, where the student has started working on level 7 topics. A reasonable question is, How does one combine status information about an individual student working at multiple grade levels within or between subject areas? One answer to this question is the weighting scheme depicted in table 4.4.

In table 4.4, the first pair of columns provides a weighting system to use when a student is working on a measurement topic that is two grade levels below the student's chronological grade level.

TABLE 4.4: Weighting Scheme for Students Working on Topics at Different Grade Levels

Measurement Topics Two Levels Below Grade Level		Measurement Topics One Level Below Grade Level		Measurement Topics One Level Above Grade Level		Measurement Topics Two Levels Above Grade Level	
Earned Score	Weighted Score	Earned Score	Weighted Score	Earned Score	Weighted Score	Earned Score	Weighted Score
4.0	1.0	4.0	2.0	4.0	7.0	4.0	8.0
3.5	0.5	3.5	1.5	3.5	6.5	3.5	7.5
3.0	0.0	3.0	1.0	3.0	6.0	3.0	7.0
2.5	0.0	2.5	0.5	2.5	5.5	2.5	6.5
2.0	0.0	2.0	0.0	2.0	5.0	2.0	6.0
1.5	0.0	1.5	0.0	1.5	4.5	1.5	5.5
1.0	0.0	1.0	0.0	1.0	4.0	1.0	5.0
0.5	0.0	0.5	0.0	0.5	3.5	0.5	4.5
0.0	0.0	0.0	0.0	0.0	3.0	0.0	4.0

Source: © 2021 by Robert J. Marzano.

The second pair of columns provides a weighting system for topics one grade level below the student's chronological level. The third pair weights scores for measurement topics one grade level above, and the fourth pair weights scores for topics two grade levels above.

To illustrate how this system is used, assume that a student who is in fifth grade is working on ten measurement topics during a grading period for a specific subject area. Seven of those topics are at the fifth-grade level and three topics are at the sixth-grade level. At the end of the grading period, the student receives a current summative scale score for each of the ten measurement topics. Figure 4.12 (page 146) shows what scoring in this scenario looks like.

The first column in figure 4.12 lists the ten measurement topics in abstract form (that is, topic 1, topic 2, and so on). The second column depicts the grade level of each measurement topic. The first seven topics are at the fifth-grade level, and the last three topics are sixth-grade level. The third column depicts the student's score on the associated proficiency scale. For the first seven topics, the student received relatively high scores; two scores were 4.0, three scores were 3.0, one score was 3.5, and one score was 2.5. However, on the last three topics, the student received much lower scores: 1.5, 1.0, and 0.5. This is because the student is just being introduced to the content at the sixth-grade level. One would expect his or her initial scores to be relatively low for that reason. The simple average for these ten scores is 2.6, which translates to a grade of B using the conversion table in

Measurement Topic	Grade Level	Unweighted Score	Weighted Score
Topic 1	5	3	3
Topic 2	5	3.5	3.5
Topic 3	5	4	4
Topic 4	5	3	3
Topic 5	5	2.5	2.5
Topic 6	5	3	3
Topic 7	5	4	4
Topic 8	6	1.5	4.5
Topic 9	6	1.0	4
Topic 10	6	0.5	3.5
Total		26	35
Average		2.6	3.5

Source: © 2021 by Robert J. Marzano.

FIGURE 4.12: Example weighted scoring scenario.

table 4.3 (page 142). However, the fourth column in figure 4.12 lists the weighted scores, according to the weighting scheme presented in table 4.4. The student's scores for the fifth-grade topics stay the same, but the last three scores for sixth-grade topics are weighted to account for the fact that they are above the student's chronological grade level. The weighted average using this scheme is 3.5, which translates to a letter grade of A. In effect, reporting in a CBE system where students are working at different grade levels in different subject areas can be adapted to retain many of the characteristics of a traditional grading system.

High Reliability Leadership for School-Level Indicator 14

The reporting and grading system in a CBE school is an important tool for generating student agency, as well as ensuring the learning process itself is efficient and meaningful. When a school moves away from traditional point-based grading toward a CBE reporting system, that school provides students, teachers, and parents alike with a more robust platform to analyze a student's academic status, areas of strength or weakness, and ability to work concurrently at different levels and subject contents.

The previous discussion on school-level indicator 14 emphasizes the following elements of reporting and grading.

- Reporting for CBE
- Communicating the tenets of a CBE system
- Converting to traditional grades

Figure 4.13 depicts possible lagging indicators for this school-level indicator. Figure 4.14 depicts the customized high reliability scale for this school-level indicator.

School-Level Indicator 15: Collective Responsibility

In the Marzano Academies model, teachers interdependently provide students with instruction, assessment, and general support regardless of whether a given student is assigned to their class. As the following discussion illustrates, this is accomplished by teachers sharing decision making and responsibility in areas that teachers traditionally approach individually. We refer to this approach as *collective responsibility*.

Programs and Practices	Lagging Indicator Data	Potential Standard for High Reliability Status
CBE reporting	A CBE reporting system is in place that determines each student's status and growth on the various topics available to him or her	100 percent of teachers understand and accurately employ the CBE reporting system
Communicating the tenets of a CBE system	Systems are in place to provide parents and students with detailed information as to students' status and growth	90 percent of parents receive the information explaining the CBE reporting system
Translations to traditional grades	If required, conversion systems are in place to translate scores from the CBE reporting system to traditional grades	100 percent of teachers accurately employ the conversion systems
Perceptions of students, teachers, and parents	Surveys of teachers, students, and parents	90 percent of teachers report that the CBE reporting system has been beneficial to them 80 percent of students report that the CBE reporting system has been useful to them 70 percent of parents report that the CBE reporting system has been useful to them

Source: © 2021 by Robert J. Marzano.

FIGURE 4.13: Potential lagging indicators for school-level indicator 14.

Evidence	
4 **Sustaining** **(quick data)**	Quick data like the following are systematically collected and reviewed. • Examination of report cards generated by the LMS • Quick conversations with teachers, parents, and students about reporting and grading
3 **Applying** **(lagging)**	Performance goals with clear criteria for success like the following are in place. • 100 percent of teachers understand and accurately employ the CBE reporting system • 90 percent of parents receive the information explaining the CBE reporting system • 90 percent of teachers report that the CBE reporting system has been beneficial to them • 80 percent of students report that the CBE reporting system has been useful to them • 70 percent of parents report that the CBE reporting system has been useful to them
2 **Developing** **(leading)**	• A comprehensive CBE reporting system is in place • Systems are in place to inform parents and students with a clear understanding of the CBE reporting system
1 **Beginning**	• Report cards depict status and growth on a few measurement topics only • The school has a plan for a reporting system that depicts status and growth but does not implement that plan
0 **Not Using**	• The school has no written plan for a reporting system that depicts status and growth • There is no reporting of status and growth on any measurement topics

Source: © 2020 by Marzano Academies, Inc. Adapted with permission.

FIGURE 4.14: Customized high reliability scale for school-level indicator 14.

The school-level indicator of collective responsibility might be thought of as a first cousin to the concept of collective efficacy, which was popularized in 2018 by education scholars Jenni Donohoo, John Hattie, and Rachel Eells in an article titled "The Power of Collective Efficacy." The authors explained that the concept of collective efficacy can be traced back to the work of psychologist Albert Bandura in the 1970s. In 1977, Bandura observed that a group's confidence in its abilities seemed to be associated with greater success (Donohoo et al., 2018). In other words, the assurance members of a team place in their teammates affects the team's overall performance for the better. Researchers have since found this to be true across many domains (Eells, 2011). When a team of individuals share the belief that they can overcome challenges and produce desired results through their unified efforts, such teamwork is more effective than the actions of those competent individuals working independently. Bandura (1997) referred to this phenomenon as *collective efficacy*, which he defined as "a group's shared belief in its conjoint capability to organize and execute the courses of action required to produce given levels of attainment" (p. 477).

Since then, there have been a number of studies conducted on the topic (see Eells, 2011), along with the development of instruments to measure the collective efficacy of educators in a school (Eells, 2011; Goddard, 2002; Goddard, Hoy, & Hoy, 2004). Perhaps the most noteworthy aspect of the reported research on collective efficacy is that in 2015, Hattie ranked it second among 195 variables in terms of its relationship to student achievement. This is noteworthy not only for its high ranking, but also because the variable was not even mentioned in the previous lists of variables reported by Hattie (2009, 2012) as important correlates of student achievement.

Most of the discussion about collective efficacy has focused on what educators believe—do teachers believe, as a group, that they can advance student learning? In the academy model, belief is considered an important first step, but those beliefs must turn into concrete actions to rise to the level of collective responsibility. There are a number of ways leaders using the academy model can engage in such concrete actions, which we describe in the following sections.

The "We" Mindset

One simple approach to developing collective responsibility is to adopt the "we" mindset. To develop such a mindset, a principal should frame his or her communications to the school community through a "we" and "us" lens instead of "I" and "me." It is common to hear principals use first-person pronouns when describing school operations. For example, "*My* school uses a block schedule . . ." or "*My* teachers worked hard to ensure . . ." or "*I* made the decision to welcome students . . ." These first-person pronouns, although appropriate, do not support a culture of collective responsibility. Collective responsibility is supported by using collective pronouns: "*Our* school uses a block schedule . . ." or "*We* worked hard to ensure . . ." or "*We* made the decision to welcome students . . ." Focusing on pronoun usage may seem trivial, but even subtle language choices affect the culture of a school. If the principal desires teachers to abandon the idea of "my students" in favor of "our students," he or she must lead by example and eliminate "my school" from his or her own lexicon.

With this said, if the principal wants to ensure every student benefits from collective action, he or she must systemically design concrete situations in which collective responsibility is required, including recording evidence scores and summative scores, transitioning, providing support for individual students, and planning instructional units.

Submission of Evidence Scores and Summative Scores

One powerful way to manifest collective responsibility is to have multiple teachers submit evidence scores for students on specific proficiency scales. To accomplish this, a principal would designate various teachers to enter evidence scores on specific measurement topics for any students working on those topics. For example, consider mathematics measurement topics at the fifth-grade level. In addition to the teacher of record who is responsible for fifth-grade mathematics instruction, other teachers who have been vetted for their knowledge of fifth-grade mathematics could enter evidence scores for these topics.

Another version of collective responsibility for entering evidence scores is to set aside time during the school day when students can work with teachers of their own choice on specific measurement topics. These teachers would provide instruction to those students who come to them and would enter evidence scores based on their interactions with those students.

Schools can also expand this practice to assigning current summative scores to students. Specifically, groups of teachers who share responsibilities for teaching and assessing students on common measurement topics can periodically meet to examine evidence scores. Based on the evidence scores, teachers come to agreements on the specific summative scores that should be assigned to specific students. Specifically, in the discussion of school-level indicator 13 (page 125), we emphasized the fact that assigning a current summative score for a specific measurement topic should involve an examination of the patterns of evidence scores a student has exhibited and the mathematical evaluation of those patterns by the LMS. When employing collective responsibility, all those teachers who have entered evidence scores for a particular student can be part of the decision as to the most appropriate current summative score to assign.

Transitions From Level to Level

One of the most important decisions teachers in an academy school must make is when students are ready to move up to the next level of a specific subject area. Teachers who have been involved in entering evidence scores or determining current summative scores should meet periodically to determine if specific students should move up to a higher level of content (for example, from fourth-grade mathematics to fifth-grade mathematics). For some students, deliberation might focus on whether they should be moved down a level in the rare situations where a student does not seem to have mastered the content at the next lower level.

The decision to move a student to the next level in a given subject area should be made after a robust analysis of the available data. Certainly, the student's scores on the various measurement topics at the current level will be a major consideration. A student must have already achieved a score of 3.0 on each topic at the current level. However, other considerations factor in as well, such as the psychological impact the transition will have on the student and the extent to which support for the student is in place if the transition is made.

Support for Individual Students

Collective responsibility also manifests as deliberations about support required for individual students. This commonly takes the form of response-to-intervention (RTI) activities. Within the RTI model, Tier 1 instruction refers to general classroom instruction that all students experience. This is sometimes referred to as *core instruction*. Tiers 2 and 3 represent interventions that do not apply to all students. Tier 2 interventions supplement what students receive during regular Tier 1 instruction. This is typically accomplished in small-group settings. Working in collaborative teams, teachers identify groups of students with specific needs and ensure those groups receive adequate and targeted instruction in their common areas of need. Such instruction might occur during focused instructional time (see page 154). Finally, Tier 3 interventions are for students whose specific needs require one-on-one interaction, such as students who have fallen so far behind in a subject area that they require one-on-one support to catch up. In many cases, such interactions require the attention of teachers who do not have whole-class responsibilities. Again, teachers working in collaborative teams would determine which students need Tier 3 instruction. Given the extent to which teachers share responsibility for students in a CBE system, the decision as to which students require Tier 3 interventions can be made with input from all teachers who worked directly with the students in question.

Unit Planning

Unit planning is one of the more robust areas for demonstrating collective responsibility. This follows logically from the idea of a guaranteed and viable curriculum. Instead of individual teachers making their own curricular decisions and creating their own idiosyncratic unit plans, teams of teachers collectively engage in this activity. In the Marzano Academies model, unit plans can and should be a vehicle for bringing together a number of the school-level indicators. To this end, teachers responsible for content at the same grade level might meet and design units. The collective unit design process should be guided by questions like the following.

- What proficiency scales will we address? (See school-level indicator 9, page 83.)

- What specific instructional activities will we employ for various elements within the proficiency scales? (See school-level indicator 5, page 49.)

- What vocabulary clusters will we address? (See school-level indicator 11, page 104.)

- What knowledge maps will we use? (See school-level indicator 8, page 74.)

- Which cognitive and metacognitive skills will we address? (See school-level indicator 10, page 91.)

- What topics will we address during cumulative review? (See school-level indicator 7, page 70.)

- What types of assessments will we use? (See school-level indicator 13, page 125.)

The idea that teachers should work collaboratively in making planning decisions is certainly not new. This type of collective unit planning is similar to the often-cited practice of lesson design made popular in Japan. In Japan, the collaborative development of lessons is a fundamental aspect of *kounaikenshuu*, or in-service training, a comprehensive set of activities that formed the crux of school improvement in Japan at the end of the 20th century. Regarding this form of collaboration, psychologist James Stigler and education scholar James Hiebert (1999) wrote:

One of the most common components of *kounaikenshuu* is lesson study (*jugyou kenkyuu*). In lesson study, groups of teachers meet regularly over long periods of time (ranging from several months to a year) to work on the design, implementation, testing, and improvement of one or several "research designs" (*kenkyuu jugyou*). By all indicators, lesson study is extremely popular and highly valued by Japanese teachers, especially at the elementary level. It is the linchpin of the improvement process. (pp. 110–111)

Lesson study has caught on in the United States. Education researchers Richard DuFour and Robert J. Marzano (2011) explained that, since the introduction of the concept of lesson study to U.S. educators, a number of adaptations have been developed (see, for example, Jalongo, Rieg, & Helterbran, 2007). DuFour and Marzano (2011) noted that collaborative teams within PLCs are perfect vehicles for developing and vetting effective lessons, and those teams should engage in their own form of *jugyou kenkyuu* (lesson study) at a very detailed level.

Within the Marzano Academies model, the concept of *lesson design* is expanded to *unit design*. This has a number of benefits. First and foremost, common unit design helps ensure that students receive well-crafted and vetted instruction that is similar from teacher to teacher. Second, focusing on unit design as opposed to lesson design provides individual teachers with day-to-day flexibility to meet the specific needs of their students while still operating within a well-defined structure.

Within a school, teachers at the same grade level tasked with addressing the same content can jointly answer the unit-design questions for specific units of instruction. That is, they would agree on the specific proficiency scales they will include in the unit, specific instructional strategies they will use, and so on. With these decisions made, teachers would employ this initial unit design but not wait until the unit is completed to share perspectives on its success. Rather, cooperating teachers would meet once a week to discuss successes and issues they have experienced with the unit as designed. When they have completed the unit, the cooperating teachers would meet to formally make changes in the unit based on their joint experiences and perspectives.

High Reliability Leadership for School-Level Indicator 15

In the Marzano Academies model, collective responsibility refers to the general attitudes of teachers regarding their potential impact on students. Perhaps most important, collective efficacy involves specific areas of shared decision making and responsibility, including transitioning students to the next level of learning, supporting individual students, and planning instructional units.

The previous discussion on school-level indicator 15 addressed the following topics related to collective responsibility.

- The "we" mindset
- Submission of evidence scores and summative scores
- Transitions from level to level
- Support for individual students
- Unit planning

Figure 4.15 (page 152) depicts possible lagging indicators for this school-level indicator. Figure 4.16 (page 153) depicts the customized high reliability scale for this school-level indicator.

Programs and Practices	Lagging Indicator Data	Potential Standard for High Reliability Status
The "we" mindset	Protocols are in place for engaging the "we" mindset	90 percent of teachers utilize the protocols for the "we" mindset
Assigning evidence and summative scores	Protocols are in place for teachers to collectively assign evidence scores and summative scores	100 percent of teachers engage in collective assignment of evidence scores and summative scores
Transitions from level to level	Protocols are in place for teachers to collectively make decisions about student transitions from one level of learning to the next	100 percent of teachers engage in collective decisions about student transitions
Supporting individual students	Protocols are in place for teachers to collectively make decisions about individual students' needs	100 percent of teachers engage in collective decision making about individual students' needs
Unit planning	Protocols are in place for teachers to collectively develop unit plans	100 percent of teachers engage in collective unit planning
Perceptions of teachers, students, and parents	Surveys of teachers, students, and parents	90 percent of teachers report that they participate in and benefit from collective responsibility activities 80 percent of students report that they see their teachers working together when making decisions and believe this benefits them 70 percent of parents report that they see the teachers working together and believe it makes the school better

Source: © 2021 by Robert J. Marzano.

FIGURE 4.15: Potential lagging indicators for school-level indicator 15.

School-Level Indicator 16: Flexible Scheduling

One of the most profound and sometimes complex structural changes in schooling effected by the Marzano Academies model is the creation of flexible scheduling. The leader of an elementary academy should ensure that the school employs scheduling practices that allow students to receive instruction, support, and evaluation on measurement topics at any level and in any subject area. To accomplish this commonly requires substantial changes in how a school is organized.

Flexible scheduling begins with the operational decision that students will not be limited to a single classroom throughout an entire day. This is counter to many existing scheduling preferences at the elementary level, but it is a critical step toward achieving collective responsibility, as well as equal learning opportunity for all students. A simple reality in most schools is that some teachers are more effective at improving student learning than others due to more years of experience, varying degrees of motivation, or even natural abilities. This is just a mathematical fact. At any given point in time,

Evidence	
4 **Sustaining** **(quick data)**	Quick data like the following are systematically collected and reviewed. • Records from Empower indicating multiple teachers are providing evidence scores for measurement topics • Quick conversations with teachers and students about the extent to which multiple teachers are engaged in decisions about individual students
3 **Applying** **(lagging)**	Performance goals with clear criteria for success like the following are in place. • 100 percent of teachers engage in collective assignment of evidence scores and summative scores • 100 percent of teachers engage in collective decisions about student transitions • 100 percent of teachers engage in collective decisions about individual student needs • 100 percent of teachers engage in collective unit planning
2 **Developing** **(leading)**	• Protocols are in place for teachers to collectively assign evidence scores and summative scores • Protocols are in place for teachers to collectively make decisions about student transitions • Protocols are in place for teachers to collectively make decisions about individual students' needs • Protocols are in place for teachers to collectively develop unit plans
1 **Beginning**	• The school has written plans to facilitate collective responsibility but those plans are not specific enough to be actionable • Some teachers attempt to work with each other to implement their own versions of collective responsibility
0 **Not Using**	• The school has no written plans to facilitate collective responsibility • No teachers try to implement aspects of collective responsibility on their own

Source: © 2020 by Marzano Academies, Inc. Adapted with permission.

FIGURE 4.16: Customized high reliability scale for school-level indicator 15.

the teachers within a building will differ in terms of their professional expertise. Unfortunately, this has consequences for students. When a principal assigns a student to a single classroom all year, the quality of that student's education will largely be dictated by the quality of his or her assigned teacher. This can create winners and losers amongst students simply because of the classroom roster to which they are assigned (Nye, Konstantopoulos, & Hedges, 2004). Although instruction and teacher development (school-level indicator 5, page 49) can help mitigate this, flexible scheduling can immediately address the heart of the problem.

Flexible scheduling can manifest in many different ways, but at its very core it allows students to receive instruction from multiple teachers throughout the school day. On one end of the scheduling spectrum is the complete elimination of homerooms, or even subject-based class groupings, opting instead for a collective teaching approach. In this situation, the principal utilizes a strengths-based model to determine teaching responsibilities. Some teachers are naturally inclined to whole-class direct instruction, while others might excel in small-group settings, and still others are best at individualized instruction. In this scenario, the principal designs a flexible schedule that assigns some teachers to direct instruction of large groups of students, while other teachers conduct small-group instruction, and still others preside over individualized instruction. Teachers are assigned to topics not only based on their knowledge of the topics, but also based on their expertise at teaching large groups, small groups, and individuals. Students who require the most support are assigned to small-group sessions or individual sessions as their needs dictate. This type of scheduling requires a complete overhaul of the traditional school schedule, and logistically can be difficult to achieve with the current confines of many collective bargaining agreements and existing norms. This notwithstanding, there are other types of flexible scheduling options for a principal to adopt that do not completely rewrite how schools operate but still achieve the larger goals of competency-based education. We present a few of these options in the following sections.

FIT Block

A *focused instructional time* (FIT) block is a popular way to employ flexible scheduling. As mentioned previously, this is also known as *what I need* (WIN) block. Regardless of name, the tenets of this type of scheduling remain the same. A FIT block is a dedicated time each day when students are provided focused instruction that targets their personalized learning plan. For example, a special education student might receive pullout instruction as dictated by his or her individualized educational plan (IEP), or an English learner student might receive his or her language acquisition support during this block of time. Similarly, a gifted and talented student might work toward the learning goals established in his or her advanced learning plan, while other students who are behind in reading would work with an instructional paraprofessional.

Finally, the classroom teachers who share a FIT block can coordinate efforts to work with targeted groups of students from all of their classrooms who need to review or relearn previously instructed content. This provides students who have not demonstrated competency on a particular

	8:00 a.m.	8:05 a.m.	8:10 a.m.	8:15 a.m.	8:20 a.m.	8:25 a.m.	8:30 a.m.	8:35 a.m.	8:40 a.m.	8:45 a.m.	8:50 a.m.	8:55 a.m.	9:00 a.m.	9:05 a.m.	9:10 a.m.	9:15 a.m.	9:20 a.m.	9:25 a.m.	9:30 a.m.	9:35 a.m.	9:40 a.m.	9:45 a.m.	9:50 a.m.	9:55 a.m.	10:00 a.m.	10:05 a.m.	10:10 a.m.	10:15 a.m.	10:20 a.m.	10:25 a.m.	10:30 a.m.	10:35 a.m.	10:40 a.m.	10:45 a.m.	10:50 a.m.	10:55 a.m.	11:00 a.m.	11:05 a.m.	11:10 a.m.	11:15 a.m.	11:20 a.m.	
Kindergarten A	Breakfast and Attendance 8:00–8:15			Specials 8:15–9:05										Literacy 9:05–11:25																												R 1 1
Kindergarten B				Specials 8:15–9:05										Literacy 9:05–11:25																												R 1 1
Level 1				Literacy 8:15–9:05										Specials 9:05–9:55										Literacy 9:55–11:30																		
Level 2				Literacy 8:15–9:55																				Specials 9:55–10:45										Literacy 10:45–11:35								
Level 2				Literacy 8:15–9:55																				Specials 9:55–10:45										Literacy 10:45–11:35								
Level 3				**FIT Block 8:15–9:00**									Literacy 9:00–9:45									Recess 9:45–10:00			Literacy 10:00–11:35																	
Level 3				**FIT Block 8:15–9:00**									Literacy 9:00–9:45									Recess 9:45–10:00			Literacy 10:00–11:35																	
Level 4				Literacy 8:15–9:00									**FIT Block 9:00–9:45**									Recess 9:45–10:00			Literacy 10:00–11:35																	
Level 4				Literacy 8:15–9:00									**FIT Block 9:00–9:45**									Recess 9:45–10:00			Literacy 10:00–11:35																	
Level 5				Literacy 8:15–9:30															Recess 9:30–9:45			Recess 9:45–10:30									Literacy 10:30–11:35											
Level 5				Literacy 8:15–9:30															Recess 9:30–9:45			**FIT Block 9:45–10:30**									Literacy 10:30–11:35											

Source: © 2021 by Westminster Public Schools. Used with permission.

FIGURE 4.17: FIT block schedule.

measurement topic with additional instruction the rest of the class does not require. The possibilities of a FIT block are vast, but the results are the same: every student is provided a dedicated block of time every day to receive targeted, personalized instruction that does not interfere with or take away from his or her access to the direct instruction of the day's lesson plan.

In order to establish a FIT block, the principal needs to formally build it into the daily school schedule. The easiest way to do this is to treat the FIT block in the same way specials blocks, such as for music and arts instruction, are addressed. Depending on the size of the school and the number of classrooms, multiple teachers will have FIT blocks scheduled at the same time. Knowing this, the principal will want to ensure the teachers who share a FIT block have students at similar learning levels. This is critical for several reasons. First, it allows the intervention team to pull students from several classrooms for the same targeted small-group work. It also allows the classroom teachers to strategically group students from multiple classrooms for reinforcement and remediation. Figure 4.17 is an example of a school schedule with FIT blocks built in.

Another critical component to ensuring that a FIT block serves its purpose is the full power of collective responsibility—the expectation that every educator, regardless of position or title, who works with a particular student assumes responsibility for that student. For example, if the English-as-a-second-language (ESL) teacher wants his or her language instruction to be most relevant to the student, he or she will co-plan lessons with the student's assigned classroom teacher to ensure that language instruction is utilizing some of the same themes or topics being taught in the general education classroom. Simply being aware of the general education teacher's lesson or unit design will allow the ESL teacher to choose specific vocabulary clusters or particular topics to focus on while designing language lessons. Another example of such cooperation would be the ESL teacher and the classroom teacher collaborating on the upcoming unit assessment to provide a modified

Time columns: 11:50 a.m. – 3:30 p.m. (5-minute increments)
–12:00 · Literacy 12:00–12:45 · Mathematics 12:45–1:45 · **FIT Block 1:45–2:30** · Recess 2:30–2:45 · Mathematics 2:45–3:30
–12:00 · Literacy 12:00–12:45 · Mathematics 12:45–1:45 · **FIT Block 1:45–2:30** · Mathematics 2:30–3:30
…nch :45–12:05 · Literacy 12:05–12:45 · Mathematics 12:45–1:00 · **FIT Block 1:00–1:45** · Mathematics 1:45–2:30 · Recess 2:30–2:45 · Mathematics 2:45–3:30
Lunch 11:50–12:10 · Literacy 12:10–12:45 · Mathematics 12:45–2:15 · Recess 2:15–2:30 · **FIT Block 2:30–3:30**
Lunch 11:50–12:10 · Literacy 12:10–12:45 · Mathematics 12:45–2:30 · **FIT Block 2:30–3:30**
Lunch 11:55–12:15 · Mathematics 12:15–1:00 · Specials 1:00–1:50 · Mathematics 1:50–3:30
Lunch 11:55–12:15 · Mathematics 12:15–1:00 · Specials 1:00–1:50 · Mathematics 1:50–3:30
…cess :45–:00 · Lunch 12:00–12:20 · Mathematics 12:20–1:50 · Specials 1:50–2:40 · Mathematics 2:40–3:30
…cess :45–:00 · Lunch 12:00–12:20 · Mathematics 12:20–1:50 · Specials 1:50–2:40 · Mathematics 2:40–3:30
Recess 11:50–12:05 · Lunch 12:05–12:25 · Mathematics 12:25–2:40 · Specials 2:40–3:30
Recess 11:50–12:05 · Lunch 12:05–12:25 · Mathematics 12:25–2:40 · Specials 2:40–3:30

version with English-learner supports built in. Alternatively, an English learner student might take an unmodified version of the classroom assessment while in the ESL teacher's classroom during the FIT block to ensure that student receives the necessary supports while taking the assessment.

Classroom Regrouping

One implicit component of competency-based education is extensive use of regrouping—reorganizing the groups in which students receive instruction as their learning needs change. We addressed one version of regrouping in the discussion of school-level indicator 6, blended instruction (page 62), in relation to utilizing a target browser to create small groups inside of a classroom. The same ideas can be applied to whole classroom groupings as well. That is, the entire roster of a classroom can be periodically changed. Of course, this is almost impossible in a traditional school and, in fact, goes against the assumptions underlying traditional classroom composition.

As mentioned previously, the norm in K–12 education has been to use students' ages (and, by default, grade levels) as the primary mechanism for creating class rosters. This method of age-based groupings creates instructional challenges for the teacher, specifically in relation to the need to differentiate instruction. For example, it is intuitively obvious that not all eight-year-old students have the same reading or mathematical ability just because they are eight years old. Therefore, when class rosters are determined by students' ages, teachers are left with a well-defined bell curve of student ability levels, creating the need for differentiation if every student is to receive targeted instruction. Utilizing an ability-based grouping of students in particular subject areas mitigates this issue but requires the principal to adopt a highly flexible schedule.

Ability-based classroom groupings begin with the principal deciding what metric the school will use to determine student ability in particular subject areas. Ideally, principals should examine multiple data points to make grouping decisions as opposed to relying on a single assessment. With this said, the principal still will need to start somewhere, perhaps using the school's local assessment for a composite view of mathematics and literacy scores. The principal would begin by ranking, for example, every student's composite score in mathematics from the BOY assessment results and then doing the same for literacy. Using these lists, he or she would create class rosters of approximately twenty-five students with similar composite scores in mathematics and literacy. Remembering the importance of multiple data points, the principal would then look at other assessment scores (such as DIBELS for literacy or state assessments for mathematics) to see if the initial groupings still appear reasonable. Finally, the principal would conduct a class roster meeting with the classroom teachers and intervention teams to discuss the roster groupings as determined by the assessment data. Through this process, the principal can form tightly homogenous ability groups, lessening the need for teachers to differentiate instruction while still ensuring each student receives targeted learning opportunities. Since student learning is fluid, the initial ability-based classroom groupings created in the beginning of the year will likely become gradually less valid as the year progresses. This reality creates the need for the principal to ensure that students can switch classrooms midyear as their individual academic progression dictates.

Communication About Regrouping

When it is deemed appropriate to move a student's classroom midyear, communication with the student and his or her parents is vitally important. Since most schools operate under a grade-leveled, single-classroom assignment model, some students and parents might be wary of a midyear move. Such concerns are understandable and should be acknowledged. Student-teacher relationships matter, as do the social dynamics among students. Switching a student's classroom might cause concern with some parents or guardians in that they might interpret such a change as evidence their child is failing or something is wrong regarding the child's progress. This renders the school's communication with the student and his or her family critical.

The principal should ensure clear and consistent processes are in place to reduce any negative effects of such a move. For example, the current teacher needs to initiate contact with the student and his or her family regarding the new classroom placement. The teacher will want to explain the academic reasoning for the move by highlighting progress-monitoring data or other reporting and grading data as evidence supporting the school's decision. The teacher will also want to formally introduce the student to the new teacher, as well as offer ongoing support as the student changes classrooms. Next, the receiving teacher should also initiate contact with the student and his or her family *before* the class move is made, introducing him- or herself and offering an opportunity to meet with the family, if desired. These transition processes need to be articulated in writing and inspected for compliance, as the importance of classroom regrouping in a CBE system cannot be overstated.

Anticipating that students will make midyear classroom moves, the principal should lay the groundwork at back-to-school night. Most schools use back-to-school night as an opportunity for students and their families to meet their classroom teachers and become acquainted with the school. This is a wonderful opportunity to welcome families back from summer, but also to start the critical task of relationship building. When a school adopts a flexible-scheduling approach to classroom groupings, the principal will want to introduce this concept to students and parents during these initial back-to-school activities. He or she might begin by providing a brief explanation of the school's competency-based approach to learning, as well as why the school values an ability-based approach to classroom groupings. During this time, he or she should also communicate that a student's classroom placement will not be static, but instead might shift during the year if needed. Leaders should emphasize the fact that in all cases changes will be made to enhance each student's learning. Because students will likely be assigned to multiple teachers over the course of the year, the principal should not provide families with roster assignments and instructions to meet a sole classroom teacher, but instead should introduce families to teams of teachers students may learn from throughout the year. This early communication and assignment of students to a team of teachers helps families understand the school's flexible scheduling model from the outset.

High Reliability Leadership for School-Level Indicator 16

While scheduling might seem like a mundane aspect of an elementary school, a CBE system cannot exist without flexible scheduling. The shift to flexible scheduling is a substantial change to the most basic structures of the school system. Consequently, school leaders should have concrete strategies for moving to a flexible schedule. School-level indicator 16 addresses strategies a leader might use.

The previous discussion on school-level indicator 16 emphasized the following elements of flexible scheduling.

- FIT blocks
- Classroom regrouping
- Communication about regrouping

Figure 4.18 (page 158) depicts possible lagging indicators for this school-level indicator. Figure 4.19 (page 158) depicts the customized high reliability scale for this school-level indicator.

Programs and Practices	Lagging Indicator Data	Potential Standard for High Reliability Status
FIT block	Protocols are in place to use FIT blocks as a tool for flexible scheduling of students' instruction	100 percent of teachers follow the protocols for using FIT blocks as a tool for flexible scheduling
Classroom regrouping	Protocols are in place for regrouping of classes	100 percent of teachers use the protocols for classroom regrouping
Communication about regrouping	Protocols and procedures are in place to communicate with parents and other constituent groups about regrouping	100 percent of teachers use the protocols and procedures for communicating about grouping and regrouping with fidelity
Perceptions of students, teachers, and parents	Surveys of teachers, students, and parents	100 percent of teachers report that flexible scheduling is having a beneficial effect on students 90 percent of students report that flexible scheduling is beneficial to their learning 70 percent of parents report that flexible scheduling is beneficial to their children

Source: © 2021 by Robert J. Marzano.

FIGURE 4.18: Potential lagging indicators for school-level indicator 16.

Evidence	
4 **Sustaining** **(quick data)**	Quick data like the following are systematically collected and reviewed. • Scheduling records indicating the frequency with which students change groups • Quick conversations with teachers and students about flexible scheduling
3 **Applying** **(lagging)**	Performance goals with clear criteria for success like the following are in place. • 100 percent of teachers use the protocols for classroom regrouping • 100 percent of teachers use the protocols and procedures for communicating about grouping and regrouping with fidelity
2 **Developing** **(leading)**	• Protocols are in place for regrouping of classes • Protocols and procedures are in place to communicate with parents and other constituent groups about regrouping • Surveys are administered to parents
1 **Beginning**	• The school has written plans to create a flexible schedule but the plans are not specific enough to be actionable • Some teachers informally work together to create their own versions of flexible scheduling
0 **Not Using**	• The school has no written plans for a flexible schedule • There is no informal implementation of flexible scheduling at the classroom level

Source: © 2020 by Marzano Academies, Inc. Adapted with permission.

FIGURE 4.19: Customized high reliability scale for school-level indicator 16.

Summary

This chapter addressed four school-level indicators of the Marzano Academies model that all represent major changes in the way schools are run. Those indicators are as follows.

School-level indicator 13: Classroom assessment

School-level indicator 14: Reporting and grading

School-level indicator 15: Collective responsibility

School-level indicator 16: Flexible scheduling

Classroom assessment occurs on a frequent and sometimes daily basis in elementary schools. However, the important information gleaned from this practice is commonly not used to its full capacity. In the Marzano Academies model teachers have expanded options for assessing students and rigorous methods of analyzing patterns of scores to assign summative scores for each measurement topic. This information is also used to design a reporting and grading system that details each student's status and growth on each measurement topic using the proficiency scale metric. This can even be done in a manner that preserves traditional reporting schemes (for example, letter grades). Collective responsibility is how a Marzano Academy operationalizes the popular concept of collective efficacy. Finally, flexible scheduling allows for a system that is sensitive to the needs of every student and can adapt the schedule to meet those needs.

CHAPTER 5

Leadership for

Second-Order Change

The previous four chapters described sixteen interventions that academy schools must implement. We refer to these interventions as school-level indicators. Some school-level indicators (such as indicator 1, a safe, orderly, and supportive environment, page 14) are common in elementary schools across the country. Others (such as indicator 15, collective responsibility, page 146) represent what the literature on change has referred to as *second-order change*.

The Nature of First- and Second-Order Change

In the books *School Leadership That Works* (Marzano, Waters, & McNulty, 2005) and *District Leadership That Works* (Marzano & Waters, 2009), Marzano and colleagues applied the general research and theory on change to the specifics of K–12 schooling. The primary distinction made in those books is that there are two basic types of change: first-order change and second-order change. Using different terminology, others have made these same distinctions (Argyris & Schön, 1974, 1978; Heifetz, 1994). Table 5.1 (page 162) indicates some of the important distinctions between first- and second-order change.

Even a cursory analysis of these characteristics demonstrates that if a leader is promoting initiatives that are second order in nature, then he or she will have a much more difficult task than promoting initiatives that involve first-order changes. To determine the order of change, regarding any type of initiative that is being considered, a leader should ask the following questions.

- Is the initiative a logical and incremental extension of what we have done in the past?

- Does the initiative fit within the existing paradigms of teachers and administrators?

- Is the initiative consistent with prevailing values and norms?

- Can the initiative be implemented with the knowledge and skills that the faculty and administrators already have?

- Can the initiative be implemented with the resources and conditions that are easily available?

- Is there common agreement that the initiative is necessary?

We assert that if a school leader asked these questions about the initiatives necessary to implement the Marzano Academies model, then the prevailing answers to these questions would likely be *no*, indicating that some—if not many—of the school-level indicators require second-order change.

TABLE 5.1: Characteristics of First-Order Change Versus Second-Order Change

First-Order Change	Second-Order Change
Is perceived as an extension of the past	Is perceived as a break with the past
Fits within existing paradigms	Lies outside existing paradigms
Is consistent with prevailing values and norms	Conflicts with prevailing values and norms
Can be implemented with existing knowledge and skills	Requires the acquisition of new knowledge and skills
Requires resources and conditions currently available to those responsible for implementing the innovations	Requires resources and conditions not currently available to those responsible for implementing the innovations
Is easily accepted because of common agreement that the innovation is necessary	Is easily resisted because only those who have a broad perspective of the school see the innovation as necessary

Source: Adapted from Marzano & Waters, 2009; Marzano et al., 2005.

Our comments are not designed to discourage leaders from implementing or adapting the academy model; rather, they are intended to inform leaders so that they will be better prepared for the planning and energy required.

It is important to remember that whether something is considered a first- or second-order change by faculty and staff within a school is a subjective matter of perspective. Marzano and colleagues (2005) explain:

> The phenomenon of first- versus second-order change is an internal event. It is defined by the way people react to a proposed innovation. Whether a change is perceived as first-order or second-order depends on the knowledge, experience, values and flexibility of the individual or the group perceiving the change. . . . Depending on how they perceive the change initiative, some staff members may experience the initiative as first-order change and others will experience it as second-order change. (pp. 112–113)

With these factors in mind, we next consider some of the aspects of the academy model that have a higher probability of being perceived as second-order change.

Aspects of the Academy Model Potentially Considered Second-Order Change

Teachers and other school staff may perceive many aspects of the sixteen school-level academy indicators as second-order change. Individual teachers might feel this concern, as well as groups such as the third-grade team or the science teachers. Here we consider some elements of the Marzano Academies model that may challenge stakeholders.

Competency-Based Education

The competency-based approach is a foundational characteristic of the academy model. By definition, CBE utilizes competency-based groupings of students as opposed to groupings based solely on the chronological age of students. Students in a CBE system working on the same content are grouped together regardless of their age. Additionally, within a CBE system, students do not move to the next level of content until they have demonstrated proficiency at their current level of content. For example, in a CBE system, a chronological fifth grader is not expected to multiply fractions when he or she has not yet demonstrated proficiency at single-digit multiplication.

This approach might seem intuitively obvious in its logic, yet schools have traditionally presented new content to students simply because their age indicated it was time to do so. This practice has unwittingly created massive problems for students, teachers, and the system itself. Each year, every teacher must work with groups of students who have substantial differences in their preparedness for the content being taught, thus preserving the bell curve at every grade level. The CBE system is designed to stop this phenomenon in its tracks.

While the competency-based approach has strong logical support, age-based grouping has a long tradition dating back to the late 1800s. Parents and community members might initially find it unsettling that two students of the same age are receiving instruction in two different levels of mathematics, for example. Some parents might feel that their children are being "left behind" or labeled as deficient in some way. Of course, any deficiencies in students' knowledge and skill are reconciled over time within a CBE system and, as time goes on, all students have a solid foundation in the critical content of the curriculum. However, the differentiation of instruction while students are in elementary (or secondary) school might be jarring to some parents or students. For these constituents, the CBE system would probably be perceived as second-order change.

The Rigor of the High Reliability Approach

The high reliability approach to the Marzano Academies model inherently holds administrators and teachers to concrete and rigorous standards. Some might perceive the notion that their school should meet the criteria articulated in sixteen different indicators as undue and unnecessary pressure. For those individuals, the high reliability process would be second-order change. It is important to remember that reaching high reliability status is a voluntary endeavor that a school engages in to enhance its efficiency and effectiveness, much like an individual might voluntarily go to a gym and follow a predetermined exercise regimen to improve his or her health. So, while it is true that a school seeking high reliability status will exert extraordinary energy in this effort, the end result is perceived as well worth the effort (Marzano et al., 2018).

The Prominence of Student Efficacy and Agency

While it might seem that everyone would automatically be an advocate for the academy model's focus on student efficacy and agency, it is also true that such a focus—and more specifically the practices of student voice and choice—has not been common in K–12 education. Indeed, one might make the case that the traditional school structure is to some extent based on fostering conformity in students. To be clear, in the academy model, students must still follow rules and procedures, but these rules and procedures are commonly stated in the form of standard operating procedures that students have helped construct. The Marzano Academies model aims not to eliminate adherence to established rules and procedures in lieu of individual efficacy and agency, but to tap into the power of students' efficacy and agency to help improve the learning environment for themselves and others.

Proficiency Scales

While proficiency scales are becoming more and more prominent in K–12 education, they are still a rather dramatic departure from the norm in the perceptions of some constituents. Every state has standards intended to guide curriculum, instruction, and assessment for the schools in that state. Schools typically parse those standards into specific statements of what students need to know and be able to do in ways that make these expectations very clear. Some schools refer to these translations as *essential learnings, essential outcomes, priority standards*, or similar terms. Proficiency scales go a step further in that they not only identify the progression of knowledge and skill leading up to an essential learning, but also identify the knowledge and skill indicating progress beyond the essential learning. While this level of specificity might be viewed by some as excessive detail, it provides teachers with more and clearer guidance relative to curriculum, instruction, and assessment.

Record Keeping, Reporting, and Grading

One of the most visible aspects of the Marzano Academies model is the changes a school might make in record keeping, reporting, and grading. Observers of the academy model are frequently struck by the level of detail available about students' status and growth on a daily basis. This is commonly viewed as a great benefit of the system, but some may also view this level of detail as something of a liability, usually because it is more complex than and different from the letter grade and point system that has been used for so many decades. This notwithstanding, we have found that once the constituents of a school using a CBE reporting system understand the new system, they come to prefer it over the previous system.

Cognitive and Metacognitive Skills

Cognitive and metacognitive skills have traditionally been tacit aspects of the curriculum. However, many state-level standards documents refer to these skills more specifically, albeit using different names for them, such as critical thinking skills or higher-order thinking skills. Additionally, the world of testing has noted the importance of enhancing students' cognitive and metacognitive skills. For example, in 2006, ACT released *Reading Between the Lines*, a report warning that only 51 percent of U.S. high school graduates were ready for college-level reading, based on results indicating that high school students had difficulty with items requiring complex thinking. This resulted in a revamping of ACT's test construction protocols to include items that required more complex types of thinking.

Because standards documents and external tests already recognize the importance of cognitive and metacognitive skills, there is, on one hand, great support for these skills among constituents. On the other hand, making these skills a formal part of the curriculum that is taught, reinforced, assessed, and reported can be a very new perspective to some, making the explicit emphasis on cognitive and metacognitive skills second-order change for those individuals. Schools that believe these skills are necessary for success in an increasingly complex world must be willing to address any difficulties associated with this level of change.

Facilitating Second-Order Change

The preceding sections present components of the academy model that some constituents of an elementary school might consider second-order change. Regardless of the specifics of the list, elementary school leaders must thoroughly, accurately, and systematically address whatever concerns their constituents express. In doing so, leaders should always remember that those who are expressing the concerns are valued members of the school community who should be heard, understood, and provided with detailed information regarding their concerns. We recommend school leaders address these concerns in a methodical way. As mentioned previously, the books *School Leadership That Works* (Marzano et al., 2005) and *District Leadership That Works* (Marzano & Waters, 2009) provide detailed guidance as to how a school can navigate the process of second-order change. We present some of the guidelines only briefly here.

The first step in addressing expressed concerns is to select the primary aspect or aspects of the academy model that concerned constituents may perceive as second-order change. For example, a particular school leader might select the reporting and grading aspect of the model if stakeholders raise concerns (or the leader expects they will raise concerns) about their perceptions that schools must give up traditional methods of grading when they embrace such a system. The second step involves learning as much as possible about the selected element. This should be done with an eye toward answering detailed questions constituents might ask, making sure to have accurate and understandable answers. School leaders should take sufficient time for this step, because being able to effectively answer questions might be the determining factor in whether a school's efforts get off the ground. In this case, school leaders would become familiar with the recommendations we have made in the discussion of school-level indicator 14 and become well versed in the various options from which a school can select and still maintain a CBE methodology. With this knowledge as a foundation, a leader should then provide opportunities for all constituents of the school to ask questions, seek clarity, and raise concerns. The leader can do this through open-house meetings, town-hall-type meetings, scheduled meetings with small groups and individuals, spontaneous meetings with small groups and individuals, and the like. Finally, when the school actually starts implementing the academy model, the leader should closely follow the high reliability approach to implementation with particular emphasis on the scale for each indicator. Use of these scales will provide clear benchmarks for progress on each school-level indicator, a vehicle for forecasting problems, and concrete options for solving those problems.

Summary

This chapter has dealt with the nature of second-order change and the fact that some aspects of the academy model might be viewed as second-order change by some constituents of a particular elementary school. This noted, such a dynamic is probably inevitable when significant change is called for. Fortunately, there are concrete steps leaders can take to mitigate virtually any of the concerns that might arise. The starting point is to learn as much as possible about the particular area of concern with an eye toward being able to answer any questions that constituents might have. The discussions of the sixteen school-level indicators of the Marzano Academies model in chapters 1–4 of this book provide an initial resource.

We have written this book to provide a vision for what elementary schools can be and what we believe they should be. We have attempted to provide sufficient detail and examples for leaders to use this text as a roadmap to make the requisite changes in their schools. As we mentioned in the introduction (page 1), this book is intended for two audiences. One audience is those schools seeking official status as academies. Those schools should contact Marzano Academies (MarzanoAcademies .org) to begin this journey. The other audience is those schools who wish to implement some but not all of the components of the academy model. Those schools should select the indicators of interest and make any adaptations or alterations to those indicators they see fit. We wish these schools great success and satisfaction in their efforts.

Regardless of whether a school embraces the full Marzano Academies model or adapts the indicators in the model to meet their specific needs, we hope this book provides a stimulus for school leaders to evolve their systems into the next generation of elementary schools. We believe that the sixteen school-level indicators described in this book represent the foundational pillars of that next-generation school, and hope that our comments not only inspire elementary school leaders in this endeavor but also offer a concrete roadmap.

REFERENCES AND RESOURCES

ACT. (2006). *Reading between the lines: What the ACT reveals about college readiness in reading.* Accessed at https://www.act.org/content/dam/act/unsecured/documents/reading_report.pdf on April 22, 2020.

Anderson, L. W., & Krathwohl, D. R. (Eds.). (2001). *A taxonomy for learning, teaching, and assessing: A revision of Bloom's taxonomy of educational objectives.* New York: Longman.

Argyris, C., & Schön, D. A. (1974). *Theory in practice: Increasing professional effectiveness.* San Francisco: Jossey-Bass.

Argyris, C., & Schön, D. A. (1978). *Organizational learning: A theory of action perspective.* Reading, MA: Addison-Wesley.

Bandura, A. (1977). Self-efficacy: Toward a unifying theory of behavioral change. *Psychological Review, 84*(2), 191–215.

Bandura, A. (1993). Perceived self-efficacy in cognitive development and functioning. *Educational Psychologist, 28*(2), 117–148.

Bandura, A. (1997). *Self-efficacy: The exercise of control.* New York: Worth.

Beck, I. L., & McKeown, M. G. (1985). Teaching vocabulary: Making the instruction fit the goal. *Educational Perspectives, 23*(1), 11–15.

Beck, I. L., McKeown, M. G., & Kucan, L. (2002). *Bringing words to life: Robust vocabulary instruction* (1st ed.). New York: Guilford Press.

Bloom, B. S. (Ed.). (1956). *Taxonomy of educational objectives: Handbook I—Cognitive domain* (2nd ed.). New York: David McKay.

CCSSO. (2019). *Math: Spring 2018—Grade 7 released items.* Accessed at https://resources.newmeridiancorp.org/wp-content/uploads/2019/08/Grade-7-Math-Item-Set-2018.pdf on January 22, 2021.

Dodson, C. (2019). *The critical concepts in social studies.* Bloomington, IN: Marzano Resources. Accessed at www.marzanoresources.com/critical-concepts-social-studies.html on April 19, 2021.

Donohoo, J., Hattie, J., & Eells, R. (2018). The power of collective efficacy. *Educational Leadership, 75*(6), 40–44.

DuFour, R., & Marzano, R. J. (2011). *Leaders of learning: How district, school, and classroom leaders improve student achievement.* Bloomington, IN: Solution Tree Press.

Dweck, C. S. (2006). *Mindset: The new psychology of success.* New York: Ballantine Books.

Eells, R. J. (2011). *Meta-analysis of the relationship between collective teacher efficacy and student achievement* [Doctoral dissertation, Loyola University Chicago]. Accessed at https://ecommons .luc.edu/cgi/viewcontent.cgi?article=1132&context=luc_diss on May 21, 2021.

Goddard, R. D. (2002). A theoretical and empirical analysis of the measurement of collective efficacy: The development of a short form. *Educational and Psychological Measurement, 62*(1), 97–110.

Goddard, R. D., Hoy, W. K., & Hoy, A. W. (2004). Collective efficacy beliefs: Theoretical developments, empirical evidence, and future directions. *Educational Researcher, 33*(3), 3–13.

Graves, M. F. (2006). *The vocabulary book: Learning and instruction.* New York: Teachers College Press.

Hattie, J. A. C. (2009). *Visible learning: A synthesis of over 800 meta-analyses relating to achievement.* New York: Routledge.

Hattie, J. A. C. (2012). *Visible learning for teachers: Maximizing impact on learning.* New York: Routledge.

Hattie, J. A. C. (2015). The applicability of visible learning to higher education. *Scholarship of Teaching and Learning in Psychology, 1*(1), 79–91.

Hattie, J. A. C. (2016, July 11–12). *Mindframes and maximizers.* Paper presented at the third annual Visible Learning Conference, Washington, DC.

Heifetz, R. A. (1994). *Leadership without easy answers.* Cambridge, MA: Belknap Press of Harvard University Press.

Jalongo, M. R., Rieg, S. A., & Helterbran, V. R. (2007). *Planning for learning: Collaborative approaches to lesson design and review.* New York: Teachers College Press.

Koltko-Rivera, M. E. (2006). Rediscovering the later version of Maslow's hierarchy of needs: Self-transcendence and opportunities for theory, research, and unification. *Review of General Psychology, 10*(4), 302–317.

Marzano, R. J. (1992). *A different kind of classroom: Teaching with Dimensions of Learning.* Alexandria, VA: Association for Supervision and Curriculum Development.

Marzano, R. J. (2000). *Transforming classroom grading.* Alexandria, VA: Association for Supervision and Curriculum Development.

Marzano, R. J. (2003). *What works in schools: Translating research into action.* Alexandria, VA: Association for Supervision and Curriculum Development.

Marzano, R. J. (2004). *Building background knowledge for academic achievement: Research on what works in schools.* Alexandria, VA: Association for Supervision and Curriculum Development.

Marzano, R. J. (2006). *Classroom assessment and grading that work.* Alexandria, VA: Association for Supervision and Curriculum Development.

Marzano, R. J. (2007). *The art and science of teaching: A comprehensive framework for effective instruction.* Alexandria, VA: Association for Supervision and Curriculum Development.

Marzano, R. J. (2010). *Formative assessment and standards-based grading.* Bloomington, IN: Marzano Resources.

Marzano, R. J. (2011). Making the most of instructional rounds. *Educational Leadership, 68*(5), 80–81.

Marzano, R. J. (2017). *The new art and science of teaching.* Bloomington, IN: Solution Tree Press.

Marzano, R. J. (2018). *Making classroom assessments reliable and valid.* Bloomington, IN: Solution Tree Press.

Marzano, R. J. (2019). *The handbook for the New Art and Science of Teaching.* Bloomington, IN: Solution Tree Press.

Marzano, R. J. (2020). *Teaching basic, advanced, and academic vocabulary: A comprehensive framework for elementary instruction.* Bloomington, IN: Marzano Resources.

Marzano, R. J., & Abbott, S. D. (2022). *Teaching in a competency-based elementary school: The Marzano Academies model.* Bloomington, IN: Marzano Resources.

Marzano, R. J., Brandt, R. S., Hughes, C. S., Jones, B. F., Presseisen, B. Z., Rankin, S. C., et al. (1988). *Dimensions of thinking: A framework for curriculum and instruction.* Alexandria, VA: Association for Supervision and Curriculum Development.

Marzano, R. J., Dodson, C. W., Simms, J. A., & Wipf, J. P. (2022). *Ethical test preparation in the classroom.* Bloomington, IN: Marzano Resources.

Marzano, R. J., Heflebower, T., Hoegh, J. K., Warrick, P. B., & Grift, G. (2016). *Collaborative teams that transform schools: The next step in PLCs.* Bloomington, IN: Marzano Resources.

Marzano, R. J., & Kendall, J. S. (1996). *A comprehensive guide to designing standards-based districts, schools, and classrooms.* Alexandria, VA: Association for Supervision and Curriculum Development.

Marzano, R. J., & Marzano, J. S. (1988). *A cluster approach to elementary vocabulary instruction.* Newark, DE: International Reading Association.

Marzano, R. J., Norford, J. S., Finn, M., & Finn, D., III (with Mestaz, R., & Selleck, R.). (2017). *A handbook for personalized competency-based education.* Bloomington, IN: Marzano Resources.

Marzano, R. J., Norford, J. S., & Ruyle, M. (2019). *The new art and science of classroom assessment.* Bloomington, IN: Solution Tree Press.

Marzano, R. J., Pickering, D. J., & Pollock, J. E. (2001). *Classroom instruction that works: Research-based strategies for increasing student achievement.* Alexandria, VA: Association for Supervision and Curriculum Development.

Marzano, R. J., Rains, C. L., & Warrick, P. B. (with Simms, J. A.). (2021). *Improving teacher development and evaluation: A guide for leaders, coaches, and teachers.* Bloomington, IN: Marzano Resources.

Marzano, R. J., Scott, D., Boogren, T. H., & Newcomb, M. L. (2017). *Motivating and inspiring students: Strategies to awaken the learner.* Bloomington, IN: Marzano Resources.

Marzano, R. J., & Simms, J. A. (2019). *The new art and science of teaching reading.* Bloomington, IN: Solution Tree Press.

Marzano, R. J., & Toth, M. D. (2013). *Teacher evaluation that makes a difference: A new model for teacher growth and student achievement.* Alexandria, VA: Association for Supervision and Curriculum Development.

Marzano, R. J., Warrick, P. B., Rains, C. L., & DuFour, R. (2018). *Leading a high reliability school.* Bloomington, IN: Solution Tree Press.

Marzano, R. J., Warrick, P. B., & Simms, J. A. (2014). *A handbook for high reliability schools: The next step in school reform.* Bloomington, IN: Marzano Resources.

Marzano, R. J., & Waters, T. (2009). *District leadership that works: Striking the right balance.* Bloomington, IN: Solution Tree Press.

Marzano, R. J., Waters, T., & McNulty, B. A. (2005). *School leadership that works: From research to results.* Alexandria, VA: Association for Supervision and Curriculum Development.

Marzano, R. J., & Yanoski, D. C. (with Paynter, D. E.). (2016). *Proficiency scales for the new science standards: A framework for science instruction and assessment.* Bloomington, IN: Marzano Resources.

Marzano, R. J., Yanoski, D. C., Hoegh, J. K., & Simms, J. A. (with Heflebower, T., & Warrick, P. B.). (2013). *Using Common Core standards to enhance classroom instruction and assessment.* Bloomington, IN: Marzano Resources.

Marzano Academies. (n.d.). *School-level indicators.* Accessed at https://marzanoacademies.org /interventions-and-initiatives/slis/ on July 27, 2021.

Maslow, A. H. (1943). A theory of human motivation. *Psychological Review, 50*(4), 370–396.

Maslow, A. H. (1954). *Motivation and personality* (1st ed.). New York: Harper & Row.

Maslow, A. H. (1969). The farther reaches of human nature. *Journal of Transpersonal Psychology, 1*(1), 1–9.

Maslow, A. H. (1970). *Motivation and personality* (2nd ed.). New York: Harper & Row.

Maslow, A. H. (1979). *The journals of A. H. Maslow* (R. J. Lowry, Ed.; Vols. 1 & 2). Monterey, CA: Brooks/Cole.

National Center for Education Statistics. (n.d.). *Fast facts: Educational institutions.* Accessed at https://nces.ed.gov/fastfacts/display.asp?id=84# on August 31, 2021.

Nye, B., Konstantopoulos, S., & Hedges, L. V. (2004). How large are teacher effects? *Educational Evaluation and Policy Analysis, 26*(3), 237–257.

Oakley, B., Rogowsky, B., & Sejnowski, T. J. (2021). *Uncommon sense teaching: Practical insights in brain science to help students learn.* New York: TarcherPerigee.

Scott, M., & Scott, D. (2018). *180 Connections: Daily connections between teacher and students.* Denver, CO: Rachel's Challenge. Accessed at https://rachelschallenge.org/media/teachers _kit/180_Connections.pdf on May 21, 2021.

Seligman, M. E. P. (2006). *Learned optimism: How to change your mind and your life.* New York: Vintage Books.

Simms, J. A. (2016). *The critical concepts (Final version: English language arts, mathematics, and science).* Bloomington, IN: Marzano Resources. Accessed at www.marzanoresources.com/the -critical-concepts.html on April 19, 2021.

Stigler, J. W., & Hiebert, J. (1999). *The teaching gap: Best ideas from the world's teachers for improving education in the classroom.* New York: Free Press.

Strickland, B. (Ed.). (1992). *On being a writer.* New York: Writer's Digest Books.

Thrash, T. M., Elliot, A. J., Maruskin, L. A., & Cassidy, S. E. (2010). Inspiration and the promotion of well-being: Tests of causality and mediation. *Journal of Personality and Social Psychology, 98*(3), 488–506.

Webb, N. L. (1997). *Criteria for alignment of expectations and assessments in mathematics and science education* (Research monograph no. 6). Washington, DC: Council of Chief State School Officers.

Yousafzai, M., & McCormick, P. (2016). *I am Malala: How one girl stood up for education and changed the world* (Young reader's ed.). New York: Little, Brown and Company.

INDEX

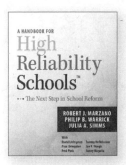

A Handbook for High Reliability Schools™
Robert J. Marzano, Philip B. Warrick, and Julia A. Simms

Usher in the new era of school reform. The authors help you transform your schools into organizations that take proactive steps to prevent failure and ensure student success. Using a research-based five-level hierarchy along with leading and lagging indicators, you'll learn to assess, monitor, and confirm the effectiveness of your schools. Each chapter includes what actions should be taken at each level.
BKL020

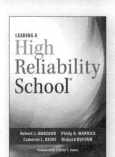

Leading a High Reliability School™
Robert J. Marzano, Philip B. Warrick, Cameron L. Rains, and Richard DuFour

How do educators build High Reliability Schools (HRS) that consistently produce excellent results? The key is to establish interdependent systems that focus on continuous school improvement. A critical commitment to leading a high reliability school is the implementation of the PLC at Work® process. This user-friendly resource provides guidance on establishing and maintaining a high reliability school.
BKF795

A Handbook for Personalized Competency-Based Education
Robert J. Marzano, Jennifer S. Norford, Michelle Finn, and Douglas Finn III

Ensure all students master content by designing and implementing a personalized competency-based education (PCBE) system. This handbook explores approaches, strategies, and techniques that schools and districts should consider as they begin their transition to a PCBE system. The authors share examples of how to use proficiency scales, standard operating procedures, behavior rubrics, personal tracking matrices, and other tools to aid in instruction and assessment.
BKL037

Scheduling for Personalized Competency-Based Education
Douglas Finn III and Michelle Finn

A challenge at the heart of personalized competency-based education (PCBE) is grouping and scheduling students according to their learning needs rather than their age. With this guidebook, you'll take a deep dive into the why and how of these foundational PCBE components. Gain clear guidance for gathering standards-based data and then using the results to create schedules that promote student proficiency.
BKL049

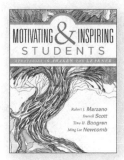

Motivating and Inspiring Students
Robert J. Marzano, Darrell Scott, Tina H. Boogren, and Ming Lee Newcomb

Bringing motivation and inspiration to the classroom is not easy. With this practical resource, you'll discover a results-driven framework—based on a six-level hierarchy of student needs and goals—that you can use to provide engaging instruction to students. The authors share comprehensive understandings of the nature of motivation and inspiration and detail specific strategies to connect with your students.
BKL025

MARZANO Resources

Visit MarzanoResources.com or call 888.849.0851 to order.

Professional Development Designed for Success

Empower your staff to tap into their full potential as educators. As an all-inclusive research-into-practice resource center, we are committed to helping your school or district become highly effective at preparing every student for his or her future.

Choose from our wide range of customized professional development opportunities for teachers, administrators, and district leaders. Each session offers hands-on support, personalized answers, and accessible strategies that can be put into practice immediately.

Bring Marzano Resources experts to your school for results-oriented training on:

- Assessment & Grading
- Curriculum
- Instruction
- School Leadership

- Teacher Effectiveness
- Student Engagement
- Vocabulary
- Competency-Based Education

LEARN MORE at MarzanoResources.com/PD